# THE GRIFTER, THE POET,
# AND THE RUNAWAY TRAIN

*Stories from a Yankee Writer's Notebook*

## GEOFFREY DOUGLAS

Globe
Pequot

Guilford, Connecticut

Globe
Pequot

An imprint of The Rowman & Littlefield Publishing Group, Inc.
4501 Forbes Blvd., Ste. 200
Lanham, MD 20706
www.rowman.com

Distributed by NATIONAL BOOK NETWORK

British Library Cataloguing in Publication Information available

**Library of Congress Cataloging-in-Publication Data available**

ISBN 978-1-4930-4148-0 (paperback)
ISBN 978-1-4930-4149-7 (e-book)

∞™ The paper used in this publication meets the minimum requirements of American National Standard for Information Sciences—Permanence of Paper for Printed Library Materials, ANSI/ NISO Z39.48-1992

Printed in the United States of America

# A NOTE FROM THE AUTHOR

These stories, all of them published originally in *Yankee,* were written over a roughly twenty-year span, from the late 1990s to the spring of 2018. They took me, as you'll see, over the six states of New England and beyond: from a tiny island twenty-three miles off the Maine coast to a hospital in Boston, a firehouse in Worcester, a horse farm in Kentucky, a burned-out town in Quebec; to homes, racetracks, police stations, churches, a mosque, a newspaper, a cemetery, a school. Some were assigned to me by *Yankee* editors (most by Mel Allen); others were my own ideas. Nearly all, at their core, are about ordinary people—a policeman, a reporter, a fireman, a mill worker, a jockey—whose lives, by choice or chance or some combination of the two, are upended in extraordinary ways.

My hope is that you will know these people. That, although you will not have lived their lives, you will recognize at least some of the plights or perils they face: the high risks truth-telling can sometimes carry in "The Conscience of a Chief"; the straddle between unthinkable choices in "A Matter of Life and Death"; or, in "Searching For Alexander," the almost unimaginable grief of losing a child.

*Yankee* being a regional magazine, of course, all seventeen stories are set in (or directly involve) New England. But there isn't one—with the possible exception of "A Break in the Family," about a community of Maine lobstermen—that couldn't be set in Florida, New York, or the Dakotas. Several of them—at least six, perhaps more, depending on how expansively you read them—involve issues specific to our times: immigration, gay marriage, school shootings, end-of-life decisions. All of them, to my thinking anyway, are about more than the sometimes narrow story-lines they follow—the core requirement, I think, of all good nonfiction writing.

———

Some thanks are in order. First to *Yankee* Editor Mel Allen, a close friend all these years, who assigned most of the stories here and worked with me, always seemingly tirelessly, through to their completion. His commitment to good writing is equal to that of anyone I know; and yet, unlike many editors, he wields his red pencil with more respect and restraint than I ever had the right to ask.

Also to Paul Marion, my old friend and colleague from UMass Lowell, who is not only the subject of one story here, but was the inspiration behind the collection itself—though he would have had me call it "Yankee Grit."

And finally my wife, Landon, who met me early in the cycle of these stories, and more than once kept me company on the road trips they required. She never turned down a request for a read-through or a listen, and always—even at the end of my longest-winded disquisitions—found the world's kindest ways to tell me to shut up. It is a skill, along with all her many others, I'm more grateful for than I can say.

—Geoffrey Douglas

# CONTENTS

# FOREWORD

Inside the pages of this book, you will find stories that rank among the most memorable in *Yankee* magazine's nearly 85-year history. Each one is by a writer with a voice so natural and compelling I'm guessing you won't stop reading for hours once you start—and even then, that you'll want to retrace your steps to reenter the lives of these people you won't have known before.

I arrived at *Yankee* forty years ago, in 1979, and have been its editor for much of that time. As any editor knows, the excitement of finding new writers with the gift of language, as well as sensibility and compassion, is why we do this work. Geoffrey Douglas is why I do this work. He is drawn to struggle and heroes. Not Hollywood's improbable heroes—but the men and women who do their best against seemingly insurmountable forces: power linemen who battle a once-in-a-lifetime ice storm; doctors and nurses who face daily, sometimes unthinkable choices; a small-town police chief who challenges the norms of response when a young man's recklessness needlessly takes two lives.

In over two decades of working with Geoffrey, I have never known him to take a shortcut. His writing begins with deep reporting, infused with curiosity and the courage to ask hard questions. Whenever we find a story we agree on, I can count on that, when he's ready—for Geoffrey takes his time—I will read a story full of tension and fully realized characters, a story that matters. I will then make suggestions, and he will listen. Then the process will work in reverse.

The first long narrative he wrote for me, in the late 1990s, was about a county-fair jockey whose luck—always short to begin with—had run out. "Death in the Homestretch" begins like this:

> FOR THE FIRST THREE FURLONGS, *he ran cleanly. Unblocked, near mid-pack, a yard or two off the rail—a patient, ground-saving ride. His mount, Highblast, a five-year-old brown gelding with six wins in 52 lifetime starts, was moving easily, barely four lengths off the*

*lead. Rounding into the stretch turn, he had to be feeling pretty good about things.*

*A win would bring him $180. That, plus another $180 for the win aboard Stage Manager in yesterday's sixth, plus the $70 in "rider's fees" for the pair of losers he'd ridden home, would give him the biggest two-day take of the year. Add to that the win he'd had opening day and a third-place finish the Friday before, plus another $300 or so in rider's fees—if he could bring Highblast home on top here, he'd be pushing $1,000 for ten days' work.*

*"That was huge money for a kid like Ray," says Sal DiMeo. "Huge money. He'd been waiting all year for those ten days."*

I knew the moment I read this: here was a writer I wanted to bring to *Yankee.* And still today, all these years later, when a Geoffrey Douglas story arrives on my desk or in my inbox, I close my office door, ignore phone calls and emails, tell others I'm not to be disturbed. Because, as much as I am an editor, I am a reader first. And I know I'm about to read a story that matters.

I'm proud to have been Geoffrey's editor when his first story crossed my desk. Twenty years later, that hasn't changed.

—Mel Allen, *Yankee* editor

# Death in the Home Stretch
## *August 1997*

*I first learned of him in a four-line Boston Globe report in early September 1996 under the heading "New England Briefs." A 39-year-old jockey, Raymond Garry, had fallen from his horse and been trampled to death during a race the day before at the Northampton (MA) County Fair. Outside of some data on the details of the accident, there wasn't much else reported—which was sad, but no surprise. Ray Garry wasn't a winner, on the track or in life. Like small armies of others before and since, he had lived in the industry's shadows: riding no-name horses for small purses at county fairs and backwater racetracks. For every triple-crown jockey, there are a thousand like him, men and women who inhabit the barns and backsides of the nation's racetracks, hauling oats, mucking out stalls, breezing horses at five in the morning to catch the eye of a trainer who—should another jockey show up drunk or fail to make weight—might give them a shot on the afternoon's card.*

*For Ray Garry, there weren't many shots. And too many of those he got, like the mount aboard Highblast in the ninth race that day at Northampton, were on castoff horses at county-fair racetracks too narrow and treacherous for the top-name riders to even go near.*

*"He didn't have the happiest or the luckiest life," a fellow jockey would say of him later. "He just kept plugging along."*

For the first three furlongs, he ran cleanly. Unblocked, near midpack, a yard or two off the rail—a patient, ground-saving ride. His mount, Highblast, a five-year-old brown gelding with six wins in 52 lifetime starts, was moving easily, barely four lengths off the lead. Rounding into the stretch turn, he had to be feeling pretty good about things.

A win would bring him $180. That, plus another $180 for the win aboard Stage Manager in yesterday's sixth, plus the $70 in "rider's fees" for the pair of losers he'd ridden home, would give him the biggest two-day take of the year. Add to that the win he'd had opening day and a third-place finish the Friday before, plus another $300 or so in rider's fees—if he could bring Highblast home on top here, he'd be pushing $1,000 for ten days' work.

"That was huge money for a kid like Ray," says Sal DiMeo. "Huge money. He'd been waiting all year for those ten days."

Sal is 63, a tiny, leathery man with an old athlete's careful saunter, who has "bumped around" the Northeast's small-track circuit for most of the past 50 years. Once, decades ago, he made his living briefly as a jockey ("A hard life," he says. "I never had much luck."), later as an exercise rider, hot-walker, and valet. Today he's the jockey-room custodian at New Hampshire's Rockingham Park.

In the old days, he explains, there used to be more than enough opportunity for the Ray Garrys of the racing world. "Brockton, Northampton, Weymouth, Berkshire, Marshfield, Great Barrington—20, 30 years ago, every one of 'em had its fair. Seventy days of fair-racing every year. Seventy days. And for kids like Ray, the guys with no racing luck, who couldn't get the trainers [at the year-round tracks] to give 'em decent mounts—well, it was the fairs, for guys like that, that paid a big part of the rent.

"The way it is now, Northampton's the only one left. Ten days. You gotta make the best of it. So believe me—Ray, he was thankful for every ride."

We're standing just outside the Rockingham jockey room, across from the paddock, on a warm September afternoon. Joe Hampshire, a coiled, dark-haired jockey in blue-and-white racing silks, comes out the door and starts past us on his way to the track. He is about to ride the favorite, Side Winding, a $4,000 claimer, his fourth of nine mounts for the day. Hampshire, at present, is first on the Rockingham money list: $563,000 in purses (the jockey's take is ten percent)—75 wins, 69 seconds, 60 thirds—in 90 days of rides. In the midlevel league of $5,000 purses, Joe Hampshire is as good as it gets.

"Hey, Joe!" yells Sal, pulls him over, then winks coyly at me: "Answer a question for us, will you, Joe? Northampton—the fair. What would you say to riding at the fair?"

Hampshire, briefly, seems bemused. Then impatient: "No," he says flatly and moves on.

"See that?" Sal says. "See that? The good riders, the guys with money, the guys who get the mounts—they won't go near the fairs. Half-mile tracks—too risky, too narrow, the turns come up too quick. You ride them half-milers, you gotta need it real bad."

Then he shakes his head—twice, deliberately—and brings up his arms, wide apart, as though delivering a blessing or remembering a long-ago trophy fish.

"And have a heart *this* big . . ."

—◦—

There's been some bunching coming out of the turn. Five horses are abreast now—jammed as tight as packed fish, crowding, bumping, flailing whips. The favorite, Premier Flag, with Henry Ma aboard, has pulled a length or so clear of the pack, with the leader another length in front of him. The lagger, Rusty Brick, is running alone at the rear.

Behind them, at their backs now, is the midway. Teenage boys in Chicago Bulls sweatshirts jostle each other across the length of dirty-grass corridors chockablock with 50¢ thrills—ball throws, dart throws, rifle shoots, miniature colored horses that advance up a track powered by water shot from pistols chained to a board. Small children tag along behind mothers, their faces sugar-smeared from chin to nose. A young man in a crew cut wipes his hands dry against his jeans to gain purchase on a mallet that will send a rubber cone the height of a shaft to ring a bell—and win a stuffed bear half the size of his girlfriend, who watches *oooh*-ingly. And over it all, like a mist, are the smells of barn animals, dried alfalfa, charred burgers, deep fat. It is late afternoon, late summer, at a county fair in New England. The farthest spot on earth from death.

Highblast, with Ray Garry aboard, is bunched with the pack: second from the rail, with three horses outside—the closest a boot's width away.

("It was crowded, too crowded—he should have pulled out," James Bell, the state racing steward, will say later on reviewing the film.) Ray is hunched low, whipping wildly. He doesn't look sideways; his straight-ahead view is of the rump of Premier Flag. It is nearly in his face now. It is the last thing he will see.

———

Around here, we call it "racing luck," says Bob Destasio, another of the old-time jockeys, today director of racing at Rockingham Park. "It's hard to put your finger on it—some guys have it, some guys don't. Ray didn't. Hell, Ray never had any kinda luck at all."

That's most of what people have to say about Raymond Garry. No luck. A big heart, a gritty spirit, and more than enough courage to go around ("He'd take the rough horses," says Sal DiMeo, "the ones no one else would ride"), but no luck. Which translates to no winners. And when you don't get the winners, the trainers forget you—no winners, no mounts. No mounts, no winners. No winners, no money. No luck.

Ray Garry had 57 rides—two winners—in all of 1994. A year before at the Rockingham meet, through roughly 60 days of racing, he rode just two horses; neither won.

So he did what all luckless jockeys sooner or later do. He hustled warm-up gallops on the backside at five in the morning for seven dollars a pop—and while he was waiting to get paid ("Getting paid can be the toughest part," says another rider, who'd rather not be named), tried to convince this or that trainer to give him a mount in the afternoon. The few he got were nearly all long shots: hopeless, over-the-hill nags who would go off at 20 or 30 to one, run out of the money, and keep the string of lucklessness alive.

He lived, with his cat Misty, in a one-bedroom walk-up off Route 28 in Methuen, just south of the New Hampshire border, 30 minutes—by bicycle—from the track. He owned no car; more often than not, he had no phone. Even his tack—his saddlery—was hand-me-down. When riding on the road, his usual bed was the rear seat of a borrowed car.

His pleasures were as modest as his life. He played chess, tinkered with old cars, old radios, and cable TVs ("He sure knew how to work those dials," says Sal DiMeo), and shot pool on Monday nights in the B division tournaments at Salem's Breckinridge Lanes. (At least once, he took home the top prize—$100—which, he told a fellow shooter, more than doubled his earnings for the week.)

"The guy didn't have much," says Sal. "Didn't have much of anything at all. But you know what? I never once heard him say 'I wish' or 'I want'—never. He never bitched. And he never turned down a mount."

His first win came on a horse named Jet Capsule—a horse his father was training at the time—at the old Narragansett racetrack in 1974. He was seventeen years old.

"It was only the second race he ever rode," his father, Al Garry, remembers. "The other jocks, afterward, they did what they do to you when you win your first time—they got him back in the jocks' room, knocked him down, pulled his drawers off, and painted his peter with shoe polish. It's kind of an initiation thing."

The pride Al feels for his son comes over the phone line intact. He is talking from his home in California, where, he says, he is "more or less retired." He is seventy-five today and between racing and training has lived and breathed horses for 56 years.

"After Ray started riding—well, he was a changed boy. When he was growing up, you'd have to say he was kinda crazy, kinda wild. His mother and I, we used to worry. But once he got to riding—yes sir, he was changed."

Ray Garry was born, the fifth of seven children, in Lincoln, Rhode Island, in January of 1957—"a redhead, like his mother, hot temper, always liked things his way." By the time he was five, he was hanging around the stables where his father's horses trained ("'Take me with you, Daddy'—he'd beg me and beg me, until I'd let him come"). He was seven when he rode his first horse.

"It was a pony, really—'Bill,' you called any pony 'Bill.' We'd go out there Sunday mornings, I'd lead him around, he'd get a feel for the movement, get a feel for the reins. It wasn't too long before he was doin' it alone.

"He was maybe twelve, thirteen when I put him on a racehorse. We'd go once around the track; I'd be alongside on a pony, just ride alongside and tell him things—'Not so much strength on the reins there,' 'Keep your hands low on his neck'—the kinda things you gotta know.

"He'd come to the track when I was racing. He'd watch me, then he'd want to know—'How'd you do this, Daddy? How'd you do that?' 'Don't worry,' I'd tell him, 'you just keep watching, keep practicing like you are. When the time comes, I'll know it—you'll be a rider soon enough.'

"When he got good enough to gallop, I'd have him breeze with some other jock. They'd breeze together—three-eighths, five-eighths, whatever it was—and I'd watch how he handled it, I'd watch him make his moves. Maybe a couple years later—he was probably fifteen—I taught him how to come out of a gate.

"He was crazy about horses, right from the first. And he took to it, too—good moves, good instincts, no fear. I'd come home from the stables and I'd be tellin' his mother. 'Doris,' I'd say, 'we got us another rider in the family, I believe.'"

By the time Ray rode his first winner, his father had been retired from racing for two years. He was fifty-three and had known no life but the racetrack since he was old enough to shave.

"I raced at just about any track you could name. Rockingham, Scarborough Downs, Narragansett, Garden State, Pimlico, Bowie—California, Canada, Mexico, all over. I rode my first race in Arkansas—a horse named Be Jabbers, at Oaklawn Park, in 1939. My first winner was that year, at Rockingham, a horse named Ethel Pair.

"I didn't get a lot of good mounts. But I got some—I had some good years. The biggest day I ever had was at Rockingham, in the early 1970s, on a horse named Handsome Flyer—a handicap, a mile and 70 yards. I told my father-in-law to bet $300 on the nose. The horse paid $68 [for $2] to win. Whoo-ee, we won some money that day."

His best year was probably 1962. At the Berkshire Downs meeting that summer, he rode 35 winners in 96 mounts—easily earning the meet's racing title—then followed with strong showings at the Weymouth, Marshfield, Northampton, and Great Barrington fairs.

"The Eddie Arcaro of the half-mile tracks," a Boston racing writer christened him late that year. "After nearly 25 years in the saddle, he has the respect of everyone in racing . . . one of the top jockeys on the smaller New England tracks."

Four years later, on September 9, 1966, Al Garry was aboard a horse named Orinoco, also at Northampton, with a half-length lead midway through the stretch.

"My horse went down. They say another horse came over the top of me, that he rolled over on my head. They say I should have wound up a vegetable. I don't know, I don't remember a thing. When I woke up, it was three months later—December 14, it was snowing outside." He has no sense of taste or smell to this day.

For the Garry family, life was never right after that. The brain damage—or the worst of it—lasted two years. In 1972, after four more years of on-and-off racing, Al Garry hung up his silks to try his hand at training.

"I've got a great home life with my wife and seven children, ranging from twenty-one down to the baby, who is two and a half," he told a reporter just months before he retired.

Two years later, his son Ray rode his first winner—the first of far too few. Six years after that, in Pawtucket, his third daughter, Nancy, was "stabbed to death by a married man"—it is absolutely all he will say. Not long after, Al and his wife split up. She remains in Rhode Island. The children are grown and scattered.

———

He was real, real loyal to his dad. He talked about him a lot. It always seemed like, to me, that his dad was a hero to him."

Gayle Murray (she is "Sandpiper," for whatever reason, to all who know her at the track) is a blond-haired, watery-blue-eyed young woman of about thirty, who sips coffee between long silences at a scarred wooden table in the jockeys' cafeteria across from the stables at Rockingham Park. She makes her living as a lead rider—a "pony girl" in racetrack vernacular—and attends classes in biochemistry at the University of New Hampshire part-time. For two years in the early 1990s, she lived with Ray Garry in a small apartment in Derry, New Hampshire, 15 minutes from the track. They split up, she tells me, in October of 1992 but stayed close friends.

"He was close to his mother in Rhode Island. But it was his dad that he talked about. He wanted to be like his dad."

She says Ray was "troubled, not happy." But she will not—or cannot—explain. "I can't tell you that," she says. "It wouldn't be loyal."

No amount of coaxing will sway her. Were his troubles about his father? Over money? Because he couldn't get rides?

No, she says. "It was different. He just wasn't happy, is all."

She talks in bursts, which end abruptly—followed by silences that seem never to end.

"We did things together. We got hot fudge sundaes. We went to movies, we played chess and Nintendo, we watched cable TV. We ate meals together. We played golf. We rode our bikes together. I miss the bike part a lot."

She drifts off. Another endless silence. And then: "He was very generous. He was good at listening, he really helped me a lot. He helped me with my pony. He'd get me a sub if I was hungry, he cooked hamburgers for my dog. If my car was broke, he'd fix it—it was this maroon 1981 Chevy we shared. He'd fix it if it took five hours. And all he ever wanted was coffee and cigarettes."

Gayle is silent once again. Stone-faced, staring at her hands. I break the moment with a question: What, in your mind, did you have to offer Ray?

She lifts her head, fastens her eyes to mine, and smiles.

"I tried to help him be more happy."

⌒⌒

It is nearing noon on a Sunday morning in late September. In a tiny, cramped anteroom off the jockeys' locker room at Rockingham, there is a church service underway. The reading is from John ("Keep us safe from danger . . ."). There are several brief, informal dialogues—about fear, arrogance, the love of money and fame. "I've done things to win that I'm ashamed of," one jockey confides. The others nod or smile. We bow our heads to a prayer for the departed, then to another that all present "stay safe through this day." We join in the Lord's Prayer, bid good wishes to one another briefly, then break up. The service has lasted 30 minutes. First-race post time is 60 minutes away.

"Ray was always with us Sunday mornings," Lee Allphen, the chaplain, tells me as she packs up her Bibles, her bag of clothing and notes. "He was a regular. He used to walk me out—tell me I ought to refer more to the gospels, tell me about some piece of scripture he'd say I left out. He was serious about the Bible. He was serious about God. And it wasn't just words with him. He lived it, he really did.

"I used to get calls from Ray, late at night from the pool hall—'This or that person doesn't have anything to eat,' he'd tell me. 'You got to help this lady, she's twenty-three years old, she's being abused.' He'd leave the pool hall, or some friend's number, as a contact. He didn't have a phone. He was a beautiful person, he really was. He cared."

She tells me then—as others, by now, already have—about how Ray plaster-boarded the altar of the little chapel on the Rockingham backstretch. And about how, as broke as he was, he wouldn't take a dime. "I'm doing it for God,' he told me. 'For God and people. I can't take money for that.'"

But as quick as you begin to think of him as some sort of beleaguered, benighted minor saint, the other side comes through. In 1985 he was suspended from racing for the illegal use of an "electrical device" on a horse. At least twice in recent years, he was taken off a mount because a steward smelled liquor on his breath. He is known—according to James Bell, the Massachusetts state racing steward—to have been suspended in California in 1978 for marijuana possession.

"You get to know the ones who have problems," Bell says. "Ray Garry was one of them. He was a troubled guy."

"He was hard to know," says Al Howarth, another of the jockeys who get by on fair riding and 5:00 a.m. gallops. "Kinda strange and weird, a by-himself kinda guy. One day he'd be up—joking, laughing, he could be a real comic sometimes—the next day he won't talk to you, he won't have a word to say.

"But he'd give you anything. He'd give you five dollars if he had six in his pocket. If he had two shirts, he'd give you one. A while back, we took up a collection for this jockey who'd got hurt. Ray had made $135 that week. He gave the guy thirty-five bucks.

"He was strange. Inside himself. There wasn't anybody who really knew him—that pony girl, maybe, that he used to hang out with. I liked him, though. You couldn't help but like the guy."

⚊⚊

For the sixty days before the Northampton Fair opened—the first sixty days of the Rockingham meet—he couldn't get a mount to save himself. The one or two trainers who'd believed in him had either lost faith, lost their horses, or moved on. His phone was cut off. He was having trouble making the rent. "I'm thirty-nine years old," he told his old girlfriend. "Thirty-nine years old, 20 years riding, and I can't get a ride."

Opening day at Northampton, he had four mounts—twice as many as he'd had through two months at Rockingham—and one winner. The next day, three mounts—no winners. Then a three-day dry spell and a canceled racing day. Then three mounts on August 30, two mounts and a winner the next day. He had money in his pocket for a change.

When he rode, he rode hard. Not always safely, not always well: "A whoop-de-doo kind of jockey," says James Bell. "Not much style, not much finesse—just whip 'em hard, give 'em rein, and bring 'em home."

"He didn't have patience," says Al Howarth. "No patience at all—he was always just wanting to shoot out."

Howarth is 37, short and wide-shouldered, with tight-cut graying hair, a handshake like a vise, and four pounds of magnesium and stainless steel in his legs.

"From falls," he says simply. "From taking falls." He grins broadly—perhaps proudly—at the thought. "You ride, you're gonna fall. It's part of the game. Don't know how many falls I've had—I've lost count. A lot, though." And he smiles his wide smile.

Two or three days prior to the Highblast race, according to Howarth, Ray took his penultimate fall: "He just flipped right off his horse on the turn—maybe brushed the rail or something, I'm not sure. But he came down on his head. I thought for sure he was hurt, maybe bad. But no. He beat me back to the jocks' room."

"Ray took a lot of falls. Always got up. Nothing scared him, nothing fazed him. He was one tough jockey, that guy."

⤙ ⤚

THERE IS A FURLONG AND A HALF LEFT TO ride. Highblast, still second from the rail in a five-horse knot, remains locked onto the heels of Premier Flag—forelegs linked to hind legs, a dance step waiting to come undone. There is danger here. A need for patience, for prudence, for the small instant judgments that measure risk against reward.

But Ray does not wait. He sees or feels—or thinks he sees, or wants to feel—an atom's worth of running room to his right. He yanks the bit. Highblast veers briefly, then seems to straighten. For the briefest instant—a hoofbeat of time—his head pulls even with the rump of Premier Flag.

Then he stumbles, pitches, but does not fall—and Ray Garry, the next instant, is on his back on the ground. Ten feet from the inside railing, a furlong or so from the wire, not 100 feet from where his father had lain unconscious 30 years before.

A second or so passes. He makes a move to rise. There is a flash of brown and gray, a small sound—like a click—and he is gone.

"Mr. Garry's horse stumbled, and he lost his balance," reads the official accounting from James Bell's office. "Mr. Garry fell to the ground and was stepped on by the #4 horse, Rusty Brick."

"He was right in front of me," says Al Howarth, who was riding Rusty Brick. "Right in my path. It all happened so fast—my horse stepped on him, stepped on his jaw with his back foot. Broke his neck. I knew he was dead when I heard it—there was a snap. I kept riding. There was nothing I could do. It was just a freak thing, is all."

A jockey, Linda Fields, was watching the race along the stretch rail when Ray went down. She leapt the rail and ran toward him; he half-sat, opened his mouth once to speak, then collapsed. He never moved again.

"He broke his neck. He ripped his carotid artery," says Trooper Steven Hynes, the state policeman assigned to the death. "You could say he died of a broken neck, or you could say he bled to death. He was dead either way."

"This is an accident of the ultimate degree," concludes the steward's accounting of the race. "No one person is to blame for this tragedy. This is a very sad time for all racetrack people and is the most devastating accident I have ever experienced in almost 30 years of experience."

The next morning at Rockingham, there was a memorial service for Ray Garry in the little track-side chapel whose altar he had helped, only months before, to build. Later in the day, as post time for the first race neared and the track's flag remained at full mast, the jockeys sent a message to the steward—they wouldn't ride until the flag was lowered and a moment of silence was observed. Both wishes were granted. The first race went off, on time and fully staffed.

The official service took place three days later, in St. Jude's Church in Lincoln, Rhode Island. Al Howarth was there, and Henry Ma, and Sal DiMeo, and a small army of other jockeys, grooms, valets, and trainers, active and retired. Ray's father was there, of course, and his mother and brother Albert, and the four sisters who survive. And an old groom known only by his nickname, "Piece o' Meat."

Ronnie Fischer, a retired jockey, delivered the eulogy. "He said Ray hadn't had the happiest or the luckiest life," Sal remembers. "He said that he worked hard to fill his old man's shoes. That he was a good kid. And that he just kept plugging along."

Gayle Murray, too, was at the service—although, as she explains it, she had paid her homage already, days before.

"I heard he was dead from a trainer. I drove to D'Angelo's— the one we used to go to—and got a vanilla sundae, with the nuts under the hot fudge. That's how he used to like it—with the nuts under the fudge.

"I ate it. And I thought of him. And I cried."

# A Break in the Family

## *September 2011*

*Its name is Matinicus, Abenaki for "far out place." It is a tiny island, two miles from end to end, 23 miles by ferry off the coast of southern Maine—the most remote inhabited island on the Atlantic seaboard. Fewer than 60 people live there, most of them descended from the same eight or nine families that took possession from the Penobscot tribe more than 200 years ago. There are no year-round stores, or doctors, or policemen, and only one road; the ferry comes once a month in winter. It is a place where change comes slowly, where old loyalties run deep and tradition binds tighter than law. The world across the water— "America" to long-time islanders—is as remote as a foreign land.*

*But ten years ago this coming summer—July 2009—when Vance Bunker shot Chris Young in a dispute over lobster traps, "crossing a line that had never been crossed before" and bringing a flood of reporters and cable-TV news crews to the island, its generations-old, clan-based culture was suddenly on display. The result, as the story unfolded, pitted islander against islander in a test of whether the old loyalties—and the island itself—could long survive.*

Vance Bunker, just turned seventy, is a large, grizzled man with broad shoulders, ham-size hands, and a weathered face. He's hard of hearing and walks arthritically. Once, nearly 20 years ago, he was the captain of a lobster boat, the *Jan-Ellen*, that pulled three doomed tugboat sailors out of a January sea on a night when the storm swells were eight feet high and the wind chill was 50 below. Medals followed, and media stories, a standing ovation on the floor of the Maine State House, a citation in the *Congressional Record*. For 17 years after that night—and more than 30 years before it—he was a lobsterman on Matinicus Island: one of its most esteemed, remembered by some for his cussedness, by others for the size of his hauls, and by at least a few for the sick children he sometimes flew, in his private plane, to medical care on the mainland. ("[He] was my personal hero," blogged journalist Crash Barry, a former Matinicus lobster-boat sternman. "A gentle, funny giant... He drove a boat like it was an extension of his body... Kind and generous, tough and strong...")

Today, two years after putting a bullet into the neck of another lobsterman, in defense, he says, of his daughter, Vance Bunker is a pariah on the island: legally acquitted but privately unforgiven, widely but quietly reviled. Although he still does business on Matinicus and hauls traps in its waters, he lives year-round on the mainland now, his island home of 30 years up for sale, his life there—a lifetime—now behind him. He says he isn't angry, but it's hard to believe him, and his wife says no such thing. Even the few who defend him, including parents who recall what he did for their children, are too fearful of their neighbors to say so publicly.

And it doesn't end with him. Three families have been fractured. A man is partially paralyzed. Old wounds have deepened. A fragile, prized way of life, unchanged for generations, has never seemed more in peril. And on this little island, where a brooding sort of silence has settled over things, it's hard to find anyone who doesn't fear for the future.

"A saddening has happened here," Suzanne Rankin says. "It's happened to me, to the island—it's happened to us all. We're living it, every one of us, every single day. Vance and S.T. [Vance Bunker's wife, Sari] don't see that, I don't think. How could they possibly, with all their troubles? My heart goes out to them—but they don't see it at all."

Rankin lives, with her husband, Tom, in a 200-year-old farmhouse along a gravel road, the only through road here, midway between the school and the church. She's in her late sixties, an attractive, courtly woman with frosted gray hair and blue, intelligent eyes. Though not born here herself—she arrived with Tom less than 30 years ago, which makes her almost an interloper by the island's way of seeing things—she can trace her own ancestry here back nearly to the settlement's beginning: to Phebe Young, who came with her husband in 1763. She is the island's historian, the clerk-secretary of its church, and a member of its school board. Her devotion to the place seems almost ingrown.

It's the same with everyone here. You have to be devoted to choose to live in such a place: some 15 miles off the coast (23 miles by ferry from Rockland); no year-round stores, or bars or eateries, or doctors or policemen or paved roads, and only one industry; where the fog drops around you like a curtain for days at a time, the same three families have been fighting the same fights for 200 years, and the ferry comes once a month in winter. As the natives are fond of saying: You live here because you love it, or you don't live here at all.

But lately, since that July morning two years ago, when Vance Bunker shot Chris Young—and the island's clan-based, sometimes brutish culture was suddenly the stuff of cable-TV news—the islanders' devotion, while no less total, has stiffened and turned fearful.

"A line has been crossed that was never crossed before," Suzanne Rankin says. "There's no going back. The question is: Where will the next line be?"

Walking the length of the island—two miles, an easy hour's walk—the main thing you feel is the stillness. Even on the softest, sunniest midsummer afternoon, with a stiff little breeze and the lupines in full color on either side of the road—the way it was the day I first walked it—there's something desolate about the place. The gravel road, the island's spine, runs its dusty, almost unbending course through the old-growth spruce interior: from the tiny dirt airstrip in its clearing at the northern tip (shorter by 50 feet at high tide, they say), past the empty church and schoolhouse, the sad little pile-of-stones monument to the island's first white settler, Ebenezer Hall ("Killed by Indians, June 6, 1757"), and the two dozen or so hardy, mostly modest homes that cluster at uncertain intervals at the intersections of dirt side roads. The day I walked it, the only movement I saw was a woman feeding an animal at her back door.

The yards are large and flat; a few have small gardens. In many of the rest, scores of green or yellow lobster traps are stacked head-high, sometimes alongside the scraped-clean hulk of an old boat or dory. Fish crates, firewood, and rope coils are piled about. Lobster buoys hang like Christmas balls from the branches of a spruce. Old pickups sit in driveways, their six-year-old license plates bearing witness to their last presence on the mainland—which some here call "America."

A mile and a half down, past all but the last of the houses, where the island starts to narrow and you begin to think you can smell the ocean again, you come to the cemetery. It's larger than you'd expect, and more formal: probably two or three acres, a fenced-off square of grass and old granite, with its tiers of headstones—several hundred—giving way to a small, shaded bench in the rear. The dates begin in the early 1800s, though most are later, between 1850 and 1910, growing fewer with each decade after that. Some of the newer stones are engraved with a lobster boat.

More than half the graves belong to the same eight or nine families, the island's anchor names, which I'd come to know by this time: Ames, Young, Philbrook—the three surviving "alpha families," as one islander calls them—as well as Hall, Condon, Bunker, Tolman, Crie. Not all are grouped together; a cluster of Condons might be resting in a corner among Youngs. It's hard to guess what order was applied.

"There's a sense of history here like nowhere else," a lobsterman's wife, Lisa Twombley-Hussey, had said to me weeks before. As a child, she spent her summers on this island and now has returned here with her family. "It's all around us, layers and layers of it. 'This is Aunt Belle's house,' [someone will say]. 'She was a Ripley, she had a store here once, she was married to an Ames.' It goes on and on: this person, that house, this husband, that wife. Memories, connections, personal histories. All those generations. It's always been that way here. You don't see that other places. Not anymore, anyway."

⸺

The shooting happened over lobster traps: who has a right to them, and where. But the deeper causes had more to do with other things: pride, greed, progress, family, what it means to claim a place as home.

Matinicus is one of a vast necklace of islands, more than 3,000 in all, spread out along the Maine coast as far north as the Bay of Fundy. A century ago, 200 or more of them were fishermen's communities; today, only

14 are inhabited year-round. Of those, Matinicus is the most seaward, and the most indigenous. It is also, by an accident of topography—its distance from the mainland, which makes for less freshwater runoff, plus the mix of shoals and deepwater channels that surround it—the site of the richest lobster grounds on earth. "They're the best there is, hands down," says Marty Malloy, who's been buying lobsters for a living since he got out of the Navy 10 years ago. "There's no runoff, the water's colder, the trenches are deep around the island. If I'm buying for my own table, I guarantee you, they're going to come from Matinicus."

There was a time when that wouldn't have mattered much; 50 or 60 years ago, with an island population just shy of 200, there were other ways to make a living here. You could row out in the harbor and catch as many cod as you wanted; there were cattle here then, and horses, geese, and pigs. A few families raised potatoes; almost everyone had a garden. Lobstering was a tougher business in those days: The boats were slower; you couldn't set your traps more than a few miles out from the island; and you had to haul them up by hand. Two hundred traps, maybe 250, were the most a man could manage. Enough to make a living, but never much better than that.

Then the big trawlers came, with their drag nets and sonar, and depleted the groundfish—so that was the end of that. And the land got farmed out. And the old gasoline engines got traded in for diesels; the boats were faster now, so you could set your traps twice as far out. And with the new hydraulic trap haulers, all you had to do was twist a handle and up they came. Five hundred traps was now a manageable load. Some men began to do well.

By the early 1990s, at least a few were getting rich. With the cod and haddock now gone as predators, the Maine lobster harvest had more than doubled: from 20 million pounds a year to close to 50 million. A two-man boat would come in with a three-day haul of 4,500 pounds, worth $14,000 or more. Matinicus boat owners began wintering in Florida, or buying second homes on the mainland. Some traded up to 600-horsepower diesels that could make it to Rockland in an hour or less. They began buying their groceries there—and the island store, open a century, went under. Whole families moved away entirely, but still showed up to haul their traps. It was somewhere along this cycle that the first real damage was done.

There were 188 people living on Matinicus in 1950, roughly half that 20 years later. There are probably not 35 today. The little one-room K-8 schoolhouse, viewed by just about everyone as the island's truest pulse, has rarely had more than 10 or 12 students; in recent years the average has been more like half that. (In 2001 it had none at all, but stayed open officially—absorbing the costs required—to avert the bureaucratic death knell that closure would have meant.)

Those still left, their lobstering grounds now within range of any mainlander with a diesel engine, began drawing the lines tighter around the island—"protecting your bottom," it was called. Threatening notes were left in bottles; trap buoys were tied with half-hitches to warn away encroachers; and sometimes, trap lines were cut.

Five years ago, a member of the Ames clan, who'd left Matinicus years before but never stopped lobstering its waters, began hiring someone else to work his traps. They warned him, then cut his traps. He responded by threatening a ramming; they put two shots across his bow.

"You have to understand: This bottom, for these guys, it's like the family farm. It's their legacy; they've been working it for generations," says Marty Malloy, the lobster buyer, who lives on the island with his wife and twin boys. "You don't just let someone come in and take that away from you."

More time passed; the economy soured. By the summer of 2009, the price of lobster was at a 12-year low. On Matinicus, where the lines were drawing tighter, they told Vance Bunker that his son-in-law, a mainlander, was no longer welcome to set his traps.

———

"It used to be you fished here, you lived here," Clayton Philbrook says. "That was the way it worked—before the boats got fast enough so a man could live in one place and fish in another. So now we got problems. We've had problems ever since."

He's in his late fifties, a big man with thick arms, a droopy, graying mustache, and a warm but very certain way of saying things. He is descended, he tells me, from a family of shipbuilders who first settled in Bath in the 1770s, migrated to the Penobscot Bay islands, and have been on Matinicus for just under 200 years.

There was a time, Philbrook says, when he had thoughts of leaving the island: He went to college, took courses in aerospace engineering ("I thought maybe I wanted to go into space"), switched to biology, then to photography—but nothing clicked. He came home and got a job as a sternman—an assistant—on another islander's lobster boat, then other boats after that. Thirteen years ago, he bought his own. Along the way, he married an Ames girl. ("Some people talk about family trees; what we have here is a wreath.") Their son, Nick, now 30 years old and a captain himself, has been lobstering since he was 8.

All this Philbrook explained to me one rainy spring morning, as we sat together in the cab of his pickup, parked that day at the Matinicus dock, the site of the shooting in July 2009. His boat, the *Samantha J.*, was tied up alongside. For most of the morning, he'd been working on the engine, but the rain was a torrent now, so we were waiting it out in the truck.

At one point as we talked, another pickup pulled up in front of us, and a woman—June Pemberton, once a teacher on the island, now one of two women to captain a lobster boat—got out and began unloading traps. Without a word, Philbrook was out of the cab, and for the next several minutes the two unloaded traps together in the rain.

Mostly, he talked about the business of lobstering: how the cost of bait and fuel had gone through the roof while the price being paid for a pound of lobster was making it hard to get by. ("It's cruise ships and casinos that drive the lobster market," Marty Malloy would say to me later, "and we're in a beer-and-salad time.")

In 2009, Philbrook said, he'd sold more lobster than he'd ever sold before, yet barely covered his costs. "It's hard times for everyone," he said.

He tried his best, as they all do here, to stay clear of the subject of the shooting. But it was never far away.

He said he worried sometimes that with the way things were going, his son, Nick, could be the last Philbrook to make a living here: that if people kept leaving for the mainland and just coming back to haul lobster off the bottom ("taking and taking, and never giving back"), the island, like all those others, could die a lingering death. "And I'd do about whatever I had to do to see that doesn't happen," he said. "We all of us out here would."

I asked Philbrook about the "fishhouse meetings" I'd heard about that had been going on the last several years: all the lobstermen on the island, gathering every springtime in the schoolhouse or church basement to set the rules that would govern, among other things, who could lobster and who couldn't. There was nothing legally binding in anything they decided; a licensed lobsterman, as far as the law is concerned, can set his traps anywhere he chooses. But that was never the point.

There's a way of doing things, Philbrook told me, and it just seemed as though the time had come to get things clear once and for all. And so they'd made it formal: "If you're born here, you can fish here—or if you're the child of someone who was. If you marry one of our daughters, you can usually fish here, too. And if you fish here, we want you to live here. That isn't the law. That's just how it works."

It was a while before either of us mentioned Alan Miller. But there was never any doubt about whom we were talking. Miller is Vance Bunker's son-in-law; he married Bunker's daughter Janan several years ago, bought a house on Matinicus not long after, and had been lobstering island waters ever since. But the couple's primary home was on the mainland; some said their island house wasn't even winterized. There's a name among islanders for people like that: "fuel savers." It isn't a good way to be known.

"He's not a part of the community; he never has been," Philbrook said to me. "You want to be a part of the community, put your kids in the school here, support the island, pay into it—that's one thing. He didn't. He rubbed people wrong. He had a` bad reputation. And in the end, your reputation is all you have. Anyhow, we voted him off."

⁎  ⁎

They voted him off the island—out of island waters. He defied them: set 400 traps around Matinicus, reportedly with his father-in-law's blessing. When half of them were cut two weeks later, he was sure he knew by whom: a pair of stepbrothers, Chris Young and Weston Ames, both in their early forties, with 400 years of island ancestry between them. So he cut theirs. Or maybe Vance Bunker cut them, or maybe both of them did, or neither; it can be foggy off Matinicus in the early mornings.

However it happened, traps were cut, tempers flared, violence was threatened. And then, at a little before 6:00 on the morning of July 20, 2009, one of the men, Chris Young, boarded Vance Bunker's boat, accused him of cutting his traps, and, Bunker would say later, threatened to kill him. The two men wrestled. Bunker repelled Young with a can of pepper spray.

Most of this is pretty certain. A good part of the rest, including the bigger questions of background and intent, and who was right or wrong, depend mostly on whom you ask. It's also at this stage of things that the silence sets in. Or you get your answers off the record.

"Vance and Chris getting into it, there's nothing new there," one islander tells me. "The Bunkers and the Youngs feuding—that goes back. It could have been something their grandfathers were fighting about."

This from someone who recalls the days, 30 and 40 years ago, of church suppers, bingo nights, and community softball games; when times were so tight that most of the men fished year-round (the norm these days is April through December) and still went out at night with herring nets; and grudges, no matter how bitter, were nearly always trumped by need.

"I cut a few of yours [traps], you cut a few of mine—that was always going on—until the time came when somebody lost their boat or their roof blew off in a storm," the islander says. "Then it didn't matter if it was your worst enemy; you were there for them—because you knew you'd need the same if it was you. That's how things are when you have to fight to survive. And we did...

"But no more. Now you've got the big fishermen with their fast boats—Alan Miller, he's got two boats, he's not a young guy anymore, he's already made his money—who come in not caring about anything, just looking to fish some sweet waters."

When Miller arrived at the Matinicus dock that morning, Ames and Young were awaiting him. So was his wife, Janan, Vance Bunker's daughter—who had seen from her window the men converging on the harbor, and had brought with her a 12-gauge shotgun she would claim she didn't know how to use. Vance Bunker was there himself; he'd arrived with his sternman in a blue pickup with a .22-caliber handgun and an AK-47 assault rifle with nine loaded magazines.

There was some shouting. At some point Janan Miller yelled "Hey!" and pointed the shotgun at the stepbrothers. "Shoot me, you stupid bitch!" Weston Ames may have said, at about the same instant he grabbed for the gun. Bunker fired his handgun and missed. His second shot hit Chris Young in the neck. He collapsed in a pool of blood at his stepbrother's feet. He would survive: his hands mostly paralyzed, his left arm no longer of much use, his lifetime earning power reduced by $2.4 million, according to the lawsuit he would file.

⌒

"Greed, that's what's behind all this," Vance Bunker would tell me months later. He wasn't talking about the lawsuit. "It used to be, you had to work for every dollar you got. No more. Today, there's not a lobsterman on the island under fifty who's ever had to scrape for a living. It's all come easy to 'em. So now they think they got a right to it. And as soon as things get a little tough, they get all pissed off and start setting up rules—about property, and family and whatever, and who can fish and who can't—and writing them down and passing them out. Then at the next meeting, they go and change the rules."

It was mid-April 2010, a little more than a month since a jury had taken a day and a half to acquit him of all charges stemming from what had happened on the island dock that day. ("What type of father would pull the trigger?" his lawyer had put to the jurors. "The real question is *What father wouldn't?*") We were sitting together, he and I and Sari—known by most on the island as "S.T.," short for "schoolteacher," which is what she was when they met here more than 20 years ago—in the living room of the modest, red-shingled house they've shared seasonally for 17 years in a small coastal town just across the water from Matinicus.

I'd heard by now the story of his family's early years: how his grandfather had been a rumrunner on the island during Prohibition, hiding the bottles in deepwater puddles; of his father, a lobsterman, and how he'd met Vance's mother, who'd come there to work as a nurse; how he'd started pulling traps as a teenager and never stopped; how it used to be that when you had an argument with a neighbor, "you got over it real quick, 'cause you needed each other more than you needed to stay mad."

Working his way around Sari's occasional outbursts ("Yes, I'm bitter—I don't expect my closest friends to go against my family, and do it publicly . . ." "Easy now, you're getting yourself worked up . . ."), he'd told me his story of how it had all come to pass: how his son-in-law had played by the rules—"He married my daughter, they bought a house there"—and had still been run off the island; how he'd gone to see Chris Young's stepfather, futilely, to try to settle the dispute; how he'd feared for his life, and later for his daughter's ("The man threatened to kill me"); how Young's and Ames's civil suits, (the former settled this year, the latter still making its way through the courts) could take most of what he and Sari had; and, finally, how the island was no longer home to him, and his friends were no longer his friends. "They won't even talk to me," he said.

He seemed at a loss. It had all changed so fast. One day life was good: full, straight-ahead, uncomplicated. There was plenty of money, a close family, a lifetime of friendships, a job you were good at, the respect of almost everyone you knew. Things had been the same a long time. The next day, a day you couldn't have seen coming, you back the wrong horse, play chicken with a couple of kids who aren't 16 anymore, then pull a trigger in anger or fear. And now it's all about "the old days" and "the way it used to be."

"He had so much to lose," an islander would say to me later. "He's the last guy on the island I would have expected this from. But things were changing, and he couldn't deal with that, I guess. I feel for him, I really do. But a bad hurt has happened. And he's the one who brought the guns to the argument."

The summer before the shooting, the island got together and threw itself a high-school prom: men, women, and teens, many in 30-year-old tuxes or too-tight, floor-length dresses—one guy even in white tie—rocking out to "Boogie Fever" in the church basement under crêpe paper and string lights, popping flashes, selling raffle tickets, drinking spiked punch from a bowl in a neighbor's yard. You can watch it on YouTube: "Starry, Starry Night: Matinicus Prom 2008."

Three months earlier, the island's post office had burned down. It was the community's heart; it had begun as a chandlery a hundred years before, and later was a general store. Every man and woman on the island showed up with an ax to clear a fire line, a shovel to dig trenches, or a box of sandwiches; old men too feeble to swing axes strapped packs on their backs and sprayed down nearby trees.

Then, in October of the same year, just two months after the prom, a young lobsterman, Chris Whitaker, went missing in the waters off Matinicus; only a boot, a lunch pail, and an oil can would ever be found. Every boat on the island, and Vance Bunker in his plane, worked the sea for days, while the island's wives walked the shore in search of clues. ("He was no angel," remembers Suzanne Rankin, who walked the western shore herself. "But he was one of us.") The money raised from Prom Night would go to Whitaker's family.

There are a thousand stories like this. Of fires, drownings, lost boats, sea rescues, church suppers, roof raisings, shared food, every neighborly act you could think of. But also of cut traps, knife fights, boat rammings, death threats, and ancient feuds.

They're archetypes, all of them: Rugged Individualism, Frontier Justice, The Good Old Days. Just about any Matinicus story you read (and there have been dozens, especially since the shooting) is going to have you believe that it's either a rogue outpost of inbred, gun-happy cowboys—"Pirate Island" is a common reference—or a quaint little throwback to some simpler time. "There's a war going on in coastal Maine, where renegade crustacean gangs are forcing people to grope for their guns," was how one national magazine painted the scene, ludicrously, the year after the shooting. And its antithesis: "An out-of-the-way summer idyll... a world apart from bustling Bar Harbor," was a typical depiction several years ago.

There's no war going on, and no one I met is "groping for their guns." But other than that, there's at least some truth to most of it. Matinicus is a remote, largely forgotten island community of defiantly independent souls. "We've got no use for police out here; we're just fine policing ourselves," one local told me. "A man drives too fast, we tell him to slow down. He don't slow down, he wakes up one morning, looks out his window, and sees he's got four flat tires. He drives slower after that."

This isn't a place that could exist on the mainland—or, probably, even 10 miles closer to it. Its remoteness accounts for much of what it is: its history, its preciousness, its peril. Probably also its future, whatever that may be.

"You have to *want* to be here, really want it," Nat Hussey said to me early in my first visit. "You have to shovel the snow, sit on the school board, go to meetings, do the work—you have to share the load. There [on the mainland], when you want your car fixed, you go to the garage. Here you do it yourself, or you get a neighbor to help you. I'm forever getting helped, by this person or that. But you need to find ways to help *back*. If you can't do that, or you won't, then there's no place for you. That's the way we're built here. And I'm a guy who *wants* to be here."

Hussey is a lawyer in his forties, a slight man with thin features and tousled, receding brown hair. He used to work for the Maine Department of Corrections. Thirteen years ago, on his honeymoon, he came to Matinicus for the first time; his new wife, Lisa, had spent her childhood summers here. They began spending parts of their own summers. In 2005, for three days, he signed on as a third man in a lobster boat, and, he says, "a gene flipped on in my head." He left his job; she left hers. Today he makes his living on the island, doing carpentry jobs and occasional legal work, collecting taxes, helping out at the schoolhouse, and hauling lobsters from a motorless, oak-and-cedar "peapod"-style rowboat he calls the *Sweet Pea*. It's a boat no serious lobsterman has worked from in probably 60 years, but it leaves no carbon footprint, and that's important to Hussey. On summer Saturday nights on the boat dock, Hussey and his guitar lead dance parties that turn out the whole island. On Prom Night three summers ago, he was the one in white tie.

The day we talked, a warm May day in the front yard of the couple's island home, he'd just put his boat in the water for the season. A few yards away, alongside the traps still piled by the garage, two of the three Hussey children took turns dousing one another with a garden hose. Lisa, busy readying her Matinicus Island Store for its spring opening, just days away, came and went from the conversation. (The tiny store, launched in July 2008, lasted three seasons, but with too few patrons to cover costs, would finally close at the end of last summer.)

Out on the water, Nat said, "You're close to your work, you're wet, it's noisy, it's real, sort of like farming must have been at one time." Lisa, for her part, talked about the silence—"You listen carefully, you hear individual things: the wind, the bell buoys, the generator at night"—and the spareness of day-to-day life: "That whole Walmart mentality, there's none of that out here. You learn how little you need. You learn what *real* need is. Lots of stuff like that, stuff they lost 50 years ago on the mainland, it's still the same way here."

It was a long while before any of us mentioned the shooting. When Lisa finally did—she'd been talking about neighborliness and the response to the post-office fire—it was so unexpected, and came in such a half-whispered seethe, it felt almost like an eruption:

"It's such a fragile system we have here. Just so delicate. And then the fire, and the center of our community is gone, just like that. And then that last thing—*a man opening fire on the public dock*. I got *sick* when they told me. Literally, physically *sick*."

⌐—∾

In the end, though, it is the island's willfulness, more than anything else—more even than its isolation—that sets this place apart. Two hundred years' worth of clan-based survival—six or seven generations of Youngs and Ameses and Philbrooks, and the few who have joined them—fighting, marrying, burying, and working with one another, on a 700-acre island, has built up a very thick crust.

"It's the big dogs who've kept it going," Nat Hussey says. "It's like the way they know their bottom: The trenches and channels and rocks, they've known them since they were boys. They know the island the same way. It needs them, it's always needed them. The system here relies on clans. If they died out, I don't know where we'd be."

You hear this a lot on the island: that the old ways are the best ways, that the surest route to the future leads through the past. It's as though the clans in their way were a sort of monarchy: a continuum of ascendant families whose generations of canny, devoted stewardship will somehow see the way through. As a belief, it's a hopeful, uniting force. It's also the biggest reason why, whenever there's an event at the school—just about any event at any time of day that involves the five or six kids there—30 people are apt to show up.

"Everyone knows that the kids are the future of the island," Heather Wells told me when I met with her last summer. She had just finished her second and final year as the island's teacher; her six students had ranged from kindergarten through sixth grade. We were sitting together in her schoolroom, surrounded by books, wall maps, crayons, and computer tables, talking about all the people on the island who had helped create the projects her students had shared. She told me about how, when an octogenarian member of the Ames clan had died not long before, a local writer, Eva Murray, had come to the school to talk to the children about his life, "so they'd understand something of the history of this person they'd known." I asked about the shooting: Had she discussed it with the children? She looked at me coldly. "It doesn't come in here," she said, and that was the end of that.

She told me about a social-studies exhibit the islanders had planned: "Captains of Matinicus," put together by the captains of the island's lobster boats. "Twelve or 13 of them, I guess, came in and told stories, showed photos, shared their memories," she said. "One of them brought in some old buoys, maybe from when he was a kid, I'm not sure, and showed us how they were made. I loved seeing that. It's about building long-term memory—like the way farming used to be, when the kids still learned from their elders. Not like today, with computers, where the process works in reverse . . .

"And you know what? It works. I had two 10-year-olds this year already laying traps. There's a strong dedication in this classroom, I can tell you that, to continuing this way of life."

Donna Rogers is seventy-one. She lives with her husband, Charlie, a lobsterman, in a home overlooking the harbor, from where, in a small studio/gallery she calls "The Fisherman's Wife," she designs handcrafts and paints island scenes on postcards for the summer people who sometimes come around. On my last day on the island, I went to see her there and bought a small, dreamy photo, taken years ago, of a rainbow over Matinicus Harbor.

She's a little like a rainbow herself: stout and graying but full of wonderful old stories that paint pictures and cast spells. Many of them are included in the thin, typewritten, hand-stapled book she wrote a decade or so ago: *Tales of Matinicus Island: History, Lore and Legend*. It tells of Indians, settlers, famous storms, and old shipwrecks, as well as a long-ago girlhood of apple fights and ice-cream making and "homemade kites made of brown wrapping paper and miles of trawling line." Nearly every home on the island has a copy.

She told me about how she'd first come to the island, as a nine-year-old girl—"a thousand years ago"—when her mother married a Young. Then she'd left, and returned again as a young wife and mother when her husband first took up hauling traps: "We've always had to fight to hold on to what we had, always. When Charlie first came here all those years ago, they cut *his* traps, too. Well, he just put more in, and they cut them again. So he put more in. He was new. He had to pay his dues. It's what you had to do."

Then she stopped. "But now with *this* . . ." She tilted her head back, hard, almost violently, toward the open window behind us and the dock and harbor beyond.

"Vance and I were kids together. He's my family. All of them, everyone, the whole island—my family. So it's hard, what's happened. It's very hard. It's a break in the family . . .

"I don't know what to think anymore. When Charlie and I were coming up, it was a different time. A gentler time, I guess you'd say. You had to fight then, too, but it seems like the rules were more moral. Does that make any sense? Now, with all that's happened—I don't know. It just seems like right and wrong mean different things today."

All that was many months ago. The little photo I bought that day, of the rainbow over the harbor, hangs now over my desk at home. It seems almost of a different world.

It's hard to account for why exactly. It's more, I think, than the perfect calm of the water in the photo, or the hazy, purplish light that must have followed the rain that day. The harbor boats seem smaller, and humbler, than I remember. They float at their moorings comfortably apart, not much more than a dozen of them, gentle neighbors under an early-evening sky. I can't make out their engines, but I feel certain they were smaller, too—and slower, built for a lazier, more generous time.

On Matinicus Island, until that July morning two years ago, it was still that time. A fight was still just a fight, was still among family, could still be atoned for. The world across the water—"America"—had not yet quite arrived.

Now, I fear, it has.

# "The Town Is Gone"
## *July 2014*

*This is a story about the connections we have to the places we call home—and how it can happen that those connections are severed in an instant.*

*The meaning of home cuts deeper for some people than for others. For the people of Lac-Mégantic, Quebec, most of whom measure their roots there in generations, there's not much of importance that home doesn't mean. When you've lived your whole life in one place, and the names on the stones in the local cemetery include those of every close relative you know of—as well as scores of neighbors you've loved— and the railroad job you work at is on a track your grandfather helped lay, and there's hardly a soul in your church on Sunday at whose house you haven't shared a meal—then home is everywhere you look, and most of what you know.*

*And when all of this is destroyed in the space of seconds, as it was when a runaway train derailed, exploded its load of crude oil and wiped out most of the town, killing 47 of its people, in early July of 2013, the loss for those left behind—as they described it to me, some of them still waiting to bury their dead—is incalculable, and will be felt for decades to come.*

It was the tail end of the first warm day of summer.

And it was a Friday, the crowd was young, the weekend was just ahead—and on the outside terrace of the Musi-Café on rue Frontenac in Lac-Mégantic, Quebec, even as Friday turned to Saturday, there was still not an empty table.

Or inside, either, where singer/guitarists Guy Bolduc and Yvon Ricard, both now in their forties, hadn't been off the stage since 9:30.

The two, who had gotten their starts in the town's more honky-tonk bars two decades before and were loved here now as native sons, were playing together tonight for the first time in years. They'd begun the night with a love song—"Rosie" (*"Oh Rosie, tu est blanc / Tes yeux m'éclairent / De t'avoir eu un instant / j'étais telle-ment fier . . ."*), a Québecois favorite—then moved to the dance tunes that had kept the floor filled for most of the past three hours.

"A perfect evening," Karine Blanchette, one of the waitresses, would remember later. "Everyone was floating."

It was a local crowd. There was Stéphane Bolduc's birthday group—he was thirty-seven, a widely loved car salesman, nearly destroyed by bereavement only two years before, there tonight with his new girlfriend, Karine Champagne; Geneviève Breton, twenty-eight, a green-eyed blonde who "sang every hour of the day," had found brief fame on *Star Académie*, Quebec's version of *American Idol*, and was now working in a jewelry store down the street; Gaétan LaFontaine, his two brothers, his wife Joanie Turmel, and Joanie's aunt Diane Bizier, also there to celebrate a birthday; Natachat Gaudreau, forty-one, a single mother who worked for the town's school board, and was lately talking of opening a hostel; Mathieu Pelletier, twenty-nine, a local math teacher, hockey coach, and father of a three-year-old. And a secretary, an art teacher, a drummer; a French teacher and a daycare worker out tonight on their first date; a pharmacy worker, a stonecutter, a steeple-jack, a second daycare worker; two waitresses, at least three students, and several employees of the particleboard factory and door manufacturer in town.

At ten minutes after 1:00 in the morning—July 6, 2013—the two musicians announced to the crowd that they'd be taking a half-hour break. Guy Bolduc looked briefly at his old friend as the two left the stage together: "Man, it's fun to play with you." Then he moved off toward the bar.

More than two hours earlier, on a rail track in the village of Nantes, seven miles northwest, Thomas Harding, an engineer for the Montreal, Maine and Atlantic (MM&A) Railway, was putting his train to bed for the night. It was a big train: five locomotives and a car just behind to house the radio-control equipment, followed by a loaded boxcar and 72 carbon-steel tanker cars, each carrying 30,000 US gallons of Class 3 petroleum crude—10,300 tons in all, nine-tenths of a mile front to back, bound for the Irving Oil refinery in St. John, New Brunswick, roughly 300 miles east.

There were plenty of trains just like it—some as long as two miles—most of them coming from the same place: North Dakota's Bakken oil fields, where a boom in shale-oil production (the result of what has come to be known as "fracking") has created a massive, nearly overnight run on rail freight. Roughly 400,000 carloads of crude were shipped in 2012 on US railroads, much of it through New England to refineries in Canada or the Northeast US—up from fewer than 10,000 five years ago. Some 7,400 carloads went across the state of Maine alone—through Jackman, Greenville, Brownville Junction, and other small towns forming an east/west belt across the middle of the state. More than half of those carloads were transported behind MM&A locomotives headed east to Irving's St. John refinery.

The tide of oil hadn't gone unnoticed. Just a week before, on the night of June 27 in the central-Maine community of Fairfield, protesters had erected a large wood-framed sign—*Stop Fracked Oil*—across the tracks in the center of town, to block a train carrying nearly 100 carloads of crude to the same St. John refinery. Six of the group were arrested. "Our concern is [that] the rails aren't safe," one of them, a sixty-four-year-old protester from Verona Island, told the press.

Tom Harding, as permitted by MM&A's work rules, was the train's only crew member that July night in Nantes. By the time he had parked it, shut down four of its five locomotives—the lead engine left on to keep pressure supplied to the air brakes—and applied hand brakes on what would later be claimed were 11 of the 72 tanker cars, it was probably around 10:45. His work done, he phoned a taxi to take him the seven miles to Lac-Mégantic, where he had a room reserved for the night. As the cab pulled away, its driver would tell police later, the lead locomotive was spitting black smoke.

At 11:30, a 911 call was received: in Nantes, a passerby reporting fire in the train's lead locomotive. The village fire department responded to the call, shut down the lead engine, extinguished the blaze, and then phoned to notify MM&A of what had taken place. Not long after midnight, two of the railway's track maintenance crew arrived from Lac-Mégantic. They confirmed that the train was secure. At a few minutes before 1:00, the firemen left the scene.

It's not clear why what happened next happened. One theory is that the air brakes were disabled when the firemen shut down the lead locomotive. Others claim that the hand brakes, not the air brakes, are the critical safety system on an idled train: that if they're set properly (and enough of them are set), the train will stay in place, even on a grade.

And there *was* a grade—a barely perceptible, 1.2 percent grade. Nantes is 1,690 feet above sea level. By the time you reach rue Frontenac in Lac-Mégantic's downtown, you're at a little less than 1,350 feet. And somewhere around 1:00 a.m., unseen on the darkened track, ever so slowly at first, the big train began to roll.

❧

Yves Laporte, sixty years old, is a window on both a region and a time. In the living room of his home in Marston, on the northwest shore of Lac Mégantic, sits a crude, one-hundred-year-old rocker, probably made of birch limbs. "It's not the most comfortable chair in the world," he says, "but I like to look at it sometimes."

The chair was made by his grandfather, Joseph Cliche, and sat on the porch of the home his mother grew up in, on Lac Mégantic's northeast shore a little less than a century ago. The lake, from which the town gets its name, is nine miles long by roughly two miles wide. In a photo he keeps of the house, the chair sits empty on the porch next to his grandmother, who is standing, while the rest of the family—his grandfather in work clothes and broad-brimmed hat; his mother, who appears to be around nine, in braids and leggings with a book on her lap; and several younger brothers and sisters—look out at the camera from their spots at the front of the house. It's summer, with tall birches overhanging the scene.

Yves lived in that house for several years as a boy. He lives today across the lake from it, in the two-story home, surrounded by birches, that he built with his first wife 38 years ago. His grandfather Joseph, with a brother, Yves' great-uncle Philibert Cliche, started a broom-handle factory here around 1912, then expanded into clothespins and plywood; by the 1930s it was the largest employer in town. Joseph lies buried in Lac-Mégantic's Sainte-Agnès Cemetery. Yves' paternal grandfather, Henry Laporte, set up shop here as a baker around 1900, then owned a livery stable and a general store. He also is in Sainte-Agnès. His father, Henry Paul Laporte, ran a sporting-goods store in town, sold gas, and rented out cottages.

"The lake is in my blood," Yves says, as he finishes recounting the last of his ancestors. "It is in my family's blood."

Most people you meet here will tell you a similar story. This isn't a place you just end up in or pass through. If you're here today, it's likely because your father was here 50 years ago—was a logger or a barber, or worked in a pulp mill or the railyards—and his father 50 years before that. It's a hard place to live, on the northern slopes of the Appalachians in southeastern Quebec, the largest town for 60 miles in any direction, where the temperature can drop to 40 below in January and the snows that come in October last sometimes into May.

The earliest white settlers, most of them fishermen and farmers, from Scotland, England, and French Canada, didn't come until the early 1850s. Next came the loggers, drawn by the vast swaths of old-growth forest that surround the region on three sides (its eastern border is the lakeshore), and by the Chaudière River, which has its source in Lac Mégantic, then flows north 115 miles to end at the St. Lawrence. In 1884, when the Canadian Pacific Railroad began construction of the last leg of its rail line linking Montreal with the port of St. John—and chose the lake region as the link point of its two legs—the town was formally christened. The railroad has been its heartbeat ever since.

Yves' father used to tell him stories, he says, about the war years, the early 1940s, when trainloads of Canadian soldiers, bound for Halifax and from there to the Western Front, would come through Lac-Mégantic on their way east: "It was their last stop before the US border. They'd get off and party all night, then leave again in the morning. There were five or six hotels here—it was a big, happy town in those days."

The last passenger train stopped here 20 years ago—but the freight traffic increased almost yearly: lumber and farm products, pulp and paper, local granite. Factories grew around the sawmills and quarries; today, on the north edge of town, an industrial park houses a door manufacturer, a furniture maker (where Yves has worked for 35 years), and a maker of particleboard, and employs nearly a fifth of the town's population.

The region prospered modestly, with Lac-Mégantic always its hub. Over time, a natural division took place: the southern bank of the Chaudière, anchored by the parish of Notre-Dame-de-Fatima, became home to the town's working class—its factory workers, loggers, and jobbers—while on the north bank, the business owners, store clerks, teachers, and bank tellers built their lives around l'église de Sainte-Agnès.

But for all that, it was a small town: 2,600 people at the close of the 19th century, still fewer than 6,000 today. Its growth was slow, its hardships were shared; and even between the two shores, from the earliest days there was the sense of a common lot.

"You have to understand how it is with us here," says Gilles Blouin, a local native who heads the region's genealogical society and claims as many as "thirty, forty, fifty cousins" in the area. "I may not know Jacques, but I know Jacques' parents, or I know his grandparents, and probably some of his cousins. So in that way I know him, and I honor him. We all of us here, we stem out of the same few peasants."

⌒ ⌒

Driving southeast out of Nantes along Quebec Route 161, you follow the railroad tracks through six miles of scrub forest. The road is flat—or seems so—and mostly unbending. There are no houses to be seen, and rarely any cars; here and there a narrow dirt side road will curve off into the pines. Every mile or so, a disused boxcar, ancient-looking and smeared with graffiti, will appear to your right on a rusty strip of siding.

Then you pass through a crossroads and things begin to change. A U-Haul place. Then a gas station. A garden center, a body shop, a car dealer. The road widens, the cars increase, there are stoplights now and side streets: a Walmart, a hospital, a motel, a McDonald's; a cemetery (Yves' family's resting place), its front row of gravestones only feet from the roadside on your right. The road has become a strip now—but not for long, and just as quickly it changes and narrows again: The stores become smaller, more modest, spaced more widely, as though the planners had somehow changed their minds in the middle.

Near the end of it all, on your left, its pair of Gothic spires dwarfing everything in sight—nearly everything in town—is the century-old l'église de Saint-Agnès.

You've been traveling rue Laval, the road into Lac-Mégantic, running southeast along the lakeshore toward the river. A quarter-mile before it gets there, it bends ever so slightly to the south; this is rue Frontenac, which will take you two more blocks to the river. These last two blocks just past Sainte-Agnès, this quarter-mile just before the river meets the lakefront, is the core of the old city. And as anyone here will tell you, it is still the city's heart.

It was here that you came, from Nantes or Lac-Drolet or Stornoway or any of a dozen other villages, long before the city spread north to the strip you drive in on today, to buy your tools or your groceries, check out a book, or listen to music. The library never left here, nor the local bank. Small restaurants and specialty stores—a bistro, several cafés, a chocolate shop, an antiques store, a lingerie boutique—replaced the businesses that moved to the strip, filling the storefronts of the century-old red-brick buildings that lined both sides of the street.

The Musi-Café was one of these—by most accounts rue Frontenac's most desirable destination—with its polished-oak bar and palm-ceilinged outdoor terrace. On the sidewalk outside, each and every cement square was centered in decorative granite. The gaslight-style streetlamps sat atop raised planters, each one spilling flowers.

One morning early last summer, Yves remembers, he was sitting in his car, stopped at the railroad crossing at the head of rue Frontenac, waiting for a train to pass: "And I was just looking out the window, at the street, at all of it—the flowers under the streetlights, the potted palm trees on the porch of the Musi-Café—and thinking how nice it all was. So clean and good to look at. Just really nice. It made me proud."

— ❧ —

No one saw the train begin its slow roll on the track in Nantes. It was dark—almost moonless—there was no one around, and as slowly as it must have been moving, it wouldn't have made much noise. The first reliable sighting might have been by two teenagers, Alex Gagnon and Daniel Sivret, who were buying gas near the crossroads at the head of rue Laval in Lac-Mégantic, two-thirds of a mile from the downtown, when the train passed just north of them. It was moving faster now.

"It was going too fast," Alex would say several days later, "and there was no fire underneath, nothing to show that the brakes were on. I said to Daniel, 'Imagine if it derails.'"

The track from Nantes to Lac-Mégantic, like the road that runs alongside it, is mostly straight. The first turn comes just inside the crossroads entering the city, about where the two boys made their sighting—and the train cleared that turn. The next is a little sharper, just at the head of rue Frontenac, where the track veers east, away from the road. The train at that point, according to later estimates, was traveling between 60 and 70 miles an hour, roughly six times the speed limit. It was 1:14 a.m.

Some people talk about the noise. Others remember the smell, or the way the ground shook, or how the whole world turned orange—"brighter than the middle of the day, a blinding orange"—then black. Some people say they were paralyzed; others can recall only running. Some people say there was screaming; others say no, that no one screamed at all.

One man in town, an attorney named Robert Giguère, remembered later that he used to worry sometimes, even before it happened: "But then I would say to my wife, 'No, we're safe here. We live in a town where the trains can't just race through, where they have to stop at a station.' Who would have thought—a train without lights, without a driver, in the middle of the night?"

There were likely about 25 people still inside the Musi-Café, and another 15 or 20 on the terrace outside, when the five front locomotives

37

plowed into the turn, making it halfway around, and then left the track, pulling free from the cars behind them. (They would be found later, still intact, a half-mile east.) Those on the terrace, many of them there for a smoke between sets, saw it happen: "A black blob that came out of nowhere, no lights, no signals, moving at a hellish speed," one man would remember. They began running. Inside the bar, there was a trembling. Gaétan Lafontaine's older brother, Christian, took his wife by the arm and muscled her outside. Gaétan was headed the other way, deeper into the bar, to find his wife, Joanie; their bodies would later be found together. The lights went out. The front windows turned orange. Somebody yelled "Fire!" Geneviève Breton, the young singer, at the bar with her boyfriend to buy a bottle of water for the walk home, turned with him and ran, but lost hold of his hand somewhere in the darkness.

One by one, the tanker cars derailed. Several of them ruptured, then exploded, sending a river of molten oil through the streets. A wall of fire went up, 100 feet high, as the derailed cars piled into one another, forming a three-story mountain of steel. The Musi-Café was engulfed. Those still inside, and others escaping too late, died instantly. ("Vaporized" was the word the coroners would use.) The temperature reached 3,000 degrees.

"The entire town was on fire to my right," Yvon Ricard, the musician, who had been among the smokers on the terrace, would tell reporters later. "There was this big mushroom cloud. . . Wires were falling, transformers were exploding. . . We were running around houses, through backyards; we stopped running when we couldn't feel the heat on our backs."

There are a hundred stories like this of that night: of horror, near-death, and crazy, panicked flight. They are told by the survivors, about what they witnessed and how they survived, sometimes about someone who was with them, someone they might have loved who is gone. But these are only half the stories, and the others are less often told.

Of those who went to the Musi-Café that night, probably 26 or 27 (the exact number is hard to know) never came home. They were laborers, secretaries, business owners, waitresses, teachers, coaches, musicians, and the parents of at least 14 children. The youngest was 18; the oldest 52.

But Marie-France Boulet died that night, too, in the bedroom of her home on rue Frontenac; she was sixty-two. And Talitha

Coumi-Bégnoche, thirty, along with her two daughters, Bianka and Alyssa, ages nine and four. ("I would have preferred dying with them," their father would say later.) And Roger Paquet, sixty-one, who worked in the wood-pellet plant in town and lived alone on the lakeshore two blocks from the tracks. And nineteen-year-old Frédéric Boutin, in an apartment across the street. And a ninety-three year-old widow, a retired bookkeeper and his wife, a couple in their twenties, an accounting student and a food worker who lived in apartments above the Musi-Café, and seven or eight others.

All dead in their homes when the one and a half million gallons of molten oil swept through the downtown like a tsunami. There were probably twenty of them, in addition to the other twenty-seven: forty-seven in all. The funerals would go on for three months.

❧

I arrived for the first time in Lac-Mégantic two months later, the Wednesday after Labor Day. For weeks I'd been reading the stories: hundreds of stories from scores of news sources. Every day brought more. In the first wave were the victims' tales: the families' anguish, the orphaned children, the death toll rising by the day. (It would be July 19, 13 days after the derailment, before the number stopped at 47.) Then came the chronicling of the physical losses: businesses, historic buildings, the library with its books and family archives, the downtown under a blanket of oil. And, from the first day to the last, the stories of human kindness: letters, dollars, clothes, toys, books; a benefit concert and plans for a fundraiser in sister city Farmington, Maine; a message from the queen; the flags at half-mast, for a week, on every government building in Quebec.

But the biggest single group of stories, once the first days had passed, were the stories of the train and its people. Many of the earliest ones involved the engineer, Tom Harding, and whether he'd set enough hand brakes. Next came the ones about Ed Burkhardt, CEO of MM&A's parent company at the time, Rail World: how he'd arrived in town with a police escort four days after the derailment and been jeered by residents. There were stories about MM&A's safety record—which by most accounts was frighteningly bad—about the condition

39

of its tracks and its rules allowing one-man crews and oil-laden trains to be left unattended overnight. There were stories about oil trains in general and the hazards of their unchecked growth. "A massive, reckless increase," wrote one columnist for *The Guardian*. He called the crash site "a corporate crime scene."

Finally, and once they started, almost unendingly (and still today with no end in sight), there were the stories of the lawsuits. By the time I arrived in Lac-Mégantic in September, I'd learned of a dozen or more: against MM&A; against Rail World; against Canadian Pacific, which had contracted with it to ship the oil; against Irving Oil, Western Petroleum, the Union Tank Car Company, several North Dakota oil companies. There have been dozens more since. Some are class-action suits, some countersuits; some were filed in Canada, others in the US. The amounts total hundreds of millions of dollars. They'll be going on for years.

My first stop was at the McDonald's on Laval, the strip on the way into town. Nearly every table was filled, mostly with families, sometimes three generations. Small children chattered underfoot; adults talked between tables, loudly, familiarly, all of it in French.

From there I drove south on Laval, three-quarters of a mile, until I came to the barricades. All vestiges of the old downtown had been erased, were still being erased. What had been rue Frontenac—the town's library, post office, grocery store, a discount store, a hairdresser, a funeral home, several dozen offices, shops and apartments, as well as its three or four best restaurants—was now a quarter-mile wasteland of worked-over earth, twisted railcars, and human remains, cordoned off behind crime-scene tape and wire fencing, with police at either end. Huge backhoes plowed through four-story mountains of scorched dirt, as trucks carried off load after load. As far away as rue Champlain, 1,000 feet from the tracks, the paint on the houses was blistered and falling away. It was as though a bomb had been dropped.

I looked for the sign I'd read about in the papers, handwritten in block letters, posted alongside the tracks just outside the exclusion zone: *You— The Train of Hell. Don't Come Back Here. You're Not Welcome Anymore.* But someone had removed it.

There was to be a meeting that evening. Billed as a "public information session for the people of Lac-Mégantic," it was intended, the announcement said, to present the planners' vision for "the creation of a new commercial hub." I'd arranged for a translator, who turned out to be Yves. We'd never met before.

The meeting room, a makeshift auditorium inside the city's two-year-old, $29 million, warehouse-like Sports Center, 500 feet from the wreckage site, was packed. On a raised stage in front sat the mayor—a former schoolteacher named Colette Roy-Laroche—and three or four provincial politicians and consultants whose names and titles I never learned. Behind them was a six-foot-high display of maps and colored diagrams: streets, roads, footpaths, parkland, and local landmarks, seemingly all of it divided into "green zones" and "blue zones."

Several of the officials addressed the crowd. The old downtown, they said, had been too contaminated by oil, which had fouled the soil in every direction, to be any longer usable. The oil would be pumped out wherever possible, but that would take time. Meanwhile, the downtown would be relocated, much of it to the river's south shore, the neighborhood known as Fatima. There would be a bike path and gardens; part of the old downtown would be refashioned as a memorial park. All this, the mayor said, would serve to get businesses back on their feet, "unify the city," "commemorate the dead," and "integrate the story of the catastrophe for future generations." Sixteen million dollars was available for the job, with more expected to follow.

The crowd was polite but plainly unhappy. A man whose brother had died in the fire rose to complain that the state's coroner was still holding his body: "And now you tell me that the site of his house will be buried under a park." It wasn't right, he said. A red-haired woman said that she'd moved here years ago from Montreal because she liked the feel of a small town: "And now you're talking about making us into something we're not. I say no, no—please, sirs, keep us small!" The crowd applauded loudly.

On the way out with Yves, I asked him what he thought: Did he like the new plans, or did he agree with the red-haired woman? Oh, he said, it didn't matter what he thought: "They'll do what they want with it—and in the end it will look like the sports center, ugly and gray, like a factory.

The town will survive, but for us who grew up here, who grew up with the old buildings, it will never be the same."

— ⁓ —

There is almost no one in the region, it seems, who hasn't been touched. I asked Yves whether he'd lost anyone. No, he said, not personally—but his niece's best friend, whose birthday party he'd just attended, was among those who died in the Musi-Café, as was a co-worker, Yves Boulet. Henriette Latulippe, who'd died in her apartment next door, was the sister of a neighbor. "One way or another, I guess I knew maybe 10 of them," he said.

"If you see somebody [on the street], well, first off you know it wasn't them," a local woman told a reporter after the deaths. "So then you ask, 'How's the family?' And if they can talk, you know the family [is safe]. And then you say, 'And everybody else?' And that's when you hear, 'My son's girlfriend, my cousin, my niece . . .'"

Father Steve Lemay is the presiding priest at l'église de Sainte-Agnès. We met in mid-September at his office in the church rectory on rue Laval, 500 feet north of the derailment site. He spoke softly, in halting English. The background growl of heavy machinery would occasionally intrude.

He had just completed his 20th funeral, he said. There were 27 more still to come, with the remains of these last victims—often no more than a bone fragment or single tooth—still being held by the government coroner, awaiting identification. It was a heartbreaking process to witness, he said: "But for some people, it is hard to complete the grieving without something [tangible]. And they are willing to wait."

He told me about how he had gone to the hospital early that first morning to give comfort to any injured survivors: "But no one was there, and after a time I understood that there would be no one [coming]." So he went instead to the high school, where the people were already gathering. There were many families there, he said, and many old people. But the hardest to witness were the mothers and fathers who couldn't find their children.

"And they would come up to you with family photographs: *Avez-vous vu mon fils?*' they would say. *Avez-vous vu ma fille?*' And there would be nothing you could answer."

Later that day, he said, there began to be lists: "Lists of the lost, lists of the living—and people would look at them, and know. That was very hard. To see such pain. I was praying for myself, praying for all of us."

He feared the coming winter, he said: "It will be very hard. Winter is always hard here, the dark and the cold, and we are many miles away—but this one will be harder. We have to learn to be by ourselves, to remember that we are connected, that we are together. In that way we will help each other. . . That is the only solution to tragedy. God is present in the things we do to help each other. It is the only way."

Two days after we met, on September 21, Father Lemay would preside at the funeral of Marie-France Boulet. Another local with a century-long family history in the town—one of 11 siblings, nearly all of them still here—she had died in her home, behind the lingerie shop she owned on rue Frontenac. The searchers had found nothing to identify her, only some charred gold pieces that had once been earrings and the half-melted remains of a souvenir spoon, which the authorities handed over to her family in a Ziploc bag. But she'd been gone almost three months by then; they'd decided to go ahead with the funeral.

I'd shared a dinner with her sister Paule, as well as Paule's husband, Jacques Fortier (who served as translator) and her niece Alexe, several days before at a restaurant on rue Laval. I'd phoned her after reading a letter she'd written to the local weekly—"The right to information and the right to speak!" they'd headed it—in response to what would become known as Bill 57, an act of the provincial legislature giving the city sweeping powers in rebuilding, including the right to expropriate any home or business in the Fatima neighborhood on the river's southern bank, at a price determined by formula, to make room for the new downtown.

The concern of the city's leaders, at least as I understood it, was that if the rebuilding didn't begin right away and progress at lightning speed, the accumulation of lost dollars in the downtown, coupled with the physical devastation and the jobs lost at the businesses that had been destroyed or shut down, could result in a mass exodus that would cripple the city for decades. Although I never met anyone willing to dispute this concern on its merits, almost no one seemed able to live with its result: that Bill 57, which would pass in its final form the day after my dinner with Paule, would reverse a century of culture and demography, that it would do so more or less by fiat, and would do it overnight.

Paule's letter, in which she had pleaded that her neighbors not cede the town's future to a "group of clever people with drawing boards," was an impassioned piece of writing: wounded, uncrafted, almost a written cry; I was anxious to meet its author.

She was cautious at first—she hadn't know many writers, she said—polite, but only barely acknowledging me as she directed her words, always in French, toward her husband. It went this way for the first half-hour or so, the two of them talking mostly to each other, but always in answer to my questions: first about that July night and early morning, how they'd dropped Marie-France off at her house around 10:15 after returning from a family event, then been awakened at 2:00 a.m., "the sky bright as morning," by Jacques' son banging on the door; then about the family's night-long vigil at another sister's house as news came in and worry turned quickly to despair; and finally about the pain of having nothing of her sister, "not even a tooth," to bury or say goodbye to.

"We are not alone, of course," Jacques said at one point, almost as if to apologize. "In so many families today, in so many homes, there is pain."

"It is true," Paule's niece said now, surprising us all. She was young, about twenty, and had barely spoken up to this point. "For the first month after it happened, everybody cried," she said now quietly, in perfect English, looking at me across the table. "It was all they did. They just watched the news and they cried."

When the talk turned at last to the subject of her letter—the city's seeming indifference to its people—Paule's tentativeness was suddenly gone. She is fiftyish, dark-haired and pretty, and when she gets emotional her voice grows quicker and her green eyes seem sometimes on the edge of tears.

*Who is deciding these things?* she was asking of us suddenly, referring now to the architects of the city's new plan. "Where do they live, these people who tell us where to work and where to live, who tell us what to do with our town? In Montreal? In Ottawa? Who are they? How can they say this to us, or to the people of Fatima: *'Move your town, forget what is past'*? *'Here, we give you money, now go away'*? How can you ask a people to forget their history?"

It was something I'd been hearing a lot in the week just past. I'd heard it from Yves, who was clearly saddened by it, even angry at certain moments, but in the end seemed more resigned than anything else. "I'm not really a fighter," he had told me one day over lunch. "So my opinion isn't going to matter very much in the end." I'd heard it from a sixty-eight year-old retired poll worker named Louis-Serge Parent, who compared it to the rebuilding of postwar Berlin: "The politicians in the end, they're always going to take over. It all happens behind the scenes . . ." And I'd heard it, maybe most succinctly, from a reporter for the local weekly, Claudia Collard, who simply registered its sadness: "It's too big, what's happened to them—too big to even think about. First they lost their people; now they're losing their town."

But no one I'd met seemed more personally afflicted than Paule. "The town is my earth," she told me now. "It is where I was born, it is where I have lived my life—and now they tell us to move it. *No!* I would rather they lay down a big slab of concrete [in the old downtown] and let us live our lives there, do our business there, and leave the people in Fatima alone. . .

This thing they are doing, I cannot imagine it. *The town I was born in, where my sister died, where all these people died, a big gray hole without life.*"

⌒

I returned three months later, a week before Christmas. It was cold now, below zero both days I was there. The city seemed empty: the locals indoors, the roads mostly carless, the gawkers and reporters long departed from downtown. At the wreckage site, now under half a foot of snow, the workers toiled on, but the work was different from before. Much of the ground had been leveled, the wrecked tanker cars and old dirt carried off; newly poured concrete risers marked the contours of future streets, heading southeast off what remained of rue Frontenac toward the river and, once across, to what will be the new downtown.

On the northern riverbank, in what used to be a part of the Sports Center's parking lot, its beginnings were already in place. Four modular concrete buildings, to house a liquor store and other tenants still to be announced, were largely complete: the core of what will be a 45,000-square-foot strip mall. Across the river in Fatima, in the snow in front of the now-shuttered l'église Notre-Dame-de-Fatima—which after 67 years had celebrated its last Mass in September—a sign informed passersby that the site would soon be the home of the city's new supermarket.

But there was grace, too, to be seen—even what might be called hope. In the snow along the triangle of land at the foot of l'église de Sainte-Agnès, a small forest of lighted Christmas balsams, one for each victim (including a 48th for the volunteer firefighter who had taken his own life shortly after), most with photos or other mementos in their branches, tapered gradually downhill toward the river. Donated by a local tree farmer, they'd been planted in irregular rows, then lit together by the families three weeks before Christmas in a ceremony after evening Mass. Seeing them there, their lights shimmering like colored fireflies at the base of rue Laval—a stone's throw from where those they remember had died—I couldn't help but be reminded of what Gilles Blouin, the local genealogist with "fifty cousins," had said to me three months before: "We will come out of this closer, I think. It has happened already, I have seen it. The sorrow of losing someone loved—a brother, a son—today reunites a family that was estranged, that had hardly talked in years. Shared loss can be powerful that way."

I met with Yves my second morning in town. Nothing much had changed, he told me; nearly everything they'd announced at the town meeting in September was coming to pass. He seemed despondent. I said so, and asked him why. He talked for a few minutes about the coming of winter, then about the new buildings going up in Fatima: "Just metal and concrete, it's so impersonal."

He grew quiet before he spoke again. "The town is gone," he said. "It was gone the morning of July 6th, no matter what they do."

That night, my last in Lac-Mégantic, I had dinner with Paule and Jacques at a small restaurant across the street from Sainte-Agnès. Both seemed more subdued than I remembered. At some point, mostly to make conversation, I asked Paule whether she'd written any more letters to the paper since we'd met. She shook her head no. I asked whether she thought she would. Jacques translated the question. She shook her head again, more vigorously this time. For a moment I thought I had upset her.

"I have stopped writing," she said. "I have stopped talking. I just want to go."

I was confused. Jacques clarified: She meant that she wanted to leave the city. She wanted to move away.

I asked why. Where would she go? Jacques passed on her response: *"This is not the city where I was born. My earth is not here anymore."* She seemed about to cry.

She excused herself then, and Jacques and I were alone. He had tried to talk to his wife, he told me; her family had tried as well: "Her brother tells her she's just running away from things, that that can't be the answer." But none of it was getting through, he said: "Her whole family is here. Her friends, her whole life. But she says she wants to leave. For me, I love it here, the people, the lakes, the big mountains. But she wants to go. I don't know. I don't know what to say anymore."

It was close to 9 o'clock. Outside, in a lightly falling snow, we stood in the doorway of the restaurant, drawing out our goodbyes. Across the street in front of Sainte-Agnès, the twinkle from the 48 clusters of tree lights cast a bluish glow. I would be leaving in the morning. I said again how sorry I was for their loss and that I hoped the new year would be brighter. I shook their hands and turned to go. Paule pulled lightly on my sleeve: "Please, before you go, come see my sister's tree."

We walked together across the street, then climbed the slight grade onto the snowfield where the cluster of trees had been planted. Crude footpaths in the snow, some more well-trodden than others, crisscrossed around and among them. Marie-France's tree was near the center. For a minute or so we stood around it, none of us speaking, as Paule dusted the snow off its upper branches, removed a small photo, caressed its glass briefly, then returned it to its place.

# Epilogue

At last report, MM&A was still hauling freight through the city, though with shorter routes now, smaller trains, safer loads, and far more restrictions. Its assets had been sold at auction under bankruptcy rules. The train's engineer, Tom Harding, as well as two other railway employees, were arrested and charged with 47 counts of criminal negligence.* While the US Department of Transportation is reportedly working with the rail industry on voluntary safety measures, local demands to reroute the rails around the town remain unaddressed.

The lawsuits continue to amass. They are too many and too dispersed to put a number on—against railroads, oil companies, lease holders, tanker-car manufacturers, and individual CEOs, in Canada as well as the US—and will no doubt drag on for years. The largest suit alone, a class action on behalf of Lac-Mégantic's survivors, names 52 defendants.

More than $400 million is estimated to have been spent so far on the city's rebuilding. The total, some have said, could go beyond $1 billion. In Fatima, the residents of expropriated buildings were mostly gone by late March 2014, leaving behind clusters of denuded homes and businesses, some stripped even of their window frames. The new liquor store, already in place, was slated to be joined soon by a pharmacy, a supermarket, and a refurbished Dollarama store. The town's library, following donations of 100,000 books and $90,000 in cash from as far away as Germany, also has reopened.

In December 2014, a rebuilt Musi-Café opened on a site in the relocated downtown.

"It is much more than just another restaurant or another bar," said the head of the construction company in charge of the rebuilding. "It's not just a building anymore. It's a spirit. It's the hope of the people of Mégantic."

---

*(Following a long-delayed trial, all three men were acquitted in early 2018.)

# The Night the Bandit Dog Came In: A Memoir

## *March 2001*

*Years ago, in my twenties, I used to hang out at the track. Almost any track, really: classy, seedy, thoroughbreds, trotters, greyhounds, whatever was around. You could say I had a problem (and there were some who said just that) — but the rush it gave me, at the time, was impossible to see past.*

*One of the tracks I went to, on the seedier end of the scale, was the old Wonderland Greyhound Park in Revere, Massachusetts. Even by then, it was a fading relic of a place, first opened in the Depression summer of 1935. Its heyday-years—the '50s and '60s, when 10,000 bettors would crowd the macadam on race nights, a band playing in the infield, to watch the dogs being led to the start by tuxedoed "lead-out boys"—were long behind it by the time I came along twenty years later. The crowds were smaller by then, and older, the fanfare long gone. There was a sadness about the place, especially acute at the end of a losing night.*

*On my last return, nearly 20 years ago—the setting for this story—the track was a derelict: half closed-off, the other half nearly empty, a few knots of old men shuffling around what felt like a disused warehouse. I looked for the past, but couldn't find it. So instead, with a bartender and four strangers in a trackside bar, I tried hard to reinvent it—and almost managed to for an hour or so.*

*Today the place is a parking lot.*

The night the Bandit dog won for me must have been in March or early April—there was still old snow on the ground. I don't remember the odds he went off at, or the race distance, or even the exact year. Just that his name was Bandit-something (or something-Bandit), that he had the longest odds in the last race of the night at the Wonderland dog track in Revere, Massachusetts, and that he came out of the pack like a car in the stretch to win by a nose at the wire.

The perfecta paid about $300 on a two-dollar bet. I had $10 on it. We took a cab from the track straight to Logan, Frannie, my girlfriend, and I (betting the Bandit dog had been her idea) caught the late-night plane to San Juan and were in the La Concha Hotel casino before they closed the tables at four. I won $2,000 that trip playing blackjack, close to $4,000 total if you counted my night at the dogs. Lyndon Johnson was in the White House. I was between colleges. That was a lot of money in those days.

Frannie's long gone now. Married, divorced, remarried, somewhere on the West Coast. We've lost touch. But oh, could she pick greyhounds. She picked them just by looking, mostly—through these little red leatherette binoculars she'd bring to the track in her purse. She'd sit there squinting, elbows propped up on the table in the clubhouse restaurant where we used to sit between races, straight black hair falling down both sides of her face. All you could see was her mouth and those little red glasses homed in on the greyhounds as they were paraded in front of the clubhouse on their leashes on the way to the starting box.

"The three dog. See how his ears are pinned back? See how he's pulling at the leash? I think the three's ready to run."

So I'd check the form to see if the three dog looked like he had a chance. And if he did, and usually even if he didn't, I'd put at least five bucks on him. Or I might tie him up in the perfecta with some other dog I liked. Which is how it went the night the Bandit dog came in.

Anyway, that's how we did it. I was the analyst; Frannie just went on looks. I don't know which of us had more winners. But I know I never had a bigger score at the greyhounds than the night the Bandit dog came in on the front end of a $300 perfecta and we ended up, the pair of us, howling at the moon and stacking $100 bills at 4:00 a.m. on the beach outside the La Concha Hotel.

There are four patrons, all of them men, at the clubhouse bar, which I'm almost sure is where our restaurant used to be. But there's no sign of a restaurant now: just a large, brightly lit barroom with a dozen vacant wooden tables, a wall-mounted TV tuned to a football game that only the bartender is watching, and four men drinking beers.

It is a Sunday night in September and it's starting to rain. I am fifty-six years old with a job at a college in the morning and a good woman waiting in a sweet-smelling kitchen outside Boston 30 minutes away. The fourth race is an AA sprint. I bet the seven dog, a two-year-old brindle named Kodiak Kim, $20 across the board, and order a bourbon and some buffalo wings. Outside the barroom on the floor of the clubhouse, small knots of old men (there aren't many under 70 and barely a woman in sight) squeeze around TV monitors that carry the odds and races from tracks in Arizona, Florida, Rhode Island, anywhere that greyhounds run on Sunday nights. The old men don't cheer or jostle or talk to one another. They just stare up at the monitors in tight little huddles until a race is done, then shake their heads, make tired, disgusted faces, turn and shuffle away.

Beyond the clubhouse is the grandstand where, on the nights that Frannie wasn't with me, I used to base myself. It was dirty and crowded and busy in those days, and smelled of onions and beer. Outside on the asphalt apron that overlooked the track, every 20 minutes or so as race-time approached, the crowd would press out to watch: retirees, off-duty sailors, middle-aged men in baseball caps, college boys with their dates—two or three thousand on a good night—clotted together the length of the stretch run, rooting home greyhounds that passed so close you could hear the dirt scrunch and smell the sweat on their flanks. The grandstand, I used to like to think then, was where the *real* gamblers passed their nights.

It is dark tonight, empty behind closed-off double doors. Outside along the railing, under the lights from the stanchions overhead, a single couple sit alone: a man in a wheelchair and woman in a small chair beside him who seems, from a distance, to be reading aloud from a book.

Kodiak Kim is blocked in the first turn and never recovers. I finish the last of my buffalo wings, order a second bourbon, and watch as Jamaica Princess, my choice in the fifth, gets bumped off-stride and finishes next to last. Behind me on the clubhouse TV monitors against a background of palm trees, plastic flamingos and an Arizona sky, a dog named Baby Cakes B is caught and beaten a step from the wire. An old man spits and throws his program at the screen.

Outside on the strip of asphalt that separates the clubhouse from the track—the same place where, decades ago, Frannie and I screamed ourselves blue as the Bandit dog caught the leader at the wire—the only spectator is an empty Adirondack chair.

— ❧ —

The memories. It's always the good ones that stay. Like the winning seven-one perfecta on my birthday—I was born on the first of July. Betting $200, more than a month's rent—the biggest bet I'd ever made—on an even-money favorite named Johnny's Surprise that led from wire to wire. A ten-to-one long shot named Miss Lone Star (I was in love with a girl from Texas at the time and would marry her three years later, as husband number two). The winning tip I once got from a woman in a Chinese laundry. The long, wet kiss I got from Frannie the night the Bandit dog came in.

But memory is selective and tends to be kind. The truth is, of course, there were far more losses than wins—at the horses, the casinos, but nowhere more than at the dogs. At first, during my college years in the 1960s, they were nothing to worry about: an occasional afternoon at the track with a roommate, a night or two at Wonderland. Then over time, the pace picked up and the days took on a rhythm: classes all morning, horses in the afternoon, the dogs or trotters at night. Then the classes stopped mattering. Bills went unpaid. There were loans from bad places. Then telephones cut off, a car repossessed, books and luggage pawned or sold. More lost afternoons at the horse track, more nights at Wonderland. Then a college expulsion. A psychiatrist. Lost girlfriends. A worried family. Then a family at the end of its rope.

The end came later, a year after college, on a Tuesday in the fall of 1971. It was close to midnight. Wonderland was emptying; the last race of the night had been run. I had $3 left in my pocket, the cost of the shuttle ride back to Boston, where I lived and worked. I was twenty-seven, tired, depressed, and worried about the rent. My mouth was stale from too many cigarettes. I could smell myself. It was like five hundred other nights.

The cars they used as shuttles in those days were beat-up black Caddies from the 1950s, the kind with jump seats. They were built for seven passengers—plus the driver—though the company sometimes squeezed in eight. If you'd lost and were broke and had no better plans for tomorrow, the Wonderland shuttle at midnight was not a place you wanted to be.

I was in back, between two men in worn-out suits who smelled worse than I did. I would have said they were old, in their mid-fifties probably, about my age today. They were talking across me; it was as though I wasn't there.

They had lost and were angry: cursing trainers, cursing dogs, cursing their lousy f-ing luck—the f-word flew and flew. One of them said the last race had been fixed, that the dog he'd bet had been doped. You could tell, he said, by the way his head bobbed when he ran. The other man said he wouldn't doubt it, that he figured it happened all the time. Then they began trading stories—other races, other tracks, other years—nearly all of them about losers and the ways they'd found to lose. The first man told one about a dog he'd bet once who'd been leading ten yards from the wire, "but then he stopped to take a leak." You could tell it was an old story and that the other man didn't believe him, but he went along just the same. "If a dog you bet don't lose one way," I remember one of them saying, "he'll f-ing lose another." Both men shook their heads and agreed it was a lousy business. Then one of them took out the form that previewed the next night's entries and they began their talk about those.

I saw myself. I saw the future, and I was nearly sick. I got out at the first stop in Boston, a hotel that hasn't been there for years now, and walked the two miles home. It was five years before I went inside a racetrack again.

Frannie used to have this theory. She swore by it: if a dog pulls at his leash during the parade (which doesn't happen often), it's a sure sign he's ready to run. And if he pulls hard—really tugs so that his handler has to work to restrain him—no matter his odds or his record, he's worth the maximum bet.

There's a dog in the sixth—the number-one dog, Zemonella—who's pulling to beat the band. I bet him. He breaks first from the box and never trails. In the space of 30 seconds, I'm $300 to the good.

Then I do the dumbest thing. It's a kid thing and I know it, but there's no way I can help myself. I order a sidecar, Frannie's old drink, from the bartender and hoist it in the air. And then I tell him: "Hey," I say. "My old girlfriend, her name was Frannie. I haven't seen her in 25 years, but she just picked that winner for me."

The bartender nods and does his best to smile. "Here's to Frannie," I say then. "To Frannie, wherever you are." Then I tell him to buy a round for the four other drinkers, order another for myself, and start in on the stories: of Frannie, the tight-leash theory, the night the Bandit dog came in. By the time I leave to cash my bet an hour later, it is sheeting rain on the clubhouse apron and the six of us are friends for life.

It's close to midnight before I get to where I'm going for the night. There, in a suburban kitchen over a late-night supper of salad and warmed-up lamb, I'm asked how my night went, and whether it felt like twenty-seven again

Not exactly, I say. But I did win some money, I made some new friends, and it really took me back.

# Only Fools Were Not Afraid
## January 1999

*They still refer to it, more than twenty years later, as the Great Ice Storm of 1998. If you were living at the time anywhere along that 5,000-square-mile ribbon of land, much of it in northern New England, that felt its force that January, you know the name is deserved. And if you weren't, you've probably never seen anything like it.*

*Millions of trees, tens of thousands of power lines, thousands of utility poles, more than a thousand transmission towers collapsed under the weight of the ice. The property loss was $3 billion. Four million homes lost power. Twenty-five people lost their lives.*

*From Sherbrooke, Quebec south as far as the Massachusetts line, whole armies of linemen battled the storm that first night, climbing poles, trimming branches, chain-sawing trees off downed power lines. "It was like being in a war," one of them told me, with branches "as big as whole trees coming down around you—boom! boom! boom! And trying to stay safe was the main job you had."*

*That man, Tom Connary, then a 52-year-old, 26-year veteran lineman, did stay safe through the storm. His partner didn't. This is the story of these two men, of what happened to them that night in the woods of Sunapee NH, and of an ice storm so strong and terrible that "when you get it in winter, you think, 'Oh God, oh holy hell.'"*

Across most of New Hampshire, the rain began early Wednesday. It wasn't much to start with. If you were indoors and not paying attention, it's unlikely you would have heard it on the roof. There was no wind to speak of. The temperature—in the low 30s in Concord, a bit colder farther north—was mild for January, and not expected to dip. Here and there, dispiritedly, it tried to snow.

In Newport, at the Sunapee district office of the New Hampshire Electric Co-op, it had been a light day for the line crews—not a single outage district-wide. The men, for the most part, stayed indoors. Alan Noyes watched safety videos; Tom Connary did maintenance work on the trucks. A third man cleaned the chain-saws and checked the climbing belts and gaffs. By 3:30 in the afternoon, as the men logged off their shift, the rain was starting to fall hard.

"It was just kind of average," says Connary, a gray-haired, furrow-faced, fifty-two year-old lineman who has been with the company exactly half his life. "It was raining, but not all that hard. There was some ice building up—you could see that—but nothing more than happens all the time. I don't remember much about it, actually—I guess because of what happened later. But it didn't seem like that big of a deal."

The men went home. Connary fed his dogs and his sheep (he has 30 of them); then, alone at his kitchen table, ate the meat and salad his wife—who would not be home that night until nine—had cooked and left in the fridge. Noyes ate supper with his family, as he did every night of the week: his wife, Sherrie; their sixteen-year-old daughter, Aubrey; and Garrett, their thirteen-year-old son. They talked about deer season (the meat that night was venison, from Alan's first-ever buck), about Garrett's math homework, and their brand-new stove from Sears Roebuck that sat, an inch too wide for the old stove's cranny, in the middle of the kitchen floor.

The stove was the major joke of the night. Alan promised he'd take care of it that weekend. Sherrie said she hoped so—that otherwise, "we'll have to give that stove a name." Then she said she was going grocery shopping after supper. Alan said that maybe he'd come along.

Meanwhile, the rain picked up. And the temperature dropped. "Maybe two degrees" is Tom Connary's best guess. "Not so you'd even notice." But it was an important two degrees.

"Freezing rain and freezing drizzle developed over portions of New Hampshire during Wednesday, January 7, 1998," the National Weather Service would report five weeks later.

At a few minutes before 6:00 p.m., the call came to Tom from the company's Plymouth office: The ice was building up. Limbs were down, the outage calls were coming in. Tom in turn called Alan, who was helping his wife with the dishes at the time. He saw Garrett through the last of his homework, took a change of work clothes from the closet, and kissed Sherrie goodbye at the sink. The rain was coming down harder now. Both men must have known it was apt to be a long night.

"There's no way of knowing when he's going to come back," says Sherrie, a tall, pale, pretty woman with thick auburn hair and a smile that seems never to leave. "He could be gone an hour, eight hours, three days, you never know how long. You just know he's out there somewhere, climbing poles—that he's tired and wet and hungry, that he hasn't slept since the night before last. Or the night before that.

"It's never been my favorite thing in life, being the wife of a lineman. You feel like a widow sometimes."

The rain by now was a beating force: loud, heavy, and straight to the ground. It sheeted the trees, froze nearly instantly, then hardened and clung like shellac. The topmost limbs took the worst of it and were the first to go. If you stood still and listened, says Tom Connary, you could hear them cracking—"like little gunshots"—against the drumming of the rain.

At 6:30 p.m. or a little after, Tom and Alan arrived in their truck at the first major outage of the night. It was the "main-five" line off North Road in Sunapee, feeding power to parts of three towns, 800 to 900 homes in all. A branch had iced and snapped, falling across a pair of 7,200-volt lines, "cooking" them instantly and causing the fuse to blow. The lines themselves were intact.

From the ground, the two men cleared the branch with a telescoping stick—retractable fiberglass, 35 feet fully extended—then replaced the blown fuse with a new one from the truck. It was an easy job. By a little after 7:00 p.m., the power was back on.

For the next nine hours, it was more of the same. Downed lines, blown fuses, freezing rain. The two men jumped from outage to outage—one an hour, more or less. Around 10:00 p.m., the main-five blew a second time; before that, it was a tap line—feeding a handful of homes—on Sunapee's

Spring Hill Road. But they were small jobs, all of them. No trees down, only branches, no severed lines or damaged poles. All that would come later, as the rain wore on and the ice grew thicker on the trees.

Tom can't recall what they talked about in the truck between outages. "Sports and women, they're the usual topics," he says. "But I can't really say; it could have been anything at all. The one thing we must have talked about was the storm. It was building up pretty good. I probably said to him, 'This is going to be a beaut.'"

Alan was thirty-eight at the time, but looked younger. Tall, dark-haired, and lightly bearded, built like the high-school miler he'd once been, he moved quickly, joked often, and talked fast about skiing, hunting, computers, his kids. He was the sort of man who was seldom still when he could be doing and seldom indoors when he could be out. The winter before, his first year on skis, he'd been 22 days on the slopes. He was proud of that. "I'm getting pretty good," he told friends.

There had been a time, ten or 12 years before, when the two men had been close. "When he first came to the company," Tom remembers, "he was pretty much a kid. Twenty-something. I was maybe forty at the time. We were partners together for awhile—this kind of work makes you close. We used to go out drinking sometimes. We used to talk about stuff."

Over the years, they'd grown apart. Alan was assigned a new partner; there were some differences, some hurt feelings, that Tom won't talk about and calls "ancient history" today. Working this storm together, in Tom's mind at least, was a first step toward mending a rift. "I was kind of thinking we'd get to know each other again."

⚊ ⚊

As the night became early morning, the temperature continued to drop. The rain turned solid and stinging; it was sleeting now. Along the roads and rights-of-way where the power lines hung, the yellow-pine poles wore a crystal sheen. Ice-caked tree limbs bent deeper over the lines. The trees themselves—the birches especially, the least brittle of the hardwoods—bowed low under the weight.

Sometime around three in the morning, from the cell phone in the truck, Tom Connary phoned his supervisor, Dick Nelson, and woke him: The limbs were going down faster now, and they were bigger limbs. Whole trees would be next. There were too many outages. There was too much work for two men.

It was happening all over the state, all over northern New England and up into Quebec. In Plymouth, 40 miles north, the first outages weren't phoned in until late Wednesday night, four or five hours later than in Sunapee. But by 3:00 a.m. Thursday every lineman in the district was working the poles.

"I had all ten of them out there, and four [tree] trimmers," says Bob Chase, operations supervisor for New Hampshire Co-op's Plymouth district. "It was bad. Bad. There were limbs coming down all over, the ice was building up so fast. I had guys who worked 24 hours Thursday, midnight to midnight, then went home, slept eight hours, and worked 16 hours the next day. Forty hours in two days."

Brenton Fysh was one of them. He's forty-three: tall, pale, square-shouldered and serious, with receding brown hair and a handshake like a vise. He is married with three children, has been 23 years with the company, and worked 93 hours the week of the storm.

"I don't know when I've been tireder," he says. "Tired like you wouldn't believe. And the tireder you are, the scarier it gets. It's raining like that, the ice is building up, there are broken branches coming down all around, and you haven't slept in two days. That's when you've got to be careful. You get careless out there, you mess up just once, and somebody's apt to get killed."

He goes on to tell about the time, in the late 1970s, when a co-worker, working a pole next to his, accidentally dropped a live wire—which then touched the pole he was on: "I took 7,200 volts in the right hand. It went down my right arm, through my body, and out my left leg. The arm was paralyzed. The skin on my leg came off in scales. They had me in the hospital two days."

Fysh's partner (linemen nearly always work in pairs—sometimes in threes, never alone) is a short, red-haired man of thirty-one named Theron Comeau, with a slow smile, sleepy eyes, and a torso that looks built to stop a truck. He's been 12 years with the company, the last two of those with Fysh. There's a good feeling between them: an easiness, a sort of half-tender brusqueness, that might seem awkward if it were any less real.

"I worked with this guy once," Comeau says now, "just like Brent here—he took 7,200 in the hand. He quit. Got reassigned to Dispatch. He swore that wasn't the reason. But he's still there, he took a cut in pay. So you tell me . . .

"There are people who say we're overpaid. The same people, though, they wouldn't do the work themselves, not for anything. Me personally, I think it's pretty neat."

Twenty miles southeast of Plymouth, in the Meredith district, the first pole went down sometime around 4:00 a.m. It was just off Route 3, outside Laconia, on the south shore of Lake Winnipesaukee; it fell when a 60-foot, ice-weighted conifer landed diagonally across the line. It was the first of nearly 20 to fall in the district; Plymouth would lose 28. In Ossipee—the hardest hit of New Hampshire Co-op's nine districts—more than 80 poles would go down.

"When the poles start going, that's when you know it's going to be a big one," says Ron Anair, fifty-six, white-haired and soft-spoken, who was in the first hours of a 38-hour stretch when the Route 3 pole went down. He'd never seen a storm so destructive. "I've been working this job 31 years. It's the biggest I ever saw."

He is sitting with his friend and fellow lineman, John Amabile, a lean, gray, grizzled, fifty-four-year-old former Marine, across a table in the Meredith district office, three months after the storm. Amabile, though by two years the younger of the two, is the senior man in the district, with 32 years on the job. "That makes me—what are they calling me these days?—'working foreman'? The title changes every year."

Both men have lived their whole lives in Meredith. Forty years ago they were schoolmates at Interlakes High. Today they are old soldiers: leathery and full of tales. And when they talk about storms, they sound like old soldiers talking about war.

"It's the birches that'll get you," says Ron Anair. "They don't break— they just bend and bend, just hang on like there's no tomorrow. You go to cut 'em, you touch 'em the wrong way—*whang!* They snap back, blow right up in your face. You've got to go at 'em easy, you've got to cut 'em like this . . ." And he makes a motion with his arm: tentative, roundabout, his body leaning away, as though imitating a boxer in a jab and retreat.

For most of an hour, they go on like this. About hardwoods versus conifers, ice versus snow versus rain; the "two fatals" in 1970, the "bad one" in 1980, the "big one" in 1969. About bucket trucks versus pole climbing ("nowadays, you can go weeks and never climb a pole"), and how, in the old days, "before all the new [safety] rules that slow you down, a man didn't have to be sitting in a bucket to rubber-glove a line."

"All those rules—it can get ridiculous," says Ron.

"Been doing this a long time," John says. "Never been hurt yet. You've got to be careful is all. It's dangerous work."

"Never worse than this last one," says his friend.

"The worst I've ever seen," the old Marine agrees. Then he pauses and shakes his head. "I worked 116 hours that storm and I don't mind telling you, there were some of those hours I thought my time might have come."

---

By 3:00 a.m., in Sunapee, the rain had peaked. "It was driving," says Tom Connary. "Straight down. As hard as it gets. The kind of rain, when you get it in winter, you think, 'Oh God, oh holy hell . . .'"

It was sheening everything—trees, poles, fence posts, windshields, the snow. If you were awake then, and watching, the world outside your window was lustrous: a craggy, shimmering, self-reflecting nightscape of silver-blue and white.

If you were a lineman in Sunapee or almost anywhere else in the state, you saw only crashing limbs and ice-weighted birches, and branches hanging half-severed from their trunks. You saw power lines sagging, and trees half down, and heard the cracks of rending wood from every side at once. And you were a fool if you were not afraid.

"It was so bad," says Tom. "You can't imagine how bad. Big, 20-foot branches, big as whole trees, they're coming down all around you—*boom! boom! boom!* It got so, after a while, you're paying more attention just watching out for your life. Like being in a war—and trying to stay safe is the main job you have."

At a few minutes before four—Tom and Alan had worked 16 of the last 18 hours—there were reports of an outage on a main-five tap line that served a dozen or so homes in a development called Sunapee Heights. The trouble wasn't hard to find: roughly 20 feet off the road, a pair of white birches, one about 40 feet tall, the other a bit smaller, were bent— "like fish poles," Tom says—over the top of the tap line, their uppermost branches only inches from the ground.

There was no freeing the line without cutting the two trees. Alan brought the chain saw from the truck and walked through the snow to the smaller birch; Tom, from the edge of the road, aimed the light. It was wide-beamed, 25,000 candle-power, and lit an area half the size of a boxing ring as brightly as a room.

Alan sawed a notch in the smaller tree—to direct its fall away from the road—then sawed the trunk through at its base. The two sections parted. He sawed through again, a foot or two higher, then again, until the top branches rolled off the line. He moved to the second tree, notched it also, and began again to saw.

There was a loud noise, like a gun going off, and a flash of white. Then nothing. Tom held the light against the spot where his friend had been. The base of the big birch was sheared in two—its interior wood a frenzy of splinters, as though it had exploded from inside. Tom did not see Alan in the circle of light.

"It blew up," he says today. "Just blew up. From the pressure. When he went to saw it, it just blew apart like a bomb."

Alan was in the snow on his back in the darkness. The tree he'd been sawing lay across his chest. It was raining on his face. His eyes were open. He was unmarked.

"The tree, when it blew, it came out and up at him—it hit him right here." Tom touches his forehead with his fingers, which are trembling. There are tears in his eyes. "It happened so fast, I never saw it. He was there—then he was gone."

Alan spoke: "Tom, I'm hurt bad." And then: "I can't feel my arms. Are they gone? Did the saw cut off my arms?"

His arms were intact, and Tom told him so. Then he squeezed them, one at a time. Then his legs. Alan felt nothing. "I can't move," he said. "Please, Tom, get my wife."

He believed he was dying. He wanted to say goodbye.

Alan's neck was broken. His spine was severed between the fourth and fifth vertebrae. He was paralyzed from the neck down. Within a day, because his chest muscles could no longer work to clear fluid from his lungs, he would blow up like a balloon. From the head blow he had taken, his face would turn black. He would look, says Tom, "like a raccoon."

For now, he lay on his back in the rain while Tom worked to saw the tree off his chest. It took less than two minutes. Then Tom left to go to the truck to call for help. When he returned, he sat down in the snow with his friend. For ten minutes or so, until the first help arrived, the two men talked. Alan said something personal—something private, that Tom would rather not share—about what had happened between them in the past. Tom said it was forgotten. When he talks about it today, he cries.

When Sherrie Noyes saw her husband, an hour later at the hospital, he was lying on a gurney, his arms spread straight out from his sides. "He looked so strange," she says. "So helpless. Nothing moving. No part of him moving, except his mouth a little when he talked. His arms spread-eagled like that, hanging out straight from that bed."

"Pray for me, Sherrie," Alan said. "This is bad."

A day later, at a hospital in Hanover, a young doctor she hadn't seen before approached her in the hall. He didn't introduce himself. She never learned his name.

"The C-5 [vertebra] is crushed," he told her. "The C-4 is flipped over on top of the C-5. Your husband is a quadriplegic, and he will be for the rest of his life."

"Then he walked away," Sherrie remembers. "I don't know who he was, and I never saw him again. But I hate him for that. I'll hate him the rest of my life."

⏤ ⏤

The rain kept coming all day Thursday, Thursday night, then Friday morning and into Friday night. The trees fell by the tens of thousands, hundreds of thousands, in every corner of the state, all over Maine and northern Vermont, all over Quebec—"and more broken poles," says Plymouth's Bob Chase, "than in every other storm in the past 30 years combined."

Everyone marks it differently. For Chase, the supervisor, the storm was poles broken, lines down, hours worked. For others, the markers are different. To Theron Comeau, it is the memory of "a 22-foot tree, as big as the truck," cracking and falling a foot from where he stood. For Brenton Fysh, his partner, it is the vision of "this 80-foot birch, draped over a line, its top stuck in the ground like a spear."

In New London, just north of Sunapee, it got so bad by early Friday that they closed the town to traffic and called in the National Guard. "The Twilight Zone" is how one resident recalls it: "The whole town's dark, nothing's moving but soldiers and trucks, and we're out there, feeding doughnuts and soup and coffee to these guys up in their buckets who look like they haven't slept in a week."

Sometime around midday Friday, Bob Chase made the decision to give up. "It had got so you'd clear a tree off one pole, and another would come right down behind. You're working your tail off, all those hours—I personally worked 118 hours that week—and there you are at the end of it, losing all the ground you've gained.

"I started sending guys home—just telling 'em, 'Go home, get some sleep. There's no beating this storm. Nothing to do but wait it out.'"

For the next 20-odd hours, the storm held the upper hand. Then, gradually in some regions, more abruptly in others, it weakened, then broke. The Weather Bureau noted: "By Saturday morning, January 10, the precipitation had ended. . . . A weak cold front early Sunday brought drier and colder air. Fair weather continued during the day Monday, as high pressure crested over the state . . ."

One town at a time, over the next week and a half, the lights in New Hampshire came back on. It was slow work: The trees were still ice-socked, the woods were choked with fallen branches; there were rights-of-way so dense and tangled you needed a chain saw to cut your way to the lines. And it was colder than before.

But the rain had ended. The ice would grow no thicker. The skies had cleared, the moon was near full, and the wind, by early Tuesday, was blowing hard from the south. It was possible now, for the first time in days, for the men to make progress, to clear a line at ten in the morning and not see it downed again by noon. In Plymouth, Bob Chase began calling his men back in. By the morning of the 16th, nine days after the first outage, the last light in the district was back on.

For Tom Connary, in Sunapee, the events of those days are more or less like a blur. "I went back out," he says, "right after Alan got hurt. I know that may sound cold—it was the only thing I could do. I just kept seeing him lying there, all screwed up like that, in the snow, and I knew I couldn't go home. So I worked, the next three days—six in the morning till eleven at night—till I got too tired to think of anything at all."

———

Alan Noyes sits, neck-braced, in a straight-backed motorized chair in a semi-private room in the spinal-cord wing of the Boston Medical Center. It is April, three months since he lost the use of his arms and legs and trunk. He is the only patient in the room. His last roommate, he tells me, a young man paralyzed in a car crash, was discharged yesterday.

"You should see what he can do." He smiles—a normal, unstrained smile, his face and head the only normal things left. "He shaves by himself. He showers. When he came in, he was just like me."

He sits, completely erect in the chair, held up by a piece of steel and a portion of hipbone grafted to his spine. Without them, he says, "I'd just flop over like a doll." He is tall: a wasted tallness, his long legs at off-kilter angles to each other and the floor. And thin—except for his stomach, which is loose and low-slung and bloated, the stomach of an old man who drinks beer. "I call it my quad gut," he says, and smiles once more.

I ask if it's possible he will walk again. "No," he says, "I'm a quad. I'll probably always be.

"I can move my arms a little." He shows me, his elbows rising slightly, with effort, from his sides. "Enough to use this joystick here, to run the chair. And I can feel parts of myself again, so that's good. I could be on a feeding tube. I could be dead."

He says then he feels lucky "that I wasn't twenty when it happened. That'd be awful—to be twenty and have done all the things you're ever gonna do." Thirty-eight, he says, is "old enough to have got married, had a family, and raised my kids. I got to do some of the things I wanted to do with my life. Not all, but some."

He has been through living hell. So has his whole family. They are living it still.

Within days of the accident, his chest muscles collapsed—he could barely breathe. Without life support, the doctors told his wife, he was certain to die. What did she want to do? "Why don't you ask him?" was her answer, though she felt she knew what he'd say.

"He'd always told me," says Sherrie Noyes, "'if anything ever happens, I don't want to be a vegetable. Don't keep me alive with those tubes.' So I figured he'd choose to die. I was prepared for that."

"Give me the tubes," Alan told the doctors. "I'm walking out of here."

For the next nine weeks, he lay on his back under a tangle of tubes that grew over and out from him like vines. Tubes that breathed for him, ate for him, coughed for him, spat, urinated, defecated, did everything but think his thoughts. When he needed to make those known, he blinked his eyes—twice for "yes"—to letters his wife would point to on an alphabet board by his bed. ("A, B, C, D . . . It could take half an hour to finish a sentence," she says.) The first time she saw him like that—"the man I love, so helpless"—she ran from the room and cried the rest of the day.

Since then, there have been only triumphs. Small ones, all of them, but each one enormous at the time. First it was breath. ("Ten minutes off the machine, then 30, then an hour, then two, three, five. When we got to 12 hours, I knew we were there.") Then speech. ("The first time I heard him speak again, I was high for three days.") Then, from the chest up, he began to feel himself. Then to raise his arms, an inch more every day. By April, on the morning of a good day—"I get weaker in the afternoons," he says—he can almost touch his chin.

His next goal is to feed himself. Then—and this, he knows, will be a while—"to drive one of those cars they have for quads." There are no goals after that.

For Sherrie, there are nothing but goals. Every day brings a new one, or some new version of the old. To earn a living: Alan's future income is uncertain, and their needs have never been as great. To be a nurse to her husband: get him from chair to bed in the "basket transfer" ("I'm building up my back muscles"), change his diapers, turn him every three hours in his sleep, prod his sphincter with her finger so his bowels can move when they need. To be mother and father to two children. To stay strong.

So there is no lack of goals. What there isn't anymore, she says, is a future. "Oh, we had it all mapped out, we had it planned so perfectly, every little detail." And here her lip trembles, and the perpetual smile she wears seems in danger of coming undone.

"The first step was, we'd get the kids through college. Then we were going to buy our dream home, a log house with a fireplace and a mountain view. Alan was going to retire—he'd have his pension by then, and I've been saving from the start—and we were going to ski, and travel to places we'd never been, and just in general have a wonderful life.

"All that's gone. Now the only thing that's important, the only thing that means anything anymore, is just getting him home."

———

Eventually, of course, the ice melted. And after it the snow. And the days grew milder, and the men's work-weeks shorter and more routine. And the trauma counselors came and went from Alan's workplace. And in New London, the roads now cleared and the damage half-repaired, they traded survivor stories and bragged to outsiders that they had been—officially—the "epicenter" of the storm.

In Hanover, then Boston, Alan slowly won his fight to keep breathing, then to talk, then to move an arm. Sherrie cried less, began fighting with adjusters over money, and went back to selling houses. Tom Connary's hospital visits to his partner, at first weekly, became monthly; and Garrett Noyes's thirteen-year-old schoolmates stopped asking, "Is your father brain-dead?" Sherrie stopped thinking about a future. Then one day, it was spring.

And by early May, across all of New Hampshire, the lakes were blue again. And the trees green, though thinner than before. There were spikes now, everywhere you looked: stripped husks, by the thousands, where oaks and elms had stood.

And along every road, white birches bent in graceful, sometimes perfect, parabolas to the ground. If you didn't know better, you might think that God had made them that way.

# The Double Life of Laura Shaw
## *May 2000*

*This story, written nearly twenty years ago, still haunts me a little. It's about a woman I never met or saw or even spoke with, who for ten years—through grand theft, doggedness and simple self-persuasion— inhabited a fantasy more real to her than herself. For this reason, because she was only half-real to begin with, and because all the information I have of her, however reliable, is second-hand, it is sometimes hard for me to fully believe in the story I've created around her. What would she have said if she'd agreed to talk with me? Would her version of things have matched up with the version I heard from those who crossed her path? Can there be any final truth at all when so much of the story is rooted in make-believe?*

*I don't know the answers to any of this. I don't know what's become of Laura Shaw, or where she is today. The last I knew, in the spring of 2000, she was an inmate in the Federal Correctional Institute in Danbury CT, serving a 3 1/2-year sentence. From there, she might have landed almost anywhere. The bigger question, I think, would be: which Laura Shaw is she living as today? Has she made peace finally with the woman she is, the now-67 year-old former claims adjuster, mother of Mark, daughter of Nell,? Or is she still sustaining herself on her shining ten-year self-invention? Or on some other fantasy entirely?*

She lives in a rented cottage on the Massachusetts shore and drives to work each morning in an old Dodge pickup to a job in downtown Boston, where she sits all day in a cubicle the size of a toilet stall. She hates it, she says, but needs the money—about $10 an hour after taxes—and has had the job 20 years.

She is timid, awkward with strangers, and is said to walk in a slouch. One acquaintance describes her as "mousy," another as "pathetic," a third as "a loser without a life." No one who knows her, when asked, can say for sure the color of her eyes.

—~—

She is rich. A millionaire horsewoman with homes in three states. Some say she's a lottery winner. Or the daughter of a Midwest jeweler. Or a supermarket heiress from old New England money. It's hard to know which story to believe.

But the horses are real. She lives for them: saddlebreds, quarter horses, broodmares—she owns as many as 30 at a time. She bids for them at auctions, then rides them in show-rings, in black tie and tuxedo, jodhpurs, and a high silk hat. She's won ribbons and trophies. She golfs with owners and trainers. She trains three afternoons weekly in a practice ring in Massachusetts, while her mother watches in a full-length mink.

She spends money like water: horses, horse vans, a camper, a Mercedes, hotel bills, riding lessons, vet bills, trainer fees, airfares to Kentucky, Virginia, Pennsylvania—wherever there is a show—$3,500 monthly in boarding fees alone. She gives ponies to children, sponsors shows, donates trophies, buys her mother anything she wants. It's all she can do to stay within her income, which averages $400,000 a year.

—~—

In the early summer of 1994, Lillian Gilpin, who trains horses on the south shore of Massachusetts, got a call from another trainer, a New Hampshire friend named Rob Turner, about a client he had.

"There was this lady, who boarded some horses with him. And there was this one saddlebred—a three-year-old, his name was New Trial—that she wanted to show. But the lady couldn't ride, Rob told me. She couldn't ride worth a damn. He asked if I'd teach her. I said I'd give it a try." Gilpin is sitting in a small tack room alongside the barn at Rocking Horse Farm in Plympton, Massachusetts, a stable she owns and runs. She is tall, blond, and small-boned—like a jockey—compact and leathery, the sort of woman you could pretty much bet doesn't make her living behind a desk.

"So she shows up here one day—it was the beginning of summer—and says she wants to learn [to ride] by the fall. . . . Well, I put her up on a horse. And yeah, she could sit him all right, but that was just about all. Rob had it right. She couldn't ride worth a damn.

"But she was just so *determined*. So willing. And she had so many questions—'Why this?' 'Why that?' 'How do you do this?' 'How do you do that?' Plus she knew a lot. She read all the magazines, whatever there was to read. If she saw a horse walking down the street, she could tell you the sire and the dam. She just flat out *loved* horses. She ate, slept, and breathed horses. No one knew more about saddlebreds than Laura Shaw."

So they began. Every Tuesday, Thursday, and Saturday afternoon, Laura Shaw would show up for lessons at Lillian Gilpin's barn. She bought a practice horse, Against All Odds, for $4,500—"a skinny, ugly, scarred-up, eight-year-old saddlebred mare," recalls Gilpin. "But she was obliging. Laura needed that. She was no natural. She wasn't athletic, she wasn't graceful. She needed an easy horse."

The lessons went on. Through the summer, fall, and winter of 1994, then all of 1995. On the weekends Laura would drive with her mother to Rob Turner's farm in New Hampshire, where she would practice her skills on New Trial—who was gentle and obliging, as saddlebreds go, but still, remembers Gilpin, "too much horse" for Laura to handle in a show.

Over time, the two women grew close, the gritty, plain-speaking trainer with dirt under her fingernails and the shy, fervent horse lover who seemed to have no other life. But it was a closeness, says Gilpin, that had more boundaries than bonds: "I liked her. You couldn't help but like her. But she was different—there was all this stuff that didn't make sense. Here she was, with all that money, all those horses, all those gorgeous [riding] clothes—but she wasn't a bit classy. She looked rough. She had those big buck teeth of hers, she never wore makeup, she wore her hair pulled back like this. . . ."

And there were other things, she says.

"I knew she worked for an insurance company. She never talked about it or anything, but I had her number at work. And anytime I'd call, she'd always answer the same: 'Laura Shaw, Claims.' I thought that was weird. Here was this millionaire horse lady, working in a claims department.

Makes you wonder. But I try to never ask questions—not as long as they pay their bills. And she paid."

The year after they met, Laura invited Lillian to a Christmas party at her house, in Marshfield, Massachusetts, on a cul-de-sac off a thickly settled country road.

"I don't know what I expected, but not that. Here was this little cottage [in Marshfield] with these two little bedrooms. *Rented.* This little old rented cottage that was only barely big enough to walk around in. And nobody else. No friends, no neighbors. Just Rob [Turner] and his wife, me and my boyfriend, and Laura and her mom. That was it. And all we talked about, the whole night—just horses, nothing else."

Laura's mother was another matter. Nell Shaw, by all accounts, was a stylish woman—or did her best to be. Small and frail-seeming, she was in her late sixties, with gray hair, stooped shoulders, and a halting, uncertain walk. But she had a presence. She was a talker, a joiner; she liked people. She lived in the moment and was happiest when the moment was hers. She was fond of her evening cocktail. She had a taste for mink.

"A fun person," Rob Turner says of her. "A classy lady, and she liked her alcohol." His wife, Hazel, puts it differently. "She wasn't like Laura. She wore the money well."

Mother and daughter were inseparable. Whether by choice or necessity, it was never quite clear.

"Where one went, the other went," says Lillian Gilpin. "She'd come here with Laura for the lessons and just sit over there and watch. It was all they had, all they did. They'd be in New Hampshire with Rob on the weekends, then here three afternoons a week after Laura got off work. I don't think Nell cared one way or another about the horses, but it seemed like she was happy that Laura was living her dream."

By this time, the winter of 1995–96, according to the records of the American Saddlebred Registry, Laura Shaw owned 25 horses, most of them stabled at Rob Turner's barn, and had bought and sold roughly 30 more. In the small, circumscribed world of show-horse owners, she was a medium-to-major player, with one certified champion to her name— Shelby Stonewall, a once-and-future third-place finisher in the three-gaited Grand Championship at Louisville's Kentucky State Fair. Several others had won ribbons at smaller events—the Eastern States Exposition, the Devon Horse Show, the Syracuse International, Virginia's Bonnie Blue—but nearly always, as with Shelby, with Rob Turner at the reins.

Laura wanted her own horse. Her own honors. More than anything else she had ever wanted—and there is no one who knows her who doesn't say the same—she wanted to ride in a big-event show-ring, on the back of a three-gaited champion, and drink in the cheers of a packed-full arena when the judges named her the best.

It's impossible to know where she came by her dream. She said nothing of its origins to anyone she knew. Even those closest to her in the horse business—Turner, Gilpin, a magazine photographer named Maureen Jenner, and two or three more—knew only that she had been born somewhere in Kentucky, had a grown son by a man she never mentioned, a day job in a Boston insurance firm, and a mother who almost never left her side. And that she was rich. And that to bring up any subject more personal than horses was, as Lillian Gilpin puts it, "to get this big, dead stare."

But maybe—and it is only one theory—maybe it had nothing to do with horses at all: "Laura Shaw is a very sad person," says Bridget Parker, a Kentucky trainer who knows her, knows Rob Turner, and sold her at least one horse. "There's no question she loved the horses. But she loved the attention more. . . . She's the sort of person, well, it could have been anything: dogs, [antique] dolls, just about anything at all. She's a sad, needy person. If someone pays her the attention, makes her feel important—that's all that has ever mattered to her."

When she wasn't working, or taking lessons, or in New Hampshire with her horses (she had rented a small place near Rob Turner's farm), she was coming or going from shows. Kentucky, Virginia, Pennsylvania, Maine, Massachusetts, New York. Sometimes she drove and stayed in a camper; other times she flew and lived in hotels. It's hard to imagine how she managed it. When someone would ask how she balanced her job with travel, she would answer only that she "planned out the year in advance."

Nearly always, her mother was with her. And so was Rob Turner, whose job it was to stable and care for the horses, then to show them in the evening or afternoon events. If it was Kentucky, it might be the state fairgrounds auditorium or Lexington's Big Red Mile; at the smaller shows, there would be tents pitched around show-rings, with the judges at long ringside tables and the audience in sun hats, bright jackets, and dresses behind them in the stands. The prize money was a pittance: $50 or $60 for a small-event win, a few thousand for a grand championship—but it was never, even remotely, the point.

A top-level saddlebred horse show is as arcane, as regimented, yet as honestly elegant, as any spectacle in sports. To the first-timer, it would seem foppish, even comic, and utterly beyond understanding: a tentful of overdressed, over-serious people sitting around watching horses doing double-jointed things with their legs. To the true saddlebred lover, a three-gaited champion, in seamless transition from walk to trot to canter—head high, left foreleg raised and stretched impossibly, bent downward at the joint as though there were elastic in there, its rider erect and unmoving, in perfect fusion with her mount—is no less sublime than ballet.

Somewhere, somehow, Laura Shaw had come to this vision of things. Perhaps it was the horse magazines she pored over or that she'd been born in Kentucky and was seeking some link to her roots. It's hard to know. But one thing is clear: that perfection on horseback and the world that it opened were, to her thinking, the only truths that held weight.

In March of 1995, after only nine months of lessons, Laura rode New Trial for the first time in a show, the three-gaited Ladies' Class at the Bonnie Blue National in Virginia. Lillian Gilpin hadn't felt she was ready. "She still rode rough, she still wasn't pretty." She'd finished third in a field of six, won $25 and a yellow ribbon. It was a start.

She was easing off on the horse buying: only six horses each in 1995 and 1996. Her focus was the riding now. In November of 1995, she showed New Trial a second time: in the three-gaited Amateur Championship at the Children's Benefit in Pennsylvania. She finished second in a field of five. She was ecstatic. Her next target, she told Rob Turner, would be the three-gaited Ladies' at the Roanoke Valley in January of 1996; and a month after that, her biggest test yet: the United Professional Horsemen's Association Amateur Spring Championship in Massachusetts.

She and Rob Turner had become close. Part of it was business. Most of her horses were stabled at his barn; she accounted for close to half his income, more than $3,000 per month in boarding fees alone. And there was Shelby Stonewall, her champion gelding that Rob just kept riding to wins—28 first-place finishes in 41 events, before Shelby would be retired, at 15, in the spring of 1997. But it was more than just that.

"She needed a lot of attention," he says. "You could see she was lonely, that she needed companionship, that she had no other life. She'd be here on the weekends with her mother; then we'd do the shows. Then during the week she'd always be calling, sometimes four or five times in a day. It got kind of exhausting. But I knew she was lonely. And she spent a lot of money. And I guess I felt sorry for her."

Rob's wife, Hazel, is blunter: "She acted like Rob was her boyfriend. I think, to herself, she pretended he was."

— ⁓ —

That December was the Christmas party at the little house in Marshfield, with just the six of them. Nell was in a gay mood—looking forward, she said, to next month's trip to the Roanoke Valley; the people in Virginia were always so friendly, it was such a lovely state. Laura talked with Rob about New Trial and about Town Memories, a five-year-old mare she'd just bought. Her son, Mark, made a brief appearance but was on his way to meet someone and said he couldn't stay. It was an early night.

They shipped New Trial to Virginia a day or two ahead. Laura was nervous. She fretted about the weather, New Trial's grooming, the judges, her clothes. She had picked out her outfit: a dark-tan riding coat with a flare in the back, matching jodhpurs, a blue-on-gray tie, and a black derby hat. (It would be an afternoon event. Tuxedo and silk top hat apply only after six.)

Laura was up at dawn the morning of the show—as she was most mornings in those days—in the stall with New Trial and Shelby Stonewall, who likewise would be showing that day. (Shelby would finish first out of five entries, with Rob Turner riding, in the three-gaited open event.) She scarcely left the barns all day. Her mother, who had met some friends the night before, came and went.

She got a smooth ride from New Trial, who was at his best that day. So was Laura. She sat straight and unmoving, kept her eyes fast forward and her hands held high on the reins. "She rode pretty," as Lillian would say. There was applause. Then she waited five minutes, stared hard at the ground as there came the judges' voting, and learned that she had won.

Five weeks later, at the UPHA three-gaited Amateur Championship—her biggest show ever, with ten entries contesting—she won again. Two championship points and $100 in cash. Her first win with a champion, a pinnacle.

That was the high point. There were other shows after that and other wins—though only one more for Laura and New Trial, in November of 1996. But when you look at the record of things after that wonderful, winning winter of 1995–96, it seems as though life, for Laura, began about then to turn sour and sad.

Relations with the Turners were growing more brittle by the week.

"She was just getting too close," says Rob Turner. "Wanting too much. She knew too much about my business and too much about my life."

That's all he'll say, though Hazel Turner adds that "there was lots of fighting going on, lots of screaming, and a couple of times she threatened to leave." She remembers one incident, at a show in Massachusetts—possibly the UPHA in February, she can't recall for sure—when Laura "threw a tantrum, just threw herself on the ground."

In August of 1996, Laura took her horses and departed Rob Turner's farm—taking all except Shelby Stonewall, whom she left behind as a gift. He was 14 years old at the time.

"I considered her a friend," says Rob today. "I thought I knew her pretty well. I guess I was wrong about that."

Laura showed New Trial for the final time at the Children's Benefit in November. They won together. She sold him three months after that.

She moved her other horses to Danville, Kentucky, to the farm of an older trainer, Bill Wise, who'd earned most of his reputation a generation before with a national five-gaited champion named Sure Fire. She bought five saddlebreds under his guidance and showed at least two of them. She began spending more time in Kentucky, where she also took up golf. She and Bill Wise played often together in the dead time during shows.

"Kentucky was the big leagues," says Rob Turner. "I think she got attracted to that. I know her mother did."

Bill Wise won't talk publicly about Laura anymore. It is his wife who answers the phone. "Laura spent a lot of time in our home," she says. "We were very fond of her. I'm sorry, but that's all I have to say."

Then, in the winter of 1997, Nell Shaw was diagnosed with cancer. It spread quickly. She died, at home in Marshfield, in May of 1998. Then came the end.

⌐ ⌐

December 17, 1998, a Thursday. Laura Shaw was in her cubicle at New England Financial, in an old, marble-lobbied building in downtown Boston that its denizens call the "Burial Urn." She had come dressed for the company's Christmas party, which was to take place at the end of that day. She got a call to come to her boss's office. It's likely she knew why.

The FBI was waiting. They showed her the canceled checks: $14,239, $16,630, $25,219, made out to the phony claimants—Jeanne Davidson, James Emory, James Worth. Dozens of them. More than $4 million, they said, embezzled over nearly 11 years.

She had begun in February 1988, with a false claim of $2,493, drawn on an older policy, which was processed manually at the time. It had been easy. Her pace picked up; the checks grew larger: $39,000 by the end of 1988, an average of $400,000 a year in the ten years after that.

No one had noticed. It might have gone on forever. But in early December of 1998, she slipped: a paperwork error, a check canceled, then—unbelievably—redeposited. When it bounced—New England Financial checks do not bounce—the FBI was called in.

By that time, her mother was dead, relations with the Turners had ended, New Trial was gone, the stream of checks had slowed, and then the dumbest of dumb mistakes. It's tempting to believe that Laura Shaw just wanted it over, that the deception had grown too heavy too carry, that ten years of two lives in the end just wore her out.

Briefly she denied it. Then she confessed. Those who questioned her reported that she seemed relieved.

"Around the horse industry, I guess I was just—I was—I felt like a human being," she told the sentencing judge in federal courts in Boston in September of 1999. "I was accepted . . . just an inward feeling of . . . just peace. I mean, there's . . . I guess you have to be a horse person to understand, and it's five o'clock in the morning and you're out there . . .

"I love horses. They were living things. They were my total responsibility. I couldn't just walk away."

Her lawyer, federal public defender Stephanie A. Jirard, appealed to the judge for a brief sentence. She spoke of a "significantly reduced mental capacity" that was the result of the "alternatively symbiotic and parasitic relationship" between Laura and her mother. She asked for clemency in view of Laura's "exceptional degree of responsibility in confessing to her crime."

Judge William G. Young would have none of it. This was "typical, garden-variety embezzlement," he said, then sentenced her to 3 1/2years.

"I did it," Laura told an AP reporter before her sentencing last September. "I'll pay the price. The old life is finished now. The horses are all gone." It was, outside of her courtroom statement, the only time she has ever spoken publicly about any aspect of her crime.

— ◆ —

Laura Shaw today is an inmate in the Federal Correctional Institute in Danbury, Connecticut. Through her lawyer and later through prison officials, she has declined all requests for interviews and has reportedly asked those who know her to do the same. Most of them have complied; it's not hard to see why. The saddlebred world is small, rarefied, and in general closed to outsiders. Laura, in the eyes of most of them, is an embarrassment—who, in the words of Bridget Parker, "has made a mockery of what we do."

And so her story has holes. Unanswered questions, problems with emphasis, unaccounted-for periods of time. Because one trainer, for instance, was willing to talk and a second was not, the importance of the first may seem outsized. How it was, exactly, will probably never be explained.

Who is the real Laura Shaw? How did she come by her dream? Is her contrition genuine? What is known, beyond what has been told already—however imperfectly—is only this: Her house in Marshfield—a weathered Cape with a small, overgrown garden—is still in her name as tenant;

her son, Mark, as of last December, was living there alone with an unlisted telephone.

Her horses were signed over to New England Financial, then put up for sale through an auctioneer; most, by now, have been sold. Shelby Stonewall remains with Rob Turner. He is 18 now; his showing days are done.

The memories and judgments of others are mixed. Lillian Gilpin is happy that Laura "finally learned to ride pretty" and that she "enjoyed ten wonderful years." Rob Turner recalls her now as "a sad, lonely woman who had only horses as friends." Bridget Parker's view is simpler: "A thief is a thief. It's just a matter of what you steal."

It's hard to guess what will become of her. She is forty-eight years old. With time off for good behavior, she'll be a fifty-year-old ex-felon—broke, jobless, and largely alone in the world, the day they turn her loose.

"I've been embarrassed," she told the judge at her sentencing. "I've embarrassed my son . . . I have no retirement. I will have some kind of civil judgment against me. I will never be able to work in my profession again. . . ."

Laura Gilpin, at least, doesn't see it that way:

"She loves the horses. She's good with them, they're all she knows. She'll be shoveling shit somewhere."

*(This story was included in the collection* The Best American Sportswriting 2001.*)*

# A Voice Against Hate

## *December 2001*

*David Moats, already when I met him, was a throwback to an earlier time. A jazz-loving former Peace Corps volunteer and for thirty-six years an editor at the same small-city daily—the Rutland Herald in Vermont—he seemed to me to embody the newsman as we rarely experience him in today's rabid times: dedicated, objective, quietly but resolutely independent.*

*This was never truer than in the months between December 1999 and April 2000. With gay marriage still years in the future, three Vermont same-sex couples, all of them together for much of their lives—one of them co-parents to a child—had for two years been fighting a legal battle, first with their towns, then with the state, over their belief that "finding a mate, and getting married, is a basic human right." The Vermont Supreme Court ultimately disagreed: marriage, it said, "consists of a union between a man and a woman"—at the same time, though, ruling that a gay or lesbian couple had "the same legal status" as a married one. How to walk this tightrope, said the court, should be a task for the state legislature.*

*David Moats threw himself, and his paper, into the thick of the madness that followed. "It was the most emotional debate Vermont has even seen," The Herald's managing editor would say later—with "Take Back Vermont" signs on barns and garages from Brattleboro north to the Canadian border and anti-gay activists from as far away as Kansas picketing the capitol with their "God Hates Fags" mantra. It was among the bitterest single battles of the early culture wars.*

*This is the story of those months: of how one man's courage, restraint and plain-spoken reason ("For each of us, it is normal to be who we are") helped restore sanity to a state. And of the historic difference it made.*

On a Sunday morning in 1993 in Middlebury, Vermont, David Moats attended his first Quaker meeting. "I was curious," he says, "and it seemed like it might be kind of a peaceful thing."

There were 20 or so men and women in the room, as he remembers it, sitting in a circle, some with their eyes closed, some not. For the first several minutes, no one spoke.

"The idea was that anyone could talk, if they felt the need to speak what was in their heart, and the rest of the group would listen and share. But if they didn't, they could just keep silent. There was a very calming mood in the room."

When the silence was broken, it was by a man David had never met who looked about his own age, forty-five. A pleasant-looking, open-faced man with light curly hair, who spoke very softly at first.

"He told us, 'There's something I want to share with you. I'm gay. And I'm coming out. [My wife] and I are splitting up.'

"It was an emotional moment. Lots of tears and hugs, just total support from everyone there. It was a very moving thing."

Moats, at the time, was the new editorial-page editor at the *Rutland Herald*, a small (circulation 22,000), family-owned daily where he had already worked—as wire editor, state editor, assistant managing editor, and city editor—for nearly 11 years. The man who spoke at the meeting was Stan Baker of Ferrisburg, Vermont, a family therapist who, after a 21-year marriage, had fallen in love with another man. ("I went through college with my secret," Baker says today. "I was an athlete. I dated girls. I got married. I kept it underground.")

The two men, the journalist and the therapist, never met again. And it was not long before Moats, distracted by his newspaper job, his three children, and his own failing marriage that would end in divorce months later, stopped attending Quaker meetings.

Four years passed. Moats moved into a place of his own in Middlebury; Baker and his partner, Peter Harrigan, moved in together in Shelburne, 25 miles north. Meanwhile, by early 1996, a group that called itself Freedom to Marry, cofounded by a lesbian Middlebury lawyer, Beth Robinson, was mailing brochures and videos to civic groups and Rotary Clubs throughout the state of Vermont.

"I'm a lawyer as well as a lesbian," Robinson says today. "I care deeply about justice. And I just couldn't bear the stories I was hearing from the couples who were coming to me. Loving, committed couples, together five, ten, 25 years. And they had no rights, no status under the law. Homestead rights, medical decisions, adoption, insurance, divorce—they had no status as couples at all. It was unfair, an indignity. I wanted to see it end."

On April 25, 1997, a lesbian couple in their early fifties—Holly Puterbaugh and Lois Farnham, who had been together half their lives—appeared before the Milton town clerk to apply for a license to marry. They were denied. Seven weeks later, Baker and Harrigan were denied in Shelburne. Six days later, Nina Beck and Stacy Jolles, who shared a young son, were denied a license by the South Burlington town clerk.

In July, in Chittenden Superior Court, the three couples sued the towns and the state of Vermont, arguing—in the words of one of their lawyers—that "finding a partner, finding a mate, and getting married is a basic human right."

The court disagreed. Five months later the lawsuit was dismissed. The couples and their lawyers—Robinson among them—had the case appealed to the Vermont Supreme Court.

Five days before Christmas in 1999, the state supreme court, by a four-to-one margin, issued a ruling that would divide Vermonters almost squarely down the middle, command the attention of the nation, and usher in an era of passions unseen in the state perhaps since the Civil War.

It was rooted in a clear-cut premise—". . .marriage under our statutory scheme consists of a union between a man and a woman"—that indicated the three couples therefore had no right to the licenses they sought. On the face of it, it was an unqualified defeat. But there was a coda, which got lead billing in most of the press accounts, that said: Because "all Vermonters" are entitled to "the common benefit, protection, and security of the law," a gay or lesbian couple had the same legal status as a married one. Married but not married. "Different but equal," as the governor would later say.

As to just how to make this happen—whether to broaden the definition of marriage or create some new form of "parallel domestic partnership"—that, said the court, was a job for the state's legislative branch. It imposed no deadline, but ordered that it be done. No state legislature in the nation had ever before done such a thing.

"I look forward to Peter and me having the same kind of relationship my parents had," Stan Baker told the celebrants at the First Unitarian Universalist Church in Burlington the afternoon the court's decision was announced. "The train has left the station. There's no stopping us now."

The next day, the Tuesday before Christmas, the story went national: news accounts on the networks, the governor on CNN and NPR. Talk radio's "Dr. Laura" led her show with the story, then called on listeners to "weigh in"—and provided the governor's phone number on the air. From Kansas, members of the Westboro Baptist Church, who had come east once already to picket the statehouse with their slogans ("God Hates Fags") before being run out of town, promised to picket again.

At the state supreme court in Montpelier, where security was added the day after the ruling, a docket clerk reported to the *Rutland Herald* the general sense of some of the calls coming in: "Do you know what those people do in their bedrooms?" and, "It's Sodom and Gomorrah all over again."

Still, within a week or so, the networks and talk shows had moved on to other stories, and the Westboro Baptists, no doubt, had found other targets for their hate. For many in Vermont, though, the issue was personal. And for these people—and there were thousands—there could be no letting go.

"A lot of people in this state feel pushed around," says Yvonne Daley, who moved to Vermont 35 years ago to live on a commune and never left. For 18 years she covered the state for the *Rutland Herald;* her husband remains a sports writer there today.

"There was Act 250 that restricted land use, then Act 60—revenue sharing for education, then solid waste, and a bunch of environmental laws. After a while, I think, the people had just had enough. They felt confounded by it all. They felt they were losing control of their lives, their destinies.

"The gay rights [issue], I think, became their lightning rod, their chance to take back control."

Which goes a long way toward explaining the opposition's three-word slogan: "Take Back Vermont." Conceived and designed by a North Country farmer, Richard Lambert, it had begun showing up—on barn sides and bumper stickers, black-and-white in block-print letters—around the time the three couples' lawsuit was filed. You couldn't drive three miles on any rural road, from Bennington north to the Canadian line, without coming around a corner to find it staring at you.

—◆—

"It was a pretty incredible time," Moats says today. "The passions were high—on both sides. A lot of people were putting it on the line."

He is a short, slight man with graying, receding hair, a nearly white beard, and thin, metal-frame glasses—none of which come close to masking an essential boyishness. He smiles often, sometimes almost shyly, and speaks with a softness that seems to define him.

"There's just no way, I think, that with the courage others were showing on this, I could have kept silent on it. To do that would have been to let myself down badly, both as a person and as a journalist."

The first in his series of editorials ran in the *Herald* on December 21, 1999, the day after the supreme court's ruling. It praised both the ruling—for its "boldness and restraint"—and the chief justice, Jeffrey Amestoy, who had written for the court:

"As Amestoy understood, the United States is in the midst of 'moral flux' regarding homosexuality and gay rights. He and his court have laid down a fixed marker of high principle within that flux."

Within weeks there were hundreds of letters—from farmers, teachers, firemen, housewives, factory workers, salesmen, and store clerks, in every region of the state. Some praised the court for its wisdom and the *Herald* for its courage; others attacked the ruling—or homosexuality in general—as irreligious or unchristian. More than a few letters were unprintable. Except for these—and a handful that became outdated as the backlog grew—the *Herald* printed them all.

"Those editorials were written in the context of the most emotional debate Vermont has ever seen. There's no question about that," John Van Hoesen, the paper's managing editor at the time, would tell a reporter. "We had more letters to the editor on that topic than on any other topic [in the 24 years] I had been at the *Herald*."

Polls revealed that a majority of Vermont's voters—roughly 52 percent—disagreed with the court: Gay and lesbian couples, they told the pollsters, were not entitled to the same rights as married ones. Thirty-eight percent agreed with the court's thinking. Ten percent were not sure.

The *Herald* knew it was swimming against the tide. "[The letters] were running against us," Moats says. "Not by much, certainly; there was plenty of positive mail. But we knew there were a lot of really angry people out there."

On the afternoon of Tuesday, February 8, a week after the second of two public hearings at the statehouse in Montpelier that had drawn thousands, divided by the slogans they chanted or wore ("God made Adam and Eve, not Adam and Steve"; "Jesus Loves All People. Why Can't You?"), Moats wrote an editorial—his sixth on the subject—that asked for the anger to end. Published in the *Herald* the following day and titled "A Charitable View," it began unambiguously with a repudiation of the haters:

"Gay and lesbian Vermonters have heard a full range of denunciations in the past several weeks. It is something they have heard all their lives, beginning with common schoolyard taunts and culminating in the passionate condemnations heard at the two public hearings. . .

"These attacks are the equivalent of the fire hoses and police dogs that were turned on civil rights workers in the South in an earlier day. They are a reminder that seeking justice exacts a price."

But with that said, the message changed direction. Noting that the antigay passions of Roman Catholic Vermonters—a core group of the opposition—arose "not from bigotry, but from a specific teaching about sexuality," Moats closed his editorial with 100 words of reasoning so simple and inarguable that they must surely, for some at least, have brought a measure of light:

"It may offer some comfort to supporters of same-sex marriage to see through to the humanity of the opposition, and to recognize that the reasons for opposition are not always founded in bigotry.

"At the same time, opponents of same-sex marriage have an obligation to see through to the humanity of a vulnerable minority. Anyone tempted to condemn homosexuality as other than normal ought to consider that it is quite normal that within our population five to ten percent—the number is not important—happen to be gay or lesbian. For each of us, it is normal to be who we are."

⌐⌐

His writings are full of such quiet, homely reasoning. He is not a man—in either his person or his work—who will seek to dazzle you.

"You ever notice the way he walks? The same way he talks—slow, steady, dispassionate, that's David. We actually made a verb out of his name. So-and-so, we'd say, he 'Moats' across the room."

Yvonne Daley is laughing at her little kitchen table in Rutland on a morning in early July. She is talking about her old colleague: his evenness, his cautiousness, the slow precision of his ways.

"But I learned from the guy. About restraint, precision, the importance of doing things right. He's a very precise guy. Very thoughtful, very deliberate. The same way in his [writings]. You rarely see a lot of passion from him ... when it's an issue of fairness, or someone is truly being wronged, he can be a pretty passionate guy. But quietly so, you'd have to say."

⌐⌐

As quiet as his passions are, he seems to have come to them early. He grew up in San Mateo, California, 30 minutes south of San Francisco, and by late high school was visiting the jazz clubs there. His big brother brought home Miles Davis records; he became a fan of Duke Ellington and Dizzy Gillespie and learned early, he says, that "when you listen to jazz, you come to know the black soul."

He stood daily on hour-long vigils outside his college library — UC Santa Barbara —in protest of the Vietnam War, and marched arm in arm with thousands the day after Martin Luther King Jr. was shot. ("That struggle was so heroic," he says, "that when I hear his speeches today, they still bring tears to my eyes.")

In 1969 he joined the Peace Corps ("I'd been an English major for four years. I wanted to *do* something with my life"), and for two years he taught English to eighth-graders in a village in Afghanistan. In 1972 he went home to the San Francisco Bay area, where he worked in a bookstore, made pizza, and was briefly an editor at the *Saturday Review*.

In the bookstore one day he met Kathy, the woman who would be his wife. They fell in love, were married in 1975, and came east to Vermont. For a year he worked as a reporter at a small paper in Bradford, then for five years as editor of a weekly in Middlebury, the town where he lives today. He joined the *Herald* in 1982. He was 34 years old.

The paper, when he arrived there, was 12 years shy of its 200th anniversary. (The earliest editions, from the 1790s, remain in the basement today.) For the last 40 of those years, it had been published by one man, Robert Watson Mitchell—Mister Mitchell, to his staff—a Vermont native and son of a storekeeper, who tended the paper with a mix of love and principle that won the loyalty of everyone there. Before his death in 1993, he had written 50 years' of editorials—more then 10,000 in all, on everything from Alger Hiss and Joe McCarthy to the left-turn signal on Rutland's Main Street. But he never sought to bend the newsroom to his views.

———

In March 2000 the hate ads began. They had nothing to do with reality, but they were repulsive nonetheless. Paid for by a Rutland insurance agent who fronted a group that called itself "Who Would Have Thought, Inc.," they accused the governor—who had promised to sign the court-ordered law for same-sex couples—of promoting pedophilia. There were about a dozen of them, placed in the state's two major papers, the *Herald* and the *Burlington Free Press*.

"It was a tough decision," says John Mitchell, Robert Mitchell's oldest son, who now sits in his father's place as the *Herald*'s publisher. "They were offensive, really tasteless, and without any truth at all. So it was a close call. But I figured maybe it was better, in the end, to just put that hate out there, to let it die of its own weight."

The ads sparked an eruption of outraged letters, which Moats answered in an editorial on March 31 that could pass as a primer in civics.

"The *Herald* does not censor the political advertising it publishes. Nor does the *Herald* endorse it...

"Suppressing extreme speech only drives it underground, where it becomes more dangerous. The free expression of extreme speech is a sign that we are not afraid of democracy, that we are confident a good idea is the best corrective for a bad one.

"Another benefit ... is that it allows the public to see extremists for what they are. A person full of hate is his own worst enemy."

By early April, the Vermont legislature had approved the outlines of the bill it was soon to pass. As the outcome appeared more inevitable, the opposition's desperation seemed to grow. In Montpelier on April 6, presidential candidate Alan Keyes warned of "an effort to destroy the foundation of marriage." A Barre school-board member claimed proof of a movement to promote homosexuality in the schools.

It was clear to Moats by this time, he says, that the mission of the *Herald*'s editorial page was simply to keep the peace. "There was a lot of craziness out there. And I felt like my first job was to try to help alter the discourse in some constructive way, to help Vermont get through this without tearing itself apart."

On Sunday, April 9, in an editorial that dismissed Keyes as "a marginal character" whose "specialty is the moralistic harangue," David reminded his readers—not for the first time—that the issue before the state was not sex, but civil rights.

"Senators are now crafting their version of a bill. The sound and fury raised outside their chamber by zealots and demagogues should not distract them from the serious civil rights issue before them...

"The senators can rest assured that policing the intimate relations of Vermonters is far beyond the scope of their job. Rather, it is their job to ensure that state government treats all Vermonters with fairness."

For Stan Baker and others like him in the state, oppressed daily by the din of pettiness and homophobia, the compassion of Moats's messages seemed a gift.

"They were such a wonderful antidote to the barrage we were getting," Baker remembers. "All those awful angry voices, the Kansas Baptists and the others, all those people venting their hate. And then to have the largest paper in the state [the *Burlington Free Press*] just stay silent on the issue, to offer no sympathy at all. That was hurtful. Peter and I, and probably a lot of others, we just felt abandoned sometimes...

"But then to read those [*Herald*] editorials, always so even-handed, with their emphasis on 'humanity'—he was always using that word—that was such a source of comfort to us. We felt, when we read them, there was at least one voice out there that got the message, that really understood."

There were more than one. In April 2000 a letter to the *Valley News* in Lebanon, New Hampshire, from the Vermont mother of a homosexual son, took on the haters with a rawness as visceral as Moats's writings were restrained. Before its course was run, it would be reprinted in more than 20 papers and preached from pulpits as far away as South Africa.

"I'm tired of your foolish rhetoric ... your allegations that accepting homosexuality is the same thing as advocating sex with children. You are cruel and you are ignorant. You have been robbing me of the joys of motherhood ever since my children were tiny. My firstborn son started suffering at the hands of the moral little thugs from your moral, upright families from the time he was in first grade... In high school, while your children were doing what kids that age should be doing, mine labored over a suicide note, drafting and redrafting it to be sure his family knew how much he loved them...

"I don't know why my son is gay, but I do know that God didn't put him, and millions like him, on this Earth to give you someone to abuse...

"A popular theme in your letters is that our state has been infiltrated by outsiders. Both sides of my family have lived in Vermont for generations. I am heart and soul a Vermonter, so I'll thank you to stop saying you are speaking for 'true Vermonters.'"

———

On Tuesday, April 25, 2000, in accordance with the ruling four months earlier of the state supreme court, a bill creating "civil unions" for same-sex couples (and all the rights and benefits that come with marriage in the state) won final approval in the Vermont General Assembly. It was the first of its kind in the nation, and it was signed, a day later, by Governor Howard Dean.

"[I]t is in the nature of who they are that they love most deeply someone of the same sex," Moats had written three days earlier, when the outcome was no longer in doubt. "And that love, at its best and most moral, takes the shape of committed relationships, which now will receive recognition from the state."

———

Stan Baker and Peter Harrigan were united four months later—seven years after the Quaker meeting in Middlebury—in a civil ceremony at St. Paul's Episcopal Cathedral in Burlington. Both of their families were in attendance, as well as more than 200 friends.

"To me, that might have been the most important part of it, the sense of our two families joining," says Baker today. "They all understood the connection—they got it right away. That's a very powerful thing. And those words, that acknowledgment—'By the power vested in me by the state of Vermont.' Just the sense of legitimacy in that. It's something I've wanted, and dreamed of, my whole life."

Beth Robinson, the attorney, married her partner last summer. They will put their home in two names now, she says, and enjoy cheaper car insurance, and have the right to represent each other's wishes to doctors should either one get sick. But the bigger victory, she says, is less tangible.

"It's just knowing you're a family, that you're part of the broader community, acknowledged by the laws of the state. . .

"I know this one [gay] man, he went through it all—the lawsuits, the court ruling, the signing, the whole thing—and he never felt that much emotion at all. Then he saw his name [and his partner's] listed in the records, under marriages, at his town meeting this year, and he just broke down and cried."

On Friday, April 13, 2001, at about five in the afternoon, *Herald* publisher John Mitchell got a phone call at his home. The caller had phoned with a leak of the news that would be announced formally three days later: David Moats and the *Herald* had been chosen over two other finalists—the *Arizona Republic* and the *New York Times*—as winners of the Pulitzer Prize. (For their "even-handed and influential series of editorials," the prize committee would later write.)

Mitchell was still crying five minutes later when he phoned Moats at work. "I was just wishing my father could have been here. I was wishing so much he could have shared in this."

Moats's first call was to his eighty-four year-old mother in Idaho. He emailed his brothers and sisters out west and his son in Austria. He then shut the door to his office and, as he remembers, "had a few tears." Later that night he shared a bottle of champagne with a friend.

It is a month later. He is sitting in his corner office at the *Herald*—books and papers stacked every which way, ancient file cabinets, bare floor, the computer perched on a biography of Ralph Waldo Emerson, yellowed news photos on the walls—talking about how it has been since he won the Pulitzer. There have been talk-show invitations and nice emails and phone calls, and calls from reporters from all over the country who want to write about the little Vermont daily that won the Pulitzer Prize. With the $7,500 prize money, he has told one reporter, he plans to buy "a nice new bed with a nice firm mattress" and a piano to practice his jazz.

"I'm not really much good at it. I just play what I play—all your basics from Ellington, and 'Misty,' 'Lullaby of Birdland,' all that kind of stuff. And people will listen, and they'll say politely, 'Oh, that's nice.'

"But that's OK. I like the music. It opens my mind up to a whole other world."

# A Question of Life and Death
## *September 2001*

*One evening over dinner in the early summer of 2000, an old and dear friend, Christine Mitchell, then chief medical ethicist at Children's Hospital in Boston, told me of a case she'd been involved with until several months before. An infant boy, Jorge Gonzalez, had been born three months prematurely; weighing less than two pounds and with a hole in his trachea, only one kidney, a malformed spinal cord and defective heart—and the near certainty of brain damage— he had survived only three weeks. But those weeks, Christine said, had been a brutal case study in all that could go wrong when good intentions collide with the almost god-like capabilities of modern medical technology.*

*Out of that dinner came the longest, most ambitious story I would ever write for Yankee. Also one of the saddest. Jorge, from the first hours of his brief life, had been the object of what could only be called a power struggle: between the pediatric surgeon who had wanted to correct his problems, one by one ("All his anomalies were repairable—I was upbeat") and the NICU nursing staff, who were witness to the little boy's daily sufferings and viewed the proposed surgeries, as well as the surgeon, through a different lens ("He just wanted to cut and paste things'). Whip-sawed between the two were Jorge's parents, whose poor English and cultural backwardness left them all but help-less in the face of the doctor's certainty ("He just talked to me in doctor words—it was like Jorge was part of a car").*

*The same story is being repeated every day, with variations, in hospitals across the country. It begs the question: Is there a place for humanity in the face of such towering technical expertise?*

The meeting begins usually at one in the afternoon, always on the last Wednesday of the month. Attendance is not required, though that seems not to matter—the room is always full. It is a drab, medium-size conference room, with a small corner window and an oblong table at its center, at the north end of the Intensive Care Unit (ICU) at Massachusetts General Hospital in Boston—one of several hubs in what is probably the finest medical complex in the world. The nurses and doctors who attend are in their thirties and early forties, a mixed lot of men and women in green hospital scrubs, khaki and flannel, sneakers and street shoes, some in lab coats, some without. A few have come with bottles of water, others with Styrofoam cups of tea.

At one end sits the group's leader, a brown-haired woman in street clothes, a little older than the rest. In front of her on the table is a blue three-ring binder, opened to a list of names. This is known by the group as the Allen Street log—named for the morgue on Allen Street, where the bodies go when they leave.

In an average month, 15 patients will have left here for the morgue. There is almost nothing that can be said about them generally: Most, but not all, were old; they died of cancer, heart disease, renal failure, head trauma, a host of other things; some died alone or only with nurses, others with loved ones by their beds. Most went peacefully and without pain—"a good death" is what is said about those. One or two, perhaps, did not. It is for these—very literally in their memories, to create an "acoustic mirror" of what went wrong—that the Wednesday afternoon meetings are held.

They begin always the same way: with a reading by the group's leader of the list of the month's dead. She reads slowly, pausing and scanning the room between names. It is a solemn process. There is the sense, to an outsider, of being witness to something very private and profound.

The first four or five names are apt to pass without comment—sometimes a headshake, other times a smile. Then a name will be read and someone around the table will speak: "That one didn't have to happen that way."

Then will come the details. They are never the same from telling to telling, except in the broad picture they paint—of patients kept alive through massive arsenals of medical technology that defeat every effort of their organs to shut down. And though the particulars differ from Wednesday to Wednesday, over the course of any six or eight meetings you would hear all the commonest tales: of ventilators that breathe for dead lungs; vasopressor drugs, dripped through IVs, that stimulate blood pressure when there is no longer a working heart; dialysis machines that run the blood through purging filters long after the kidneys have shut down; a chemical mix known as TPN (total parenteral nutrition) that takes over the jobs of the stomach and bowel. You would hear about fingers and toes turned black from necrosis while the body still technically lived; of massive doses of numbing opiates, and of neuromuscular blockers that induce total paralysis in patients who might otherwise tug at their tubes.

You would hear nurses and residents report that they had cried at a patient's bedside; that they had gone sleepless for a night or two afterward or dreamed of the suffering for weeks. Some would tell of how they had phoned the ICU on a weekend from home to learn if a wife or doctor—on whose orders a dying patient was being maintained—was ready yet to give up the fight. At least one or two would confess that they had asked to be transferred off a case.

And, most weeks anyway, you would hear the term "flog" at least once—"That was a flog," or "That was close to being a flog," or "I wouldn't call it a flog exactly, but there's no way she should have suffered so much."

There are few ICU nurses anywhere who don't know what a flog is. Almost all of them will tell you: It is the worst thing that can happen on their watch. And not because it is cruel. It isn't cruel; cruelty implies malice, and there is none of that. A flog is awful precisely because it is born of hope, possibility, and good intentions. There can't be many things worse than to be in the business of healing and to cause, on a regular basis, unspeakable suffering to those you want only to help—and to not be able to *know* the difference, even as you insert the tube. Or worse, to know the difference (or believe that you do) and—on the orders of a spouse driven by love and blind hope, or a doctor driven by zeal—to insert the catheter that will (you are sure) add days or weeks of agony to a sufferer who will only die in the end.

It doesn't happen as often as it used to. Ten years ago, there might have been three flogs a month on the ICU at Mass. General; today, thanks in part to the Allen Street meetings, the number is down to one or two. Still, as any ICU nurse would probably tell you, there remain too many doctors who view their patients only as bodies with problems, and too many parents, sons, daughters, and spouses who can't bring themselves to let go.

"I call it the '*ER* scenario'—that's where you have a dying patient, past all hope of survival. And here comes this team of brilliant, dedicated surgeons who perform heroic measures to save the person's life. He survives—'It's a miracle.' Except in real life it doesn't happen that way."

Dr. Nedda Hobbs is a specialist in childhood developmental disabilities at Children's Hospital in Boston. Several months before I met her, she had attended the case of a badly brain-damaged infant, the child of immigrants, with little chance of survival. Several times the child's organs had shut down entirely—she "declared herself," as medical people say, which means she tried to die. Yet each time, at the urging of her parents, the doctors kept her alive, sometimes through measures Nedda Hobbs describes as "nothing short of grotesque." After 16 months, the baby died.

"It was awful, awful. A classic flog. I was shaken for weeks. And there was no reason for it, none at all. It happened because no one ever told that family what they should have told them in the first place—that it would be 'all right' to let go. To just let go. To see death as an *outcome*. As the *right* outcome. Because sometimes it is."

It was Christmas afternoon when the first contractions came. She told herself this couldn't be happening—she wasn't due for another three months. Then they got closer and more intense, and later that night there was blood in her bath. At a little before midnight she phoned her sister. By the time they reached the hospital—Brigham and Women's in Boston—she was three centimeters dilated. The baby, a boy—one pound, 13 ounces, roughly the size of a quart of milk—was delivered by C-section at 12:32 a.m.

"He cried when he was born," Marisa Morales says. She is a plump, pretty Hispanic woman in her late twenties with quick, intelligent eyes. "It was the only time I ever heard him cry. Then they took him away."

Her husband, Nestor, sits across from her in a little office with four chairs in the administration wing of Children's Hospital in Boston. It is the fall of 2000, ten months since the birth of his only child. He is thirty-two, Dominican, a mechanic in a car repair shop. His English, unlike his wife's, is tentative—except for simple sentences, he speaks mostly in the Spanish they share. She translates easily, almost unconsciously, speaking sometimes only for her husband, other times for them both. He smiles often, sometimes shyly: a small man in plain, clean clothes who seems to wish equally to please and to disappear. Except when he is speaking, his eyes rarely stop circling the room.

"Nestor, he is the oldest son, his father's favorite," Marisa is explaining. "Five sisters he has, and six brothers. And all with healthy, normal kids. And this was Nestor's first. The oldest son. His first child. Everybody was waiting for this. His mother, his brothers, everybody. And his father—his father would have had eyes only for this child."

Baby Boy Morales (his mother would later name him Jorge) was born, three months premature, with what is known medically as a tracheo-esophageal fistula: a hole in his trachea that could, if not corrected, allow food to track into his lungs. Within three hours of his birth, he was moved from Brigham and Women's to Children's Hospital—five minutes away, and by almost any standards the finest pediatric hospital anywhere—where emergency surgery, performed by Dr. Rusty Jennings, repaired the tracheal hole. The operation took six hours. Marisa, meanwhile, waited in her bed at Brigham and Women's. Her husband, not expecting to be a father for another three months, was in New York with his brother and would not reach his wife in the hospital until nearly nine that night.

At a little after seven, Dr. Jennings arrived at Marisa Morales's bedside. "The first thing he said," she remembers, "was that the operation went OK, that our baby was alive. Then he said he was going to be blunt. That was how he said it—'I'm going to be blunt.' Then he went down the list."

The list was long: the tracheal hole, a partial esophagus, a missing anus and kidney, a malformed spinal cord, and "multiple anomalies" of the heart. Being as premature as he was—though Rusty Jennings may not have said so at the time—there was a good chance that Jorge would also be brain-damaged.

"The doctor said there would need to be more work. He said he would let us know, and that he wasn't promising anything. Then he left. And I cried."

When Nestor arrived from New York two hours later, Marisa told him what she knew. Then they went together, sometime after midnight, to the ICU to see their baby.

"All those wires"—it is Nestor speaking now, the first time he has spoken English. "So many wires in him. I cry when I see them. But he has long legs. Long legs, just like me."

His smile this time is more proud than shy. Then he is quiet again, his eyes once more circling the room. Then they stop, and he bends forward in his chair, his elbows on his knees now, and lowers his head to the photo he has been holding all this time: of a dark-skinned, impossibly tiny infant with saucer eyes, head swathed in white tape, mouth and nose invisible under a breathing tube, his little arms nearly straight out from his sides, as rigid as sticks, taped tight against splints no larger than tongue depressors. Father or not, it is enough to make you want to cry.

— —

The room we sit in is a tight fit for the four of us: two desks on adjoining walls that push the sitting space toward the middle, a third wall of books with titles that blend medicine, religion, philosophy, and the law: *The Rights of Hospital Patients, The Theology of Medicine, The Measure of Moral Judgment, Selective Nontreatment of Handicapped Newborns, Mapping the Moral Do-main*. It is the office of Christine Mitchell, a slight, pretty, brown-haired woman in her late forties who, 28 years ago as a young nurse trainee in Boston, was asked by a sixteen-year-old leukemia patient named Tony, whose parents had kept him from the truth: "Wouldn't it be awful if I had something really bad like cancer?" She remembers that she "ducked the question," and went back to their talk about pizza—and that there was "something very, very wrong" about that.

"I could start IVs, I could do dressings, I could give meds. I could make a bed with the patient still in it. But I couldn't figure out the right thing to do when he asks the most important question there is."

Almost since that day, "the right thing to do" has been for her both a mission and a livelihood. A former practicing nurse, college teacher, and clinic counselor, she is today director of the Office of Ethics at Children's Hospital, a faculty member in the Division of Medical Ethics at Harvard Medical School, and a consultant on ethics at three other hospitals in the state. It is Christine who leads the monthly meetings at Mass. General devoted to the Allen Street log.

She is a single mother with two sons, ages ten and twelve. The youngest was born prematurely and spent three weeks on a ventilator in the neonatal ICU (NICU) with irregular breathing and a heartbeat that came and went. He is fine today: a bright, happy, blond-haired baseball player near the top of his class. But for her, the memory of those weeks is rekindled with every sick baby she sees. "I think consciously, nearly every day, how incredibly lucky I am."

She speaks quickly and precisely, though almost always quietly—it is hard to imagine that she has ever in her life raised her voice in real anger. She smiles often. If you met her and didn't know her profession, you might well guess correctly: that she was a therapist, a social worker, or a nurse.

"I talk to people," she says simply, and smiles again when I ask what she does in her work. "That's a lot of it, really. I talk, and do my best to listen. Sometimes people just need to hear themselves say something out loud—something they may find difficult, that they may never have said or even thought before. So I try to let them do that. And to offer my reaction."

Much of the talking and listening she does—though not all, by any means—is around the issue of death. Death as a choice. Hardest of all sometimes, she says, is getting a family to see that it is a choice at all.

"Hope is a coercive power. If there's the slimmest reed of it, the slimmest chance in the world that someone you love can survive—well, that's almost irresistible. And what doc is going to fight it? What doc is going to say to a parent, 'I'm sorry, but there's no hope for your son'? There are times, though, when there isn't any, and that's *just* what he ought to be saying."

⌣

Jorge, at ten days of life, was doing as well as anyone could expect. His tiny body was tolerating the gastrostomy tube (G-tube) to his stomach. His eyes were open and blinking, and could track and follow a finger. He could blink, grasp, kick, and breathe—at least partially—on his own.

Marisa visited every day, coming over from the maternity ward at Brigham and Women's to sit in a chair by his bed. She couldn't hold him, of course—he was far too fragile and too trussed by tubes and wires—but she stroked his cheek sometimes, and held his hand, and arranged a brown teddy bear and a photo of his half brother, Andrew, by his bed.

Nestor came less often, and had a harder time—he was unable to bring himself to touch his son, to look at him closely, or to come nearer than a few feet from his bed. Nestor's parents, once so dizzy with expectation, never visited at all. Still, for all that, it was a hopeful time.

"We met with Dr. Jennings on the fourth day," Marisa remembers. "He said it would be a long process—a lot of operations. I asked how many; he said he still didn't know. He started talking and talking. I had to tell him, 'Please, don't talk to me in doctor words.' But I was still believing, still trying my best to hope."

On January 5 the Moraleses met with a Spanish-speaking social worker, Maria Carvalho, to discuss their fears and get some guidance on how best to proceed. Her report of that meeting is contained in their record:

"Parents present as tearful, engaging, and united in their efforts... [They] expressed feeling overwhelmed with the complexity of their baby's medical issues and sometimes not understanding some aspects of the problems. Father expressed a wish to not have his baby be experimented on, as he had heard out in the community that there is a lot done here that is of an experimental nature..."

A week after New Year's came a new problem: An ultrasound revealed cranial bleeding and a small blood clot creating pressure on Jorge's brain. The fluid could be drained, in the short term, with spinal taps—which would be needed at least daily—though ultimately a tube (or "shunt") would have to be implanted in the brain to relieve the pressure. This could only be accomplished through the drilling of a hole.

The condition with which Jorge had been born is known medically as VACTERL syndrome (an acronym for seven body parts and systems, any or all of which may be affected: vertebrae, anus, cardiac system, trachea, esophagus, renal system, and limbs. Of the seven, only Jorge's limbs were problem-free). At least five separate surgeries, and as many as eight or nine, all of them complex and many of them risky, would be required to correct the problems—if full correction were even possible. And this did not address the higher-than-average risks of impaired vision, cerebral palsy, and brain damage that come with extreme prematurity. Nor, of course, the blood clot.

Most of this, at least in general terms, Marisa by now understood. Nestor understood less—partly because he was around less, partly because Marisa, out of deference to his deepening despair, didn't tell him.

"I knew right at first he would never play baseball," Nestor says now through his wife. His hands still grip the photo; he is shaking his head, and looks as if he could cry. "So he will never play baseball—and that's OK, that's OK. . .

"But then it is worse. The doctor, at first he says it's only one operation—then two, then four, then six. This one here will be slicing him there, this one here, this one there—and then [maybe] he's not even OK at the end. And I think, 'Will he walk? Will he *know his brother?* Will he know *me?*' My head was so full. I couldn't listen anymore. I didn't want to know."

Marisa consulted with a nurse named Cheryl in the NICU ("She explained it all so clearly; she didn't talk in doctor words"), then gave her permission for the shunt to be inserted to drain the blood from Jorge's brain. She told her husband of her decision (omitting the detail about the drilling); he said again that he felt Dr. Jennings was looking only to "experiment" on Jorge, that his son was "not a person" to him. He refused to give his OK.

On the afternoon of January 10, a Monday, both parents met with Christine. Marisa by this time was again undecided on the shunt surgery; Nestor remained opposed. Jorge, now 15 days old, was getting two spinal taps daily to relieve the pressure on his brain, and was "requiring a significant amount of ventilatory support." Marisa continued to visit every day—most recently with her nine-year-old son, Andrew, who had never met his little brother before ("It was hard for him. He just kept asking, 'Why isn't he coming home?'"). Nestor, at this point, had not seen his son in a week.

"I met with Mom and Dad this afternoon at their request," Christine wrote in her notes of that meeting. "They wanted to express their continued concern that Jorge not be put through multiple procedures for a long time if he is going to be unable to survive into adulthood or be severely retarded and handicapped... They talked with Dr. Jennings and are planning with him to wait and see how Jorge does over the next few days."

⌒⌒

Dr. Rusty Jennings is early middle-aged, fit-looking, and sandy-haired with quick-moving, intelligent eyes and a manner that falls somewhere between indifferent and brusque. Before the week is out, I will hear his skills as a surgeon described variously as "formidable," "brilliant," and "cutting-edge." On the flip side of all these descriptions will come their qualifiers: that he is "blunt," "insensitive," "controversial," or "driven." He seems clearly aware of all these depictions, and equally at home with each.

Christine has introduced us, with the smiling assurance that "Rusty won't mince words with you." His return smile is quick and thin, but not without warmth. "Right," he says. "You can pretty much count on my candor."

He knows what I've come to talk about. Also that I'm a layman. He is patient but terse, and utterly definite in every point he makes. It is plain that he is used to being deferred to, also that there is little doubt that the deference is deserved.

He begins with the briefest sort of summary: Jorge's age and birth weight, his partial esophagus, imperforate anus, missing kidney, "head-bleed," and heart anomalies. He lists the surgeries that would be needed to correct each, counting them off, one by one, on the fingers of his right hand. He stops at five. Then he cites what he calls "the other risks"—cerebral palsy, impaired vision, brain damage, death. He says he would begin with the stomach and anus ("the gut problems"), and deal with the heart later on. Any possible "neuro problems"—he is not a neurosurgeon—would be corrected as they arose. ("The brain was the big issue," he says, "the only life-and-death issue there was.") Then he leans back in his chair and opens the palms of both hands.

"All the anomalies were repairable," he says. "Every one. I was upbeat. That was my view—that he'd be a pretty good kid, that he could be normal by the time he was five."

I ask if he had put it to Jorge's parents that way.

"No. I don't try to persuade. A doctor can convince a family to do *anything*—that's a lot of power to have. I don't take advantage of that. My job is to make sure the family gets it. That's it. Then it's for them to decide."

—•—

Connie Clauson, at the time of Jorge's crisis, was a nurse in the NICU at Children's Hospital, a job she had held for the previous six years. She is tall and thin, in her mid-thirties probably, with dark-blond hair and piercing gray-blue eyes. The morning Jorge was admitted to Children's from Brigham and Women's, on the day after Christmas, she was the nurse responsible for his care. From the first minute she saw him, she says, she felt that his chances were probably slim.

"If he'd been a regular 26-week preemie—that's tough *enough,* the youngest they've ever saved was 24 weeks—or a full-term baby with the same problems, maybe then he had a chance. But all that in one child, all those problems—it was just too much, I thought. . . He was a sweet baby, though. Very easy, right from the day he came in, an active little preemie. He'd grab hold of your finger, kick out at you with those tiny little feet. . ."

Over the weeks that Jorge was with her, she came to know the Moraleses. She tells of the night Marisa phoned her, a day or two after her baby was born, to let her know that she'd decided on a name ("She said she'd just been lying awake thinking, and that she thought 'Jorge' was perfect for him, and that she wanted us to know right away"); of how "terribly hard" the visits seemed on Nestor; the awkwardness of Andrew posing for pictures by his baby brother's side; the relatives and girlfriends Marisa brought along to support her, the stuffed animals and tiny outfits that piled up by Jorge's bed.

"She sat there every day in that chair. She didn't cry much—there were tears, but she didn't cry. She was quiet. Very brave, very serious, just focused on her son. For all the terrible problems he had, I could see that he was a person to her."

At the mention of Rusty Jennings, all trace of expression seems to leave her face at once.

"He wanted to cut and paste things," she says when I ask. "That's how he saw Jorge—as a puzzle he wanted to put together."

It has been nine months, and still the feelings are acute.

"He didn't see the big picture. He didn't see that that mother needed him to recognize her, to *communicate* with her, to try to understand the problems they faced as a family. All he cared about was *persuading* her—'You should let me do this,' he'd say. 'He'll be OK if you'll let me do that. . .'"

~∙~

No one I spoke with can remember for sure when or how exactly it was first put into words. Very possibly in the NICU, in an exchange with Connie or Cheryl during one of Marisa's daily vigils there; or perhaps with Christine, or the Spanish-speaking social worker, or between Marisa and Nestor themselves. However the words were first spoken, they probably came sometime just after the finding of the head-bleed, sometime around the start of the second week of the month.

"The first time you hear yourself say it, that can be an awfully big moment," says Christine. "It means it's *thinkable*—that's the next step to being doable, which is the next step to being done. When you're talking about your child's life ending, that's a terrifying slope to start down."

Marisa had withdrawn her permission for the shunt operation, though as late as mid-January—a week after the head-bleed was found—she had still not closed the door. The surgery remained scheduled; an operating room was booked for the afternoon of January 14.

Things were going badly between the Moraleses and Dr. Jennings. The family's confusion was growing daily; their trust had shifted toward Connie and Cheryl and other members of the staff.

"Everybody understood our side except *him*," Marisa says now. The memory of it, nine months later, is enough to cause her voice to shake. "With him, it was always just, 'We can fix this' and 'We can fix that.' It was like Jorge was part of a *car*."

"They asked me things and I *told* them, that's all. I was doing the best I could for the kid—I just thought I could have done more. This is a great hospital. We can do anything we *want* in a hospital like this. And he's not bad; he's not bad. He's breathing on his own [on the ventilator], he's active, he's looking around. . ." Rusty Jennings is more frustrated than bitter. It is a frustration aimed not at the Moraleses, but at those in whom they placed their trust.

"The NICU people [the nurses and neonatal staff]—they didn't *get* it. They didn't get the distinction between the surgeries—the surgical anomalies—and the problems with the brain. They didn't get that the *brain* was the big issue, the only real life-and-death issue involved. . .

"But *they're* the ones with the biggest input on the parents. That's never seemed quite right to me."

Connie Clauson, for her part, won't get into the issue of brain versus body, shunt or no shunt, or who is right or wrong. All she'll say—again—when Rusty's charges are quoted back to her, is: "He doesn't always see the big picture," and, "I'm not sure he understands that life at all costs is not always a good thing."

She is choosing her words more carefully now than before. It also seems clear that her reactions are genuinely mixed. "Rusty Jennings is a formidable surgeon. I've seen him save kids I never thought could live." She adds that she would at least "strongly consider" placing her own seriously ill child, if she had one, in his care.

Christine adds her voice to Connie's on this score—though her emphasis has less to do with his skills. "He's a guy who thinks and frets, and lies awake at night, and worries and worries, just like a parent would, about a sick child. That's what you *want* in a doctor. That's what you hope to get."

On January 13, a Thursday, still unable to persuade Marisa to authorize the shunt surgery, Rusty phoned Christine to ask that a team from the hospital's Office of Ethics hear the case.

"I'm sure he thought they'd come down on his side, that they'd convince her to let [the surgery] go ahead," says Connie Clauson. "There's no doubt at all in my mind."

———

"As a hospital ethicist, a large part of my job is helping staff and families distinguish between sustaining life and prolonging death," Christine wrote recently in a column published in Newsweek ("When Living Is a Fate Worse Than Death," August 28, 2000). After making her case—for "the dignified death of a child held by parents who accept their child's dying," as opposed to the death that "occurs amid technologically desperate measures and professional strangers"—she finished with this thought:

"Sooner or later, every person will die. I wish, and the hospital staff I work with wishes, almost beyond telling, that people could know what they are asking for when they ask that 'everything' be done.'"

Technology is at the root of it. The technology, unthinkable 20 years ago, that can do the work of almost any organ system, that can keep almost anyone at least technically alive—although usually, at some point, there is pain. For this there are more drugs—which reduce consciousness still further, efface personhood, demean aliveness to a series of blips on a screen.

In the old days, before all these heroics were possible, it was more or less a given that you did what you could to save a life.

"You tried everything; you didn't question," Christine says. "You had the best, the brightest people, 15 people around a patient's bed, inserting artery lines, slopping on goop, pushing on the chest, shocking the heart, yelling *All Clear! All Clear!*' That was a good death. It was good because everything you could do was being done . . . except there was no one holding that patient's hand. There was no one wiping his brow."

Somewhere along the line—around the time of Karen Ann Quinlan and her endless, media-attended, living-death coma in the late 1970s—the thinking began to change. Then in 1982 came the first "Baby Doe" case, in which the parents of a Down's syndrome infant refused permission for life-saving surgery. A second, similar case made the news—and the courts—a year later. The results of the two were different, and vastly complex, but the larger effect was clear: The issue of medical heroics was in the news to stay.

At Children's Hospital, the first ethics committee, made up of 12 members including Christine, was formed in 1984. Its first case involved a four-month-old baby born with a condition much like Jorge's; his parents, after four surgeries, had refused permission for a fifth ("Plea: Let Baby Die in Peace," read the headline in *USA Today*). The hospital threatened a court order. The parents relented, and the surgery went ahead. Six weeks later, the baby died.

"You make the wrong call sometimes," says Christine. "This isn't a hard science. You can read all the books in the world, you can look at a case from every angle there is—you're going to make the wrong judgment sometimes."

I ask if she can name one wrong judgment that stands out in her mind, that she would take back if she could. She doesn't even pause. It was a recent case, she says, in which the parents of a brain-devastated infant wanted to withhold the child's feeding tube and let her die. The ethics team advised against it; the feeding was allowed to go on. The child is alive today—two years old, in an adult nursing home (her home state has no facilities for children), unable to do much more than suck and pull away from pain.

"I think of that baby all the time. It haunts me. We condemned her to a lifetime of misery. But we couldn't starve her, either."

—◦—

Once every month, the full complement of the Children's Hospital Ethics Committee (there are now more than 20 members, including nurses, surgeons, an anesthesiologist, a psychiatrist, a Harvard Divinity School student, a social worker, a minister, and at least one parent who has lost a child) meets around a large table in a conference room on the hospital's first floor. The idea is to talk about cases, many by then already resolved, that may have raised issues at the time. The hope is to gain understanding and spare future suffering, indecision, and dispute. The mood in the room, in general, is one of collegial gravity.

On the afternoon I attended, four cases were discussed. One involved a set of conjoined twins who shared a single heart, and the ethical issues surrounding the surgery to separate them—which would result in the certain death of one twin. ("A planned intraoperative death is a very rare exception to the usual commitment of doctors and nurses not to—above all—harm patients," Christine had written to the medical staff at the time.) A second discussion surrounded the case of a two-year-old named Marybeth who had been admitted with an inoperable brain tumor that was causing massive headaches. The child was certain to die; the issue was just how much morphine to allow her—enough only to lessen her pain, or enough to sedate her completely, as her parents wished, and perhaps risk hastening her death. The case had caused concern among the medical staff, who had called for a consult with an ethics team; one resident in particular had excused himself from Marybeth's care, "rather than be in a position of ordering what he believed to be unnecessarily large doses of MSO4 . . ."

The discussion in the room that afternoon, which lasted a bit less than 90 minutes and was moderated by Christine, was brisk, choppy, informal, intelligent, 100 percent engaged—and driven, it seemed to me, by nothing so much as the most basic sort of compassion ("What is most important to Marybeth and her family? More time alive? Freedom from pain? Dying while asleep? Being conscious at the end? . . . Who should determine the quality of a child's experience at the end of life?"). At one point as I sat there, I was struck by this thought: Never before in my life had I been witness to such a thing—a roomful of men and women who scarcely knew each other, sitting in judgment on the most private, ultimate moments of particular children and families almost none of them would ever see. A remarkable thing. But the twin who had been separated from her sibling at three months now was thriving, and Marybeth had died in the end without pain.

—◦—

I had asked Christine weeks before, at the start of our time together, if there were ever any true "winners" in the ethics process—if there were ever patients for whom "a good death" was not the best that could be hoped for; if any of them ever survived as sentient people, if "a good *life*" was ever the outcome of things.

Yes, she said, there were some. And she told me about Billy. And I said at the time that it didn't sound like winning to me.

She asked if I'd like to meet him. I said I would, and she promised to try to arrange it. But then other things got in the way, and it was nearly November—a month after the ethics committee meeting, two weeks after my time with Nestor, Marisa, Dr. Jennings, and the rest—by the time we made the trip.

Billy lives in a state hospital, the Hogan Regional Center on Massachusetts' North Shore. Christine, at the time we drove out together to see him, had just come back from a weekend road trip with her boys. We talked for awhile about the trials of traveling with children, about her 12-year-old's passion for Pop Warner football and all the miles she was logging on her Toyota 4-Runner to get him from game to game, then finally about how she managed, with all the sadness and urgency around her, to be a mother at all. That was when she told me about how she'd almost lost her youngest; and about Tony, the boy with leukemia; and a "beautiful teenager named Carrie" dying of a brain tumor, who, with the help of her mother and nurses, had picked out a funeral dress ("as if it were a dress for her prom"); and about how "incredibly lucky" she felt.

It was four in the afternoon when we arrived on Billy's ward. He was clapping when we met him—in "the best mood of the day," one of the aides said: His mother was there for a visit, and it was almost suppertime. He was wearing a green sweatshirt over baggy blue pants, and bottle-thick, shatterproof glasses. His mouth hung open as his tongue explored his lips and chin.

When his mother said at one point that she would take him for a walk later, his clapping grew more frenzied, and he half-ran, half-lurched from the room; when he returned he was dragging a dark blue, knee-length New England Patriots parka. His mother laughed and gave him a long hug, then said, "After supper, Billy. Not now," and he dropped the parka to the floor and lurched toward the table where an aide was laying out plates of food.

Billy is 34 years old. Mentally he is around two. For the past ten years he has lived at the Hogan Center on a ward with other patients of both sexes and roughly equal skills. Every weekday morning at nine he is taken next door for his day program: simple puzzles, a "cooking class," rearranging food containers in the fridge. At three he returns to the ward, where, until supper, he watches food programs on TV—food, and anything to do with food, is Billy's passion in life. On weekends there are field trips to Dairy Queen, McDonald's, or a local petting zoo; at Halloween the pumpkin carving is a daylong affair. Every Thanksgiving and Christmas, and sometimes on warm-weather Sundays, his mother, who loves him so nakedly she is almost never not smiling when he is in the room, arrives early to take him home.

Billy, when he is eating, sometimes breathes when he should swallow—there is always the danger that some food will lodge in his lungs. This has happened several times. Two years before our visit, at least twice in the same year, he was admitted to the hospital with aspiration pneumonia; there were several bouts of high fever, and always the risk that he could choke to death. The hospital, after several bad scares, insisted that Billy be fitted surgically with a G-tube, to be secured by a Velcro-fastened belt. This would carry the food straight to his stomach, eliminate all sensations of eating, and mean the end of most of what he loves best: mealtime gatherings, the cooking class, the food rearranging, the afternoon shows on TV.

His mother revolted.

"They're only *doctors*, I've been his mother for 34 years. I *know* him—he loves his food; he loves his eating. They're all that make him happy. How could they want to take that away from him?"

The Hogan Center contacted a specialist at Children's Hospital, who in turn requested an ethics consult. Three members of the ethics committee—including Christine—came out to meet with Billy, then with Billy's family and the staff. For most of an afternoon, they sat around a table: Billy's parents, the three-person ethics staff, the Hogan Center's medical director, facilities director, and mental retardation specialist, two nurses, a nurse practitioner, a licensed social worker, and an occupational therapist. They talked about Billy's workshops and field trips, his swallowing problem, his love of food and eating, the recurring pneumonia and choking risks, and what a G-tube would mean to his life.

"I don't know how many years in combined education we had sitting around that table"—remembers Carol Powers, one of the ethics team who was at the meeting that day—"trying to figure out just exactly what was best for this person who couldn't speak for himself. A lot of years, a lot of opinions, everybody going back and forth, all so analytically, about someone who is [his parents'] heart and soul. They *love* this person, for God's sake..."

The ethics team wrote its opinion. It concluded this way: "In comparing the benefits and burdens, we do not see sufficient and compelling reasons to override the judgment of Billy's parents that he would not want to have a G-tube inserted."

Billy today continues to enjoy his cooking classes and TV programs, as well as his chocolate ice cream, O'Doul's nonalcoholic beer, and trips to Dairy Queen. There has been only one recent bout of pneumonia and no other serious problems, although—as Hogan Center medical director Rebekka Taratuta is careful to point out—his fatal choking remains "a possibility at any given meal." The biggest problem they've had with him came when he managed to decipher the numbers and buttons it took to run the hospital elevator—he was riding up, down, and back up again the night they found him, "with this big old grin on his face" and several other patients in tow. The maintenance staff had to reprogram the elevator. The aides all call him "the mayor." The medical director, notwithstanding her worries, concedes that he's "a pretty happy guy."

The last time I saw him, on my way out the door, he was trying to wave, clap, and chew at the same time. His mother was with him. He had his Patriots parka on. They were about to take their walk.

---

On the afternoon of Friday, January 14, three members of the ethics staff—Christine, Dr. Walter Robinson, and Charlotte Harrison, a student at Harvard's Divinity School and the School of Public Health—met with Nestor and Marisa Morales to help decide what was best for their son. Also at the meeting, which took place in a small conference room just off the NICU, were Connie Clauson, Dr. Rusty Jennings, a Spanish-English translator, a hospital social worker, and several other members of the medical and nursing staff—roughly 15 people in all. The room was crowded, with only a small table at its center; several of those present had to stand.

Rusty, who had requested the meeting, was the first to make his case. He cited Jorge's problems, argued once again that the brain-bleed was the only real "life-death issue," and that if a shunt could be inserted to drain it, the "various other anomalies" could be corrected surgically. His delivery was efficient, though often too rapid for the translator to keep pace. Christine, more than once, interrupted to ask that he slow down.

As he was speaking, the nurse standing closest to the front of the room listed Jorge's problems in marker on a white board—brain, trachea, esophagus, heart, stomach, kidney, intestines, anus, prematurity. The total came to nine.

Then the talking began. Rusty and a second surgeon talked in terms of success rates; they argued for each surgery as a separate, high-percentage risk. The nursing staff, like Connie, stayed mostly with the issue of suffering; they spoke of the surgeries as a collective, sapping siege.

Marisa and Nestor were mostly silent—"listening, very thoughtful," Walter Robinson remembers today. Nestor, at one point, asked Rusty Jennings, "What would you do if Jorge were your son?" Rusty seemed uncomfortable with the question, and declined to answer it.

It was over in a little more than 90 minutes. The Moraleses asked then for a place they could be alone. They returned a few minutes later, and asked to meet with the ethics staff. They had made their decision, they told them. There would be no further surgeries.

Christine hand-wrote the opinion at three that afternoon. It began with a brief listing of Jorge's many problems, went on to acknowledge the uncertainty of any benefit coming from "multiple invasive procedures over many months/years," then concluded this way:

"The ethics consult team advises that the parents' decision about what is best for their child should prevail ... [T]hey do not want to consent to the upcoming surgery to insert a shunt ... [They plan to] prepare for withdrawing ventilatory support..."

"Yeah, I was upset. You could say I was upset. Here was this preemie with a grade-three hemorrhage in a modern hospital with the best technology in the world. You *never* withdraw support of a child with an isolated hemorrhage like that. Never."

The case still rankles Rusty Jennings. He seems somehow to have taken it personally, though he would probably say he does not. What does seem clear, though, is that his frustration goes past simple medical zealousness—he truly believes that Jorge was savable; he truly believes Jorge could have had a life.

"Listen, I grew up on a farm. I know something about death and dying. There are times it has to happen, but this just wasn't one. There were things that could have been done [to save him]. But they had made their decision—that this kid isn't going to live."

He says he understands that there were cultural differences, that "there's no way I could understand that mom's situation in life." Still, he says, the decision that was made on Jorge "fell very close to the line. . .

"They had to give a lot of morphine. I've seen those deaths before—you have nurses and doctors in tears. It's pretty awful. I try hard not to be there."

I asked Connie Clauson, who, as an NICU nurse, has been witness to scores of ventilator withdrawals (more than half of all deaths on the NICU occur this way), if Rusty's depiction was fair. My impression was—mostly from other things she told me—that she probably felt it was not. But she was careful with her words.

"Rusty has a difficult time with kids dying. He never wants to let go. He'd say I'm being touchy-feely to say this—but he'd still be coding a baby when what that baby needs most is to be held."

On the morning of Saturday, January 15, the day after the decision, while Christine drove north to New Hampshire for a ski trip with her boys, Marisa went alone to the hospital to see her son. Some of the tape and IV tubing had been removed from his head and body, allowing her, for the first time—it was a day before his three-week birthday—to hold him in her arms. She rocked him, and told him she would miss him, and that she loved him, and that that was why she and his father had made the decision they had. When she could think of nothing more to tell him, she sang him the Alvin and the Chipmunks song.

"When I first saw him that day, I felt awful. I felt I was betraying him. Then I looked in his eyes and saw the pain, and I knew that I wanted that gone."

"The strength she showed," says Connie. "The strength to make a decision like that—the most loving, unselfish decision a parent could make for a child. To go home at night and say to yourself, 'Tomorrow I'm going to do it. Tomorrow I'm going to let my child go.'"

She came again on Sunday, this time with a bassinet and heater, and a toothbrush to wash what there was of his hair. An aunt and girlfriend were with her. One of the nurses, Ann, was joking and making faces as they took turns giving him his bath. He wriggled when he felt the toothbrush ("He didn't like that at all," says Marisa), and everybody laughed.

"Part of what we try to do," Connie says, "is to give a family some memories of a child, to help create some history for them to take away. Because it's different from when Grandpa comes into the hospital with cancer. Everyone knows he's dying, and they all start telling stories, remembering things—'Remember the time he did this? Remember how funny that was?'

"But a baby has no history. So our job is to help make one—'Look at his little hands; look how he sucks his thumb.' We try to make that happen for them, so they'll have it when he's gone. We take pictures, make memory boxes, take impressions of his little feet, or samples of his hair. We try to make the child a person, someone they'll remember in small, specific ways."

———

Early Tuesday afternoon Nestor arrived alone at the hospital for a last visit with his son. All he will say about it is that it was "very, very hard" for him, and that he didn't stay long. His head is down; his hands are gripping his knees. For the nearly two hours we have been in Christine's office, he has never seemed closer to losing his control.

Marisa arrived later, with her sisters. A nurse, Cheryl, was singing to Jorge, who was very still and calm ("He looked fine," Marisa says) in tiny green pajamas and a knitted wool hat. The sisters held him first, each briefly, then gave him to his mother, who sat with him in a rocking chair and rocked him in her arms. A small comfort dose of morphine—up to one-tenth of a milligram per kilo of body weight—had been given already by IV.

At 6:00 p.m. they removed the ventilator. For the next two hours Marisa rocked him. There were some small, short gasps near the end ("But no pain really," says Christine. "The $CO_2$ in his brain was telling him not to breathe"), and then he fell asleep. Around 7:30 Cheryl told Marisa, "He's almost gone." At 8:05 p.m. Jorge's heart stopped.

"I held him after that just a little while longer," says Marisa. "Cheryl told me, 'He's very special; we'll miss him.' Then we took up his blankets and his toys and we left."

⌐ ⌐

The funeral was two days later, January 20, at Forest Hills in Boston. Everyone was there. They took turns throwing flowers and teddy bears on top of the casket, which was about the size of a carry-on bag. A day or two later, after the hole had been filled in, Nestor and Marisa returned to plant a small child's pinwheel in the dirt next to Jorge's grave.

"We come back to visit him on the 26th of every month," Marisa says. "It is the day he was born. It is very hard for Nestor. He talks to Jorge. He asks, 'Are you cold?' He gets *so* depressed. He is sad for days before."

Then she begins to tell about the pinwheel. But her husband cuts her off. It is plain he wants to tell it himself. And with her help, he does.

The first time they returned to the grave, he says, was on a day with no wind, and from a distance, the little pinwheel was still. As they came nearer, though the air remained calm, the plastic vanes began to whirl. The closer they approached, the faster the vanes whirled. They didn't stop, or even slow, until Marisa and Nestor walked away.

I look at Marisa. Yes, she says, it is true. And it has happened every time since.

"They go, '*zzzz-zzzz-zzzz*,'" Nestor says now. "'*Zzzz-zzzz-zzzz*,' the whole time, very fast. And I talk to him. I say, 'My little Sansito, my little Sansito.' And when we go, they stop."

———

We are winding down. Marisa has shown me the last pictures—of Jorge's older brother leaning over him, a giant head over a tiny one, about to plant a kiss—and we are looking now at Jorge's "memory box": photos, his hospital bracelet, a pink satin heart, his blanket, a little outfit and cap—when I think of one final, obvious question I should have asked before.

"So," I say, "do you plan to try again?"

Nestor is still sitting, looking straight ahead; his hands have returned to their place on his knees.

The question jolts him. He sits straight up, eyes suddenly alight—and I think for a moment that I may have crossed some line. Then he beams—literally beams, as though a friend had just arrived at the door. This is a Nestor I haven't seen before.

"We're trying *now*," he says, and his hands rise off his knees and ball into fists, which he uses to pump the air. "We try always. We try every night!"

Marisa smiles a shy smile, but doesn't seem to object or disagree. Christine laughs loudly, plainly delighted. Nestor scans the room, and—apparently sensing approval—plants a mischievous look on his wife that would do credit to a ten-year-old.

"*Yes!*" he announces, still grinning widely, his hands again windmilling the air. "And we're going to try tonight, too."

Our time together ends a minute or two later. There's not much you can say after that.

*(This story was a 2002 finalist for a National Magazine Award in reporting.)*

# The Conscience of a Chief
## *September 2016*

*Sometimes, though not nearly often enough, wonderful things can grow from the worst sorts of beginnings. Character is tested; common humanity is revealed; people live up to their highest visions of themselves.*

*In Hinesburg VT on a Sunday in the spring of 2015, a seventeen-year-old boy, stoned on marijuana and driving his Honda at 80 mph through the town, went off the road and struck a bicyclist. Both the boy and the cyclist died at the scene.*

*The boy had graduated from the local high school two days before; his family were long-time residents, well-known in the town. Within hours of his death, the accident site was festooned in tributes: candles, balloons, beer cans, handwritten messages. Then came the Facebook posts, the bereavement counselors, a story in the paper noting the family's "deep roots."*

*From the town's police chief came a very different message. There needed to be more, he wrote in a column for the local paper, than just "candles and flowers by the side of the road." Had the boy survived the crash, "he would have been charged with second-degree murder."*

*The outrage was instant. As was the media coverage: "Police Chief Writes With Raw Candor About Fatal Crash," USA Today headlined its story the day after the chief's column. Overnight, the town split down the middle: high schoolers, parents, bicyclists, friends of the family, allies of the chief—to some he was callous, cruel, even blasphemous, to others a courageous spokesman for the truth. Neighbors turned against neighbors. Many feared the town would never be the same.*

*Then a remarkable thing happened. In the space of three hours on a June evening six weeks after the deaths, an evening that could be a model for any community—or country—divided, the town of Hinesburg rose above itself.*

It's been nearly nine months. The flowers and beer cans and scrolled farewells ("Smoke a bong for Joey") are long gone from the roadside now, as is the ghostly white racing bike—white-painted tires, white seat and handlebars, hung with white wreaths—that stood, somehow upright, for weeks after all the rest was gone, in the field just off the turn, on Route 116 in Hinesburg Vermont, where the Honda Civic left the road. But the hand-carved, block-printed wood sign, nailed to the tree, is still there: As YOU COME HERE TO GRIEVE THE SAD LOSS OF JOSEPH AND TO PAY YOUR RESPECTS PLEASE REMEMBER THAT A MAN NAMED RICHARD WHO ALSO WAS LOVED BY FAMILY AND FRIENDS WENT OUT FOR A BIKE RIDE ON A BEAUTIFUL SUNDAY MORNING AND NEVER CAME BACK.

It's a sunless afternoon in mid-January, though there has been no snow for days, and the ground is as gray as the sky. As we make our way south on Route 116 half an hour southeast of Burlington in the black police cruiser, to our right the flatness of the Champlain Valley unrolls itself like a carpet across a succession of fields; to the west, the land rises slowly, through a ridge of low trees, toward the foothills of the Green Mountains.

The police chief, Frank Koss, drives on without looking sideways. ("I pass here," he says, "probably three or four times a day.") Half a mile or so past the spot, he turns the SUV left onto a rutted side road, then left again, as the road turns briefly to dirt, up a hill that curves past a derelict barn, then through a thinly settled neighborhood of homes that have seen better days. There are woods on both sides now—scrub pines, a scattering of birches—and every few hundred feet a driveway cuts in from left or right. One of these is the Triple L mobile-home park, a scrum of single- and double-wide trailers packed in around narrow dirt alleyways, where Joey Marshall's family still lives. "Most of those people there, I have a lot of respect for them," the chief says. "They go to work, they take care of their homes, they're good people."

Another mile farther on, and with the woods now opening up to fields, we pass a large brick church fronted by a white cross; across the road from it, in the middle distance, is the rear of Champlain Valley Union High School, where Joey was a student until two days before he died. Just past here is Annette's Preschool, where the chief likes to come some mornings, he says, to check in with the crossing guards and "just say hi to the kids."

He drives on, taking his time, glancing up this side road, turning down that one, both hands always on the wheel. A car passes going the other way; both drivers raise fingers in greeting. "This is the best part of the job," he says now. "You're out on the road, you're seeing people, they're getting to see their tax dollars at work. After a while, you get to know the faces; you get a sense of who's who. The day comes there's a report of a domestic [problem], of some man and woman fighting, it helps that you've met them, that you have a sense of the history there."

The history with Joey Marshall wasn't so different from that of a lot of seventeen-year-olds—just a degree or so more extreme. He liked speed. ("Speed [for him] was a way of life," a high-school friend would tell the police later.) He defied limits. He chafed at authority. He smoked weed. He was young.

Hinesburg police officer Anthony Cambridge, a former high-school social-studies teacher with the gentlest manner you're likely ever to encounter in a cop, recalls an early run-in with Joey: "I was in my own car, on my way home. He came up behind me and passed me, then passed five other cars in front of me, at what I'd say was 80 miles an hour. It was the most dangerous thing I've ever seen done in a car."

Cambridge went to the Marshall home, where he met with Joey and his grandfather, then brought them back to the station. Joey cried and promised to slow down. Not long after came a phoned-in complaint: He was still at it, driving his grandfather's black Ford Fiesta way too fast on North Road—the site of the mobile-home park—"in a backward baseball cap, knocking down pylons." Cambridge brought him into the station a second time, this time with his mother. His grandfather took away the car.

"Someday you're going to thank him," Cambridge told the boy. Within weeks he was driving another, this time a teal-blue Honda Civic.

There were several more incidents, one involving a defective front license plate, another a noisy exhaust. Then, on the morning of April 26 2015, a Sunday, reportedly following an argument with his parents about his summer work prospects, he set off, driving south on Route 116, from somewhere near the center of Hinesburg—it isn't clear just where. In his system at the time, it would be determined later, were 36 nanograms of THC—the active ingredient in marijuana—seven times the lawful limit in the only two states where smoking it is legal. By the time he reached the turn near the elementary school at the southern edge of town, he was traveling at more than 80 miles an hour, according to later police estimates. Two motorists coming the other way would say it was closer to 100.

Also rounding that same turn at that moment—11:06 a.m.—pedaling south on the shoulder, was a bicyclist, Richard Tom, 47, a quiet, intensely private lover of books and bicycles who, when he wasn't leading bike tours across the US or Europe for a company in nearby Williston, lived with his dog, Annie, in a one-bedroom apartment half a mile away. When the Civic, by then nearly broadside to the road, struck him from behind, his body continued into a tree, severing his spine, then flew another 41 feet. He may never have known or felt a thing.

The Civic continued down an embankment, where it collided with a tree. Joey died of blunt-impact injuries to the head and neck, including multiple skull fractures. The two bodies came to rest 100 feet apart.

———

Frank Koss, at sixty-two, is the picture of the career cop: barrel-chested, jowly, balding, white-mustached—the late-years Gene Hackman maybe, or (if you're old enough to remember) Broderick Crawford in the old *Highway Patrol* TV series. And his life has been a mirror of the role: airport policeman, crash rescue fireman, 24 years with the California Highway Patrol. Nearly all of his career has been spent answering to disasters, many of them deadly, most of them on the road. Ten years gone from California, and he can still give you chapter and verse of the first fatality he ever worked: October 1982, father and three kids, killed in a Porsche on a

Marin County mountain road. Or what he calls his worst: July Fourth weekend, 1997, Boulder Creek in Santa Cruz County, an 18-year-old, DWI, drives broadside into a tree at 1:30 a.m., killing three friends and burning a fourth over half his body. "They left flowers around the tree after that one, too," he says.

He retired in the summer of 2006 on a California state pension, finishing as a sergeant with the Mount Shasta office at the northern edge of the state. He was 53 years old, married, with 30-odd years of policing behind him.

Some weeks before he left, with his wife, Debbie, he took a road trip east: on I-70 through the middle of the country, with no certain destination in mind, "except that we both liked the idea of living in New England." The trip took six weeks. By the time they were done driving, Vermont was the clear choice of both: "It's hard to explain why. We just liked the feel of things there."

They returned home and began surfing the Web. There was an opening in Williston for a full-time beat cop—accidents, patrol duties, handing out tickets—which he began in the fall of '06, a month after his last duty day in Mount Shasta. The Williston job led, a year later, to a similar post in Hinesburg. There was a promotion, then another. Since the spring of 2012, he's been serving as chief, on a salary of $68,000 a year. He's also trained as an EMT, whose duties—up to 200 calls a year, he says—he performs as a volunteer.

To make sense of what Frank Koss did after Joey Marshall died, it helps to understand some things. He's carried a gun throughout his career and says he's prepared to use it if needed, but it's a point of pride that he never has. ("Maybe I've just been lucky, or maybe it's the way I talk to people.") He believes that shoveling driveways and responding to lockouts are courtesies that come with the job. Andy Griffith reruns are among his TV favorites; "Welcome to Mayberry" was the greeting I got the first day I visited the station, on whose front porch are a pair of rocking chairs.

There's a story he tells. One day several years ago, a local man, who, he says, may have been "a little off, a little slow," was out walking when he stopped into the station and asked for help unjamming the zipper on his jacket. The chief, who hadn't met the man before, helped fix the zipper; the man thanked him and went on his way. Some months later there came a call for an EMT, to which the chief responded: The man had had a heart attack and died.

It's a simple story, but his telling of it seems to go to the heart of how Frank Koss thinks about his job: "If he hadn't come in here that day, he would have been just another guy who died. But he wasn't. I had met him. That made it personal for me."

*Personal.* It's a word he uses a lot. During his time in California, he says, "I worked hundreds of fatals, literally hundreds, but in 25 years I never saw the same person twice. Here, we get to know people; we get to know their families and kids. So when someone in town gets hurt or killed—like early in my time here, I lost a young man on an ATV—it's personal for me."

❧

The roadside memorials began appearing the same afternoon. Crosses, candles, balloons, beer cans, bong pipes, handwritten messages, nearly all of it—at least at first—in tribute to Joey Marshall. The account that ran online the next day in the *Burlington Free Press* described the two victims in the words of those who'd known them: a "joyous person" with a surpassing love of bicycles and "a fantastic and caring young man" who had "lived life more fully than most." Joey's high-school principal noted the Marshall family's "deep roots" in the community and reported that "counselors [were] working with students, staff and faculty to provide the support needed to deal with the loss." Joey's Facebook page, the story said, was "inundated Sunday night and Monday with messages of remembrance and mourning."

No one had known at first who the biker's body might belong to; there was no ID in the pockets and no one at the scene knew the face. When at last he was identified and the chief went to his address, a condo unit just off Route 116 a half-mile from the accident site, what he found (in addition to the dog, Annie) was a collection of bikes, bike parts, and bike paraphernalia he would later describe as a testament to "a love of bicycles beyond comprehension, like nothing I have ever known."

Richard Tom, by those who cared for him, was known for many things, none of them more telling than this lifelong love affair: "He knew everything you could know about bikes—it was absolutely uncanny. He'd see some bike somewhere and tell me some trivial little fact about it that no one could possibly have known, and I'd ask him, 'How could you know that?' And he'd just kinda look at me and smile."

Diana Nelson spoke with me by phone from California, where she's lived since not long after she and Richard Tom split up seven years ago, after 15 years together. For nearly an hour she talked about his love of dogs and books and bicycles, his "wonderful ability" to make friends out of strangers at the side of the road, balanced by a closely guarded privacy that finally, she said, caused their rift. She had learned of his death from a mutual friend's phone call, then come East for his memorial in late May.

When it became clear that his parents, who live in Alabama—where Richard was born and raised—were too frail to make the trip, she agreed to stay on long enough to close down his condo and settle his affairs: "All the stuff involved with that, the emails, the phone calls, the sorting through things—it was like being in a relationship with him again. I miss him a lot. Every time I get on a bike, I think of him. He was the most selfless person I've ever known."

❧

Nearly a month passed. The ghostly white bicycle appeared by the roadside, then was joined by a second, which just as quickly disappeared. On the Sunday after the deaths, a convoy of 400 bicyclists, escorted by police, shared a "remembrance ride" honoring both victims, through the village and past the crash site. The grief counselors came and went from the high school. The funerals took place quietly. The balloons and bong pipes dwindled, then were gone.

Then, on May 21, in the "Chief's Corner" column on page 3 of that month's 3,000-circulation *Hinesburg Record*, next to a story on the success of the annual spring Green-Up Day, Chief Koss shared his thoughts with the town. By 8:00 p.m. the same evening, the news of his words had been picked up online by the *Burlington Free Press*; within an hour, *USA Today* was tweeting it nationally ("Police Chief Writes with Raw Candor About Fatal Crash"). Within 48 hours, the story had gone viral.

Koss's column, 800 words from start to finish, began by offering perspective: "I have been investigating accidents since August 5, 1982. My first fatal crash came two months later . . ." It went on to note that in all the years since, in dealing with these many deaths, he had never departed from protocol, always remained "politically correct and sensitive, just presenting the facts . . ."

From that point on, Koss's message crackled with anger. Richard Tom, he wrote, had been "killed while riding his bicycle down the shoulder of the road on one of the first decent days after a long winter, minding his own business . . ." Joey's car had rounded the corner at "what seemed like a hundred miles an hour," hitting Tom, "hurling him into the air." The event had "crossed an unimaginable line." More needed to come from it than just "some candles and flowers by the side of the road."

But by that point in the column, the chief had already crossed a line of his own: "To be blunt, if Joseph Marshall had not lost his life, he would have been charged with second-degree murder."

---

He grew up in Colorado, just outside Denver, where his father was a service manager for Honeywell. Two months out of high school, he joined the Air Force, where he was trained in electronic communications. From there, at 22, he joined the Alaska Air National Guard, in which he served for three years—while also working part-time as an airport security guard—until his release, with the rank of staff sergeant, in the summer of 1978.

During my second visit with the chief, in mid-October—nearly six months after the deaths, five months since he wrote his column—he tells me a story about that early time in his life. Like others of his stories, it seems to serve for him almost as an allegory, as the memory of a morally defining moment.

It was during the year he was in Air Force electronics school, so he would have been about 19. He had a friend at the time, a girl, who invited him to go with her to a local golf course one night and smoke a joint. He was nervous, he remembers; he'd never tasted pot before, and smoking it, for an airman trainee, was a career-ending offense. But he agreed: "I was young. That's about all you can say."

And so they went. And they found the most secluded spot they could, and they lit their joint. Not long after, they watched as the beams of two flashlights approached them: two Air Force MPs.

"I was scared, I was terrified—you have no idea." But the wind was blowing the other way. The MPs smelled nothing and walked on. If the wind that night had been blowing in a different direction, he says, "it would have changed everything. I would have gotten a dishonorable discharge, would have driven back home to Colorado in my '49 Chevy, and tried to figure out what to do with the rest of my life."

At this point he swivels in his chair and points behind him to a large vertical frame on the wall. There, arranged in an oval pattern behind glass, against a dark-blue background, are the various insignia and shoulder patches that define the trajectory of his life: US Air Force, Loomis Security, O'Neill Security Services, Alaska Airport Police, California Highway Patrol, Williston Police, Hinesburg Community Police.

"I wouldn't have had any of that," he says now, turning slowly back toward me, placing both hands squarely on his desk, as if to steady himself. "None of that would have happened. If the wind had blown the other way that night, I wouldn't be here today."

There's a long pause, which grows longer. He turns back again toward the wall frame, then returns once more to face me before he speaks again.

"Some things are life-altering events," he says. "That was one for me. Now there's this: Richard Tom was out riding his bike, enjoying his Sunday morning. Now he's dead. He'll never have a life again. What's that going to be for the other kids? It needs to be more than just 'Smoke a bong for Joey.'"

❧

In a small town, death is always big news. When the victim is a boy from a family with strong ties and years of history, and he's charged—publicly and posthumously, within a month of his death—with murder, the news can seem cataclysmic.

Early Friday afternoon, a day after the chief's column had appeared, Alicia Marshall, Joey's mother, phoned the editorial office of the *Burlington Free Press*. On the phone with her were Joey's father, Gary, his younger brother, older sister, grandmother, girlfriend, and five friends. A staff writer, Elizabeth Murray, handled the call.

"My son was not the type of person to go out and try to murder somebody," said his mother, who, along with the grandmother, did nearly all of the talking. "He loved his car. He planned on marrying his girlfriend as soon as they graduated. He was going to turn 18. He had just finished high school that Friday." She sobbed as she spoke. Several of the others also were in tears.

The story told of how Joey and his father had planned to open a family business together—Marshall & Sons Home Repair & Maintenance—and of how sweatshirts with the company's name had been delivered the day after his death.

A friend, Lucas Aube, 19, spoke up toward the end. He used to have respect for Chief Koss, he said, but had lost it after reading the column. Alicia Marshall agreed: "[He] made Joe, a 17-year-old who loved life, a murderer," she told the reporter.

In the wider world—and especially among the law-enforcement community—the chief was drawing broad support. The chief in nearby Colchester, Jen Morrison, praised him for being "unafraid of difficult conversations." Others felt the same, and continue their support today.

"It took real courage for him to write that," South Burlington police chief Trevor Whipple said not long ago. "I'm a parent myself; I can understand the grief over losing a child. But at the same time, that young man made some horrible choices, and he took someone else with him. Sometimes you just have to stand up and speak out."

But in the village and the region around it, things only got worse. Over the two weeks that followed the column, according to the Burlington paper, there was a near-endless "back-and-forth between Koss and the Marshall family," with community members often taking sides. Alicia Marshall claimed harassment. Reports of Joey's pit bull, Tank, having mauled several visitors added further heat to the fire. Meanwhile, the chief would say later, "It seemed to me like Richard Tom was just really getting lost."

———

To the chief, there seemed only one way past the ugliness—though he must have known it was a risk. On the evening of Thursday, June 4, at his invitation—"to grant the family the opportunity to speak their mind in open forum"—between 80 and 100 area residents filled the second-floor meeting room of Hinesburg Town Hall. The Marshall family—mother, father, sister, brother—were at a table in front. A dozen or so of Joey's teenage posse, nearly all in black T-shirts sporting a stenciled image of the teal Honda, lined the back wall. The rest were in folding chairs or standing along the side walls: a mixed crowd of parents, neighbors, cyclists, reporters, friends of the Marshalls, and those of Richard Tom. The chief stood at the head of the room, with his officer, Anthony Cambridge, alone in the front row of chairs.

It began as you'd expect. The chief detailed the physics of the crash: time of day, speed, the narrowness of the shoulder, the impossibility of reacting in time: "He was traveling the length of a football field every 2.4 seconds." Then he outlined the parameters of second-degree murder: unpremeditated, "caused by the offender's obvious lack of concern for human life."

Alicia Marshall, defiant at her table, speaking sometimes through clenched teeth, argued that manslaughter was the worst it should have been: "Not murder, not murder at all; he was a kid who loved life." She charged that the chief's talk of murder was part of a pattern of harassment, that her husband, Gary (who never spoke, and barely moved, throughout the meeting, hands folded in front of him, sitting alongside his wife), had himself been harassed during a traffic stop by Officer Cambridge. Anthony Cambridge answered the charge, detailing the incident in question.

Then, as others in the room rose to speak, the feeling of things began to change. A woman in back, speaking softly, addressed the family: "Our hearts go out to you, but please understand, this is not about placing blame." A second woman had words for the chief: "When I read your article, I was moved, because it came through that you want Joseph's horrible death to try to save the lives of other people." A mother told of taking her son's license away after he was stopped for speeding; another said she hadn't, and was sorry.

An older man, a schoolbus driver, visibly shaken, rose and faced the chief: "My nephew was killed, 12 years ago, by a drunk driver. It's taken me this long to speak up . . ." At this point he broke down, sobbing. "And it's because of you. It's been 12 years, and it still hurts. But thank you."

Several friends of Richard Tom took their turns. One, a man who gave his name as Jason Reed, spoke, one would assume, for them all: "Ma'am, with all due respect . . . your son sounds like a magnificent kid, but your son broke the law. Richard Tom was following the law. Your son broke the law, and my friend is dead."

There were many more: A driver's-ed teacher spoke on the difficulty of explaining the deaths to his students; cyclists shared the fears they rode with every day; a friend of Richard Tom, standing next to a friend of Joey's who wept alongside as the older man spoke, told of the two having met at the crash site, days before, when both had come to say goodbye to their friends. At one point Joey's 19-year-old sister, who had stood quietly till then against the front wall behind her parents, broke her silence with a low cry: "I have to stand here and listen to all this! I've been listening to this week after week. I just want my brother to rest in peace!"

Alicia Marshall seemed broken. Her defiance now gone, she sat at the table next to her husband, sobbing heavily, her shoulders quaking. Then suddenly, cutting off someone else who was speaking, she blurted out a string of words, not all of them intelligible through her sobs: *I'm sorry! I'm sorry! I don't know what else to say. I'm sorry my son did this to him!. . . I say that in front of every town member, in front of every bicyclist here . . .*"

By the end of a little more than an hour (the meeting would last for nearly two), it was plain that most of those present knew that something very rare was taking place. "There's so much caring in this room," one woman told the crowd. "I feel I'm just lucky to be here." A bearded man in glasses, sitting alone in the front row, rose to say that he had been a journalist all his life, had covered many sorts of meetings, "and I've never seen anything like this." He praised the Marshalls for their courage in airing their grievance and sharing their grief; he praised the chief for "caring as much about this community as to say what you said. That took incredible courage." And then he turned and faced the room: "For everyone here to sit for an hour and 45 minutes, and talk about this and show each other respect—that's just amazing, I think."

The chief stood quietly through most of this, letting it play out. There was only one point, not long after Alicia Marshall's tearful apology, that he spoke at any length. Delivering his words carefully, hands folded in front of him, he told the room that he hadn't known Richard Tom, that he wasn't a bicyclist himself ("My wife and I, two years ago we bought bikes and they're still sitting in the garage") and had no personal stake in the issue. "But when you're chief of police in a small town, you take things personally. I don't want to be in L.A., I don't want to be in South Burlington. I love being the chief of police of this town."

Then he paused, and raising his voice along with his gaze, he addressed his words to the row of black-shirted teenagers lining the back wall of the room. Would they obey the law now? Would they respect others on the road? If so, probably something had been learned.

The message he closed with, one hopes, struck a chord with at least a few of those boys and girls (mostly boys) in the back. "Go home," he told them. "Go home safely, make it home every night," because life "isn't about sixteen, seventeen,, and eighteen," or about speed or cars or good times. It's about the years that come after, "when we're out there doing something in the world. . . That's your time that you need to get to. Get past the speed, get past all of this, and make it to where your life is sup-posed to be."

When the meeting adjourned at a little before 9:00, the sky outside was darkening. But of the 40 or 50 people still left in the room, almost no one seemed ready to leave. It was hugs and handholds now that kept them. They went around from one to the other—Richard Tom's bicyclists, the Marshalls, the parents, the police—until there was no more hugging to be done. By then the sky was dark.

It was on my last visit with Chief Koss, in mid-January, that he took me on that drive around the town's back roads. "Sometimes when I'm driving these roads," he told me, "it takes me back to being in Colorado as a kid." Three weeks earlier, a Cleveland grand jury had declined to indict the officer who had been videotaped fatally shooting a 12-year-old boy; the protests were still ongoing. Six months before, a college student in Cincinnati, also unarmed, had been shot to death by police, just days after a young black woman in Texas had been found hanging in her cell. It hadn't been a good year for policing.

"It makes me sad where law enforcement is headed," the chief said to me as we drove past the preschool on our way back toward the station. "The police don't have the support of the people anymore. It's a different world today."

Things with the Marshalls had quieted by then. The town meeting had cooled tempers; there'd been no issues with Alicia in months; Joey's pit bull, after several more attacks, had been put down.

The biggest news lately had been burglaries—a number of them, nearly all with drugs at their source, most often heroin. A family of three ("including the mom") he'd told me about at our first meeting in November, known for their thefts of catalytic converters from parked cars, had been apprehended shortly after, and were off the streets now.

More recently, he said, just two days before Christmas, two burglars had broken into a local home and stolen everything under the tree, as well as several pieces of jewelry. This had especially offended him ("You steal someone's jewelry, that's not just a piece of gold—you're stealing a piece of their past")—and he'd wanted the thieves to know that they'd been seen on camera and that their remaining freedom would be short.

So he took to the town's Facebook page: "Special holiday greetings to the burglars who robbed the house on Charlotte Rd. Besides ransacking the bedrooms for jewelry, taking all the wrapped presents from underneath the Christmas tree should be a particularly proud moment for you. If you are the two thieves that had also stopped at another residence on Charlotte Rd. and spotted the camera, we have a special message. To the vehicle passenger that looked right into the camera—yes, it was real. . . The Hinesburg Police will be working extra hard toward giving these two thieves a special new year."

He's your grandfather's police chief: a protector of kids and dogs and public safety, morally outraged at the theft of Christmas gifts. Ten years ago he retired and came East, in search of something he'd know only when he found it in a small Vermont town: "We just liked the feel of things there." He's 62 today, and soon will be retiring again. But it's different this time. He plans to stay on in this town that he and Debbie discovered, to keep the home they bought on the street behind the police station, perhaps one day to die here.

And in the meantime at the station itself, his own "feel of things" will live on in the model he's imparted to his men, Anthony Cambridge among them.

"He talks to people," the chief said to me about his officer that day we were driving around. "He relates, he cares. It's a lot like the way I do policing. It's a perfect fit for this town."

# Searching for Alexander
## *June 2018*

*This is the most personal, by far, of all the stories here. Also the most recent. It is the story of a beautiful young man who was my stepson, my wife's oldest child, until he took his life six years ago. And it is the story of what a loss like that can do to a parent, and to a family.*

*The idea to write it wasn't mine. It was suggested to me, over a breakfast meeting two years ago, by* Yankee *Editor Mel Allen, who, as a close friend, knew many of the particulars of what had happened, and believed, as he told me that day, that sharing them could be a help to other families coping with a similar loss, or with the fear of one. Judging by the responses we've had to the story, I've come to believe he was right.*

Near the peak of Mt. Mansfield on a sunny July morning, Nate Launer cradles a small grey-brown bird in his hand. He has just released it from a mist net, and will soon wrap its tiny pink leg with a wafer-thin band before letting it go.

It is a Bicknell's Thrush, the rarest and most secretive of North America's breeding thrushes, and now under threat as its natural habitat—the coniferous alpine forests of northern New England, the Adirondacks, and Canada—progressively dwindles as an effect of climate change.

"As the air warms, the deciduous trees move higher and begin to squeeze out the balsam and spruce where the Bicknell's make their nests," Nate will explain to me later. The banding he was doing that morning, he says, will help track the birds' movements as they attempt to adapt to the threat.

He is twenty-one years old, a senior at the University of Vermont's Rubenstein School of Environment and Natural Resources, where he majors in conservation biology. His morning at the top of Mt. Mansfield today—and the ten weeks of mornings on either side of it—are the result of a summer apprenticeship, the Alexander Dickey Conservation Internship, awarded by the Vermont Center for Ecostudies, to honor the memory of another young man who, a few years before, also walked these woods in search of the Bicknell's Thrush: "A mostly solitary soul," as the VCE announcement would describe him later, "who found in nature," and just as often in poetry and music, "refuge from a world that often seemed too much."

Nate concedes that he knows little about the young man in whose name he is passing his summer. "I've been a little afraid to ask," he says. "I can sense there's a sensitivity there."

—◦—

I was at work in the study of our New Hampshire home, around four in the afternoon, Saturday, October 19th, 2013, when the phone rang with a call from my wife, Landon. She had just read a text message from her twenty-eight year-old son, Alexander, written an hour before: "I've gone for a walk in the woods." She asked if I thought she should worry. It was clear to me that she knew the answer already.

It was a warm, sunny fall day, nearly cloudless, with the maples near their peak. It had been much the same the morning before, when Landon had driven two hours south to visit Alex at the small therapeutic community in eastern Massachusetts, Gould Farm, where he had been living most of the past 15 months. They had gone to a garden center, where they wandered the stalls of apple varieties and bought jars of maple syrup and apple jelly—"the sort of place he loved," she says, the sort of place he might be working today." Afterward, they had driven back to the Farm and sat in the car and talked for nearly an hour, about his illness and his fears of the future. Alex cried, overwhelmed by regrets. Landon assured him that she would support him through whatever came next. On the drive home, she remembers: "I felt encouraged. Very daunted but still encouraged. We were in a new phase, and it was going to be all right."

At 11:35 that night, Alex emailed his mother. He had been for a walk, he wrote, "with the full moon high in the sky," and it had reminded him of the work of an 11th-century Japanese poet, who had written of the power of the moon to unite loved ones separated by distance: "If looking at it, we just remember/ our two hearts may meet." It was a rambling email, like so much of what came out of Alex's mind, but seemed at least to be reaching for some fuller sense of purpose, however idealized. He wrote of his love of the Maine coast and of his yearning to live there: "to live alone for a time. . . cook healthy food for myself, play the guitar, absorb the beauty and vitality of the ocean, and hopefully find a way through my illness." It was like a cancer, he wrote, "that I have to come to terms with, accept that I may die from it, but do everything I can to keep living.

"I love you so much, Mom," he closed by saying. "I can't tell you how much you mean to me, and how essential your support and love have been."

—— ⏤

It's impossible to know when or how the pain took root. Growing up in a small town in western New Hampshire, on the edge of a soft meadow with a view of Smart's Mountain on one side and the Connecticut River on the other, he spent endless hours outdoors: "planning lots of 'missions' in the woods," says his mother. He skied, played soccer, basketball, golf and lacrosse, sang in the glee club, and for a while had dreams of being a PGA golfer or a crack skateboarder in the mold of Tony Hawk. At his middle-school graduation in the spring of 2000, he won the award for Most Well-Rounded Student—Scholar, Athlete, Friend.

He was the older brother to two siblings. His sister, Kelsey, remembers, at the age of six or seven, following his tracks across a frozen pond—"it was like we were Lewis and Clark"—and being rewarded with her first Moose sighting. "He was a good older brother," she says today, "always curious, and up for anything. And he had a really big heart."

His parents separated in the fall of 2000, the same year he went away to high school. "That was hard for him," his mother says, "I think he thought if he'd been at home he might have helped repair things." But by the end of that year life seemed to have normalized: "He made lots of friends, he played sports, he took up the guitar. He could be moody at times, but mostly he seemed happy."

His brother, Charley—younger by five years, remembers he began to notice something changing toward the end of Alex's s junior year:

"I idolized him, the way you do with an older brother. He was popular, a good athlete, good-looking, and the girls all liked him. But then around junior or senior year, you could see things starting to fall apart for him. It just seemed like he was having trouble doing the things he wanted, and he couldn't relate to his friends as well anymore."

Landon had a similar sense: "He was growing more inward. You could see it happening." She remembers a T-shirt he wore that year that had the word LOST in a big green circle on the front. "It concerned me," she says. "But we stayed in close contact, visited often, and he seemed happy enough while we were with him. He had a wonderful sense of humor, could be very un-self-consciously silly with us—and that remained intact."

He graduated from high school in the spring of 2004. An honor-roll student and member of the golf team—with special distinction in Natural Science and Orchestral Music—he was asked to speak at graduation, but declined.

Three months later, in September of that year, I shared dinner with Alex and his mom in a street-side restaurant in Saratoga Springs, New York. It was the start of his freshman year at Skidmore College. I didn't know him well at that point, and don't recall what the talk was about, only that Alex did the bulk of it (as he often did when his interests were engaged) and that we stopped afterward, before returning him to his dorm, at a performance of street musicians from which we had a hard time pulling him away.

---

Who understands
why this young man,
healthy and so full of life,
goes off alone
to read a book of poems?

It's uncertain when he wrote these lines, alone and untitled, among the jumble of writings he left behind. But their message seems painfully clear: Who am I, and why am I so alone?

He wrote endlessly: poems, essays, short stories, meditations, sometimes formless constructions you have to wonder if he understood himself. He played the guitar, often for hours. He listened to punk and folk, to Coltrane and Miles Davis, played "Rite of Spring" ritually every April, lingered maddeningly long in art museums, scribbling intently in a small spiral notebook he was rarely without.

Most of all he loved the outdoors. I remember a weekend with him and Landon in the Adirondacks, well after his Skidmore days. He had brought with him a young woman-friend named Tonya, a kindred disciple of nature. For two days, they hiked, boated and communed with birds and flora, at one point paddling up the Moose River stillwater, oblivious to all of us, floating under balsams, practicing birdcalls, examining the striations of lilies and shore plants. Later at dinner, detailing their day, they were twin geysers of excitement and delight. I never saw Alex more happy.

He seems to me one of those you could say had missed his time. It's not hard to envision him in, say, Renaissance Italy or 18th-century England, a gentleman-poet awash in ideas and great feelings, haunting the village squares and coffee houses of the day, arguing the merits of humanism or democracy or extolling the beauties of the natural world. But we live in less forgiving times.

College was a struggle. In the spring semester of his freshman year at Skidmore, he confided to his advisor (who would remember him later as "one of those who catches at your heart") that he was suffering from depression and feeling overwhelmed. He changed majors twice in two years—from English to Spanish, then Philosophy—before dropping out, never to return.

This set in motion a succession of ever-narrowing paths, each one seeded by hopes that never seemed to blossom. A semester in Spain marked the start of a love affair with Spanish guitar, but was overhung by a loneliness he couldn't shake. A transfer to the University of British Columbia in Vancouver began with an immersion in the land and birds of the Pacific Northwest ("He hiked all over the province," his mother says, "started memorizing the names of birds, trees, land masses, wherever his curiosity led him"), until he dropped out overnight, midway through his third semester, inexplicably, with no warning or notice to anyone.

He was never without friends—there was a warmth to him, and a realness, you almost couldn't resist. But as time went by, even some of these began to drop away. "I think they appreciated his sensitivity," says Landon, "but in the end they couldn't completely fathom the darkness he fought against."

I also had no clue of its depths—such as the night in Vancouver, toward the end of his time there, when, drunk in a bar, he flew into a rage and went at a stranger with a broken beer bottle. I knew nothing of this then, and might not have believed it if I had. Even today, nearly ten years later, it is almost unimaginable to me.

"A bouncer threw him out on the street," his brother Charley says. "He woke up later on a train with only one shoe. It sounded kind of funny at the time when he told it, but looking back now, it really shows how separate he was."

—

Alex returned home in the fall of 2008 and moved in with his father, an attorney and health policy analyst in West Lebanon, New Hampshire. The next four years were a succession of false starts and near-rescues: a brief part-time attendance at UNH; several semesters, also part-time, at Colby-Sawyer in New London; a three-month stint at McLean's Hospital in Massachusetts; a long, increasingly close relationship with a Dartmouth-based psychotherapist, whom Alex seemed to believe had a window to his soul.

It was toward the start of this time, in the late summer of 2009, that Landon and I were married. Our wedding, by a lake in the Adirondacks where I had spent all of my boyhood summers, culminated in a ceremony overlooking the water. Alex, as the oldest sibling, stood alongside me and my son at the makeshift altar; later, toward the end of dinner, again on behalf of the three of them, he rose to toast us. I don't remember many of his words, only how awkward and heartfelt—and unfittingly honest—they felt to me at the time. It had been painful for the three of them, he said, to endure the coming-apart of their parents' marriage; it was an "adjustment" to make space for their mother's new partner. They didn't know me well but would come to know me better. I was welcome in their family. They were very happy for her.

By the end of it all he was rambling, unsure of how to finish, and the room was far too quiet. His younger brother Charley, standing next to him, waited for a pause, then raised his glass and his voice: "A toast to Mom and Geoffrey!" And Alex, suddenly shy and thankful, sat down.

It may have been around this time, from what I can tell in reading through his writings and emails, that he began having serious thoughts about dying. In an email he wrote in the fall of 2010, to a professor he'd grown close to at Colby-Sawyer, he spoke despairingly of "a disconnect in my brain; [it] simply doesn't know when to stop thinking, stop worrying, stop asking. [It] cannot feel certain, content, appeased by anything." He was finding it increasingly difficult, he wrote, "to remain afloat in this world so often beset by these thoughts."

The professor wrote back the next day, advising Alex to not isolate himself: "If you were a hockey player, and were really good at it, you would want to play hockey all the time, and want people to play hockey with. You're a thinker; so you need to find other thinkers. . . and be with them, and talk about all these questions, [and] tell jokes and see beautiful things."

For all these dark thoughts, though, there remained an embrace of life behind Alex's daily activities that was palpable to anyone who knew him. Only a few months before that email exchange, in the spring of 2010, he had begun his work with VCE; for the next several months, right into the fall, he paddled lakes and climbed mountains in search of loons to rescue from tangled fishing lines or Bicknell's Thrushes to band and release. The work delighted him—it was much of what he talked about that summer. And for those who worked with him, the delight was mutual.

"From the moment he arrived at our office that spring, Alex won us over," remembers VCE Executive Director Chris Rimmer, who especially recalls, he writes in an email, his "probing curiosity, gentle compassion and sense of innocence. . . I don't believe I've ever known a more gentle, thoughtful soul."

His life remained a battle between poles. He would write almost daily of darkness and death, but also of hummingbirds, his grandmother's picked strawberries or the discovery of a butterfly's wing ("black-framed, white-mottled and apricot, a savior on the sidewalk"). "I know what you mean about how the flicker of a whitetail deer or the chitter of a red squirrel is sometimes all that saves you," his mother emailed him in December of 2009. "Thank you, Alexander, for letting me see that world through your senses." He kept up his volunteer work at VCE, continually composed new guitar pieces, met with his therapist regularly, and made A's at Colby-Sawyer—"the best student I ever had," one professor would remember later. To most of us rooting him on, it seemed he might be winning.

The rooting was hard, though. There seemed always a stumble after every step forward. And he was in his late twenties by now; the world was moving on without him. The reality of this, his brother Charley says, was a painful one to witness:

"It was hard to see him always gracefully explaining to people how things were with him, and always in that same light-hearted way—not that he was 'failing' exactly, just that he wasn't quite where he was expected to be. The speed bumps just kept getting bigger and bigger for him, and he just kept explaining, kept keeping it light. I always respected how he handled it. I respected his pride. But I was sad that he had to answer all those questions."

Then, in early May of 2012, came a crushing blow. Alex's father, who had long been ill with a debilitating condition that had kept him out of work for more than a year, died unexpectedly. For Alex, this marked the start of the final cycle down.

We sat together in the white church.
It was May.
The windows of the church were open.
Crab apple blossoms were falling on the grass.
It made no sense.
I prepared our last dinner on a Monday night,
cooked pork chops, summer squash and brown rice,
which we ate while watching a TV program
on Geronimo and the Apaches.

It was clear to us all now that Alex was going to need more help than a twice-weekly therapist could offer. The choice was Gould Farm, a 100 year-old, non-profit working farm in western Massachusetts that functioned as a therapeutic community. It seemed made for him: small, rural, loosely structured, built around the communal sharing of work, meals and farm traditions. We went with him to visit on a weekend in late June. He seemed to share our hopefulness, and began his stay two weeks later, assigned to a job as a member of the trail-maintenance team.

For the first several months he seemed to thrive. On the phone and on visits home, he spoke excitedly of his work on the trails and in the greenhouse, his poetry group, a band he had helped form, the music he was writing and playing. And for the first time in a while, there was talk of the future: he had applied for a transfer to UMass Amherst, and been accepted; the hope was, if all went well, to enroll the following spring.

And he was touching other lives, often in beautiful ways. On a visit to the Farm that winter, I met a little boy, four or five years old, the son of a staff member, carrying around a tiny guitar. Alex had found it in some forgotten closet, his mother told me, then restrung it and was teaching him to play; he was her son's "major hero in life." I passed the news on to Alex, who just smiled and looked embarrassed.

There was another guest at the Farm, a young woman who had lost two years to depression and had twice tried to take her life ("I don't think there was even a moment in those years when I wanted to be alive"), who would remember later "raking leaves with him, riding in the back of the pickup, making cider together. I followed him around like a lost puppy." The week before Christmas, she recalled, there was to be a tree-lighting at the top of a nearby hilltop. The staff passed out songbooks beforehand:

"Only there weren't quite enough to go around, so Alex offered to share his with me. And we started walking, singing, up toward the top of the hill on a path lit by burning candles. And at that moment, walking side by side with Alex, sharing that songbook, I finally felt a part of something. I felt like I wanted to live. After two long years, I really, actually wanted to live another day. That memory will last with me the rest of my life."

Sometime around the late spring of 2013, eight or nine months into his stay at the Farm, there came a close-bunched series of losses: the retired UMass professor who had been leading the Farm's poetry group took sick and died; another member of the group, a young woman named Gabby with whom Alex had been close, took her life not long after leaving the Farm; his therapist at home, whom he'd been seeing for nearly ten years, was diagnosed with metastatic cancer and would soon be gone too.

All this, coupled with the weight of his father's death, may have seemed too much to bear. Twice during that summer and early fall, no longer trusting himself, he checked himself into a hospital psychiatric unit. Both times he was released within a week.

In mid-September Alex joined Landon and me and two friends on a weekend trip to the Adirondacks. Much of the first day he spent in his room, too low to participate; the next afternoon, he came with us to a camp on the river, where the five of us lit a fire, talked and ate lunch together. He spoke little but smiled often. It was the last time I would see him.

Two weeks later, on September 28, Alex and his five-piece band gave an informal recital for guests and staff at the Farm, doing an on-stage arrangement of a Red Hot Chili Peppers number. Later he played a guitar solo: a slow, very tender piece he had composed himself, announcing in advance, almost shyly, that he was dedicating it to his father and to his friend Gabby, "both amazing people who made the world a better place." He seemed embarrassed by the applause that followed, and left the stage quickly.

<hr />

In his room at the Farm at 1:30 on the morning of October 19th, Alex wrote a final passage in his journal: "In other days I have wanted the world—fame, love, success, happiness... I have wanted what everyone wants, one way or another. Well, peace is enough now."

Also found in his room later that day would be a sealed envelope with a letter addressed to "Mom, Kelsey and Charley," which would apologize for the hurt he was causing and plead for their understanding of his choice:

"I've simply run out of the strength to fight it any longer. I see no open paths, and I've lost all hope. It has become unbearable. I would never want to cause you the pain I know I will cause you. You have done everything you could for me and more. Thank you with all my heart."

At 1:40 that afternoon, a Gould Farm van made its regular Saturday delivery of guests, Alex among them, to its drop-off point in Great Barrington, roughly a mile northwest of East Mountain State Forest, for an afternoon of shopping. Alex was last seen walking north from the group. A little more than an hour later his text would arrive on his mother's smartphone: "I've gone for a walk in the woods."

For most of the six months that followed, time seemed to fly, then slow. Norms lapsed, civility became as precious as love. Sometimes for days at a time, the world seemed upside-down. Other times it only seemed sad.

The call came from the Farm around six that evening: Alex hadn't showed up at the meeting-point; a note had been found in his room, and was read to us over the phone. Landon seemed numb, unreachable. I was unsure what to do.

The next morning, Sunday, we drove the three hours to the Farm. We were met there by the head staff, also the local police. They had tracked the location of Alex's last cell-phone signal: the East Mountain summit sometime after three on Saturday. The Great Barrington police and fire departments had launched a search of the area, soon to be joined by a State Police helicopter equipped with thermal imaging. By the end of the day Sunday there was nothing to report. Monday morning the story made the local paper—"Gould Farm Resident Goes Missing"—with a physical description of Alex. The searches went on.

It would continue this way for a week, then part of another. Landon remained stony, impossible to read. The more time went by, the more meagre the grounds for hope, the more resolute she seemed to become. She walked the woods. She asked help from hikers, met with a tracker, who worked from Alex's boot soles, then with the leader of the search and rescue team; she consulted with a psychic, made up posters and tacked them to trees and trailheads and bulletin boards all over the county. She contacted the police to follow up reports of sightings. At one point, she was put in touch, by phone, with a dowser from Pennsylvania; he assured her Alex was alive, that he was wandering the woods, confused and afraid. For three days, working from the Google map the two of them shared, she walked the woods for miles at his direction, circling, doubling back, along roads, along trails, across streams, keeping hope alive.

Sometimes as she walked, she sang: lullabies from Alex's childhood, songs they had sung together but now with the words changed to call his name. One was a Native American chant she remembered he had loved:

> Ancient Mother, I hear you calling,
> Ancient Mother, I hear your song,
> Ancient Mother, I hear your laughter,
> Alexander, please come home. . .

"It was like I was in another dimension," she tells me today. "Maybe like falling backward out of a plane without a parachute—not the present, not the future, just tumbling backward through space., with no ground, nothing, under your feet."

On the last day of October, the weather turned suddenly cold—into the 30s with a dusting of snow. With no trace of a body, and no new leads or reported sightings, the search team called off its efforts. It was on that Wednesday, with Alex gone 11 days, that Landon came home.

"A fifth of me, or maybe only a tenth, had believed he could still be alive. But I knew he was gone, I knew I had to let go. Mostly all I felt was numbness. When people would ask how I was doing, it was hard to answer—kind of like that feeling you get when you try to speak or smile after the dentist has shot you with novocaine. You can't work your mouth very well. It was like that, only emotionally. An emotional effacement."

⌒

Winter came. The phone calls were slowing, though the letters, more than a hundred by the end, still arrived. The day before Thanksgiving, Alex's younger sister and brother, one in New York, the other in his senior year at college, arrived home. There were long silences, quiet tears, much drinking, football on TV. "It was the worst Thanksgiving of my life," Landon says today.

Christmas loomed. It had been Alex's favorite holiday, Kelsey's and Charley's too. Now it seemed unthinkable. So we did what we could to erase it, to abandon every trapping and reminder, even the season itself. We booked the cheapest Caribbean cruise we could find, on a humongous floating city known as Enchantment of the Seas, with 2,500 passengers, and found ourselves, on Christmas Day 2013, on an artificial beach in the Bahamas listening to a piped-in rendering of "Ave Maria" as hundreds of our fellow shipmates—and eventually even Landon—lined up to glide down the length of a massive water slide. It was awful. But we laughed a lot together, ate too many salad-bar shrimps, drank too much bad champagne, and managed almost to forget why we were there.

Four months later, on April 13, a day or two after the ice went out on Lake Buel, a forested pond just east of Great Barrington, a fisherman called police to report a body on the surface. By the time Landon got the word, in a voicemail message a day later, the body had been shipped to the medical examiner's office in Boston. Dental records confirmed it was Alex. The autopsy would confirm he had drowned—we can only assume intentionally. A week later we drove to the funeral home in Winthrop, Massachusetts and made arrangements for cremation. Before leaving, Landon sat alone with the closed coffin, covered in a royal blue blanket, and said goodbye.

No one wanted a funeral. It had been too long, the grieving had claimed too much of us already. But there needed to be something, some way of marking his passing and remembering who he had been.

The internship was his grandmother's idea. Closey Dickey, by then in her late 80s, had ten grandchildren, though Alex had been her first. It was in her garden, as a child, that he had first found his love of plants and flowers. They both loved books; he wrote her long letters, she bought him his first Spanish guitar. It was she who suggested he volunteer with VCE. "She had a real sense of him," Landon says.

Closey's commitment, of $25,000, laid the groundwork. Friends and family more than tripled that. In the early spring of 2016 the call for applicants went out, mostly to the biology and environmental-studies programs of New England colleges, seeking candidates who could—among other requirements—show "a proven dedication to conservation biology. . . a willingness to work unpredictable hours in demanding field conditions, [and] a personal connection to nature that reflects the solace and delight it offered to Alexander." The winning candidate would be rewarded with "a 12-week, field-based, paid internship in conservation science."

Amber Wolf, a conservation biology major at College of the Atlantic in Maine, was the first year's intern. Nate Launer would be the second.

There could be no more perfect legacy. To walk in the woods with Alex was to experience them on a deeper level: the birdsong, the flora, the lichen on the underside of downed trees. The joy he got from his work with VCE, for those summers of his mid-twenties, whether charting migratory patterns on an overnight field trip in the White Mountains or sitting at a desk uploading data on the habits of some Hispaniolan cloud-forest bird, seemed among the very few things sufficient to liberate him from the world, and from himself.

"He just liked being there. He liked talking birds, he liked talking nature," says his mother. "He used to call it 'nerding out' on bird stuff. They didn't judge him there. They didn't care that he wasn't going the same route as other people his age. They just accepted him, they made a place for him. He was so happy there, so in his environment."

---

On an early morning in the last part of July, near the summit of Mt. Mansfield, Nate and his VCE fellows are unfurling their mist nets to release and band the captured birds inside. There are two new species today—a Black-and-White Warbler, an out-of-habitat Rose-breasted Grosbeak—as well as a Robin, a Golden-crowned Kinglet, other Warbler types and several Swainson's Thrushes. There is also a single Bicknell's Thrush. All are tiny, some small enough to sit easily on the first joint and nail of your finger.

Landon has joined the group. She is working with Nate, taking the birds in a small bag from the nets to the nearby car where they will be weighed and banded before their release. She will remember the young man's gentle sureness in handling them, his warmth and ease in talking, as well as the beauty of the morning.

"We were watching mist just clearing the ridges. Nate was taking the birds from my bags, cupping them in his hand and weighing them—and we were just talking about things, school and work and his plans for the future."

There was birdsong all around them, and from time to time the group would pause to listen and try to identify—a Cedar Waxwing, a Canada Warbler, this or that type of Thrush. There was a feeling of connection in the group, Landon says, "a sense of quiet and purpose, a sort of delicacy," that triggered memories.

"Alex had begun to teach me how to listen in the woods, how to tell one birdsong from another, to receive sounds as though your ears were a satellite dish—and that's what it felt like was going on that morning. He would have loved to have been there. He would have loved that *I* was there."

# Caught Between Two Cultures

## *January 2004*

*I first met Said Mohamud and his wife Shukri in Lewiston ME in the summer of 2003. Their journey there was unimaginable to me: separated by tribal war in their native Somalia, where their year-old daughter had been shot to death in her mother's arms, they'd been shuttled for years between refugee camps throughout sub-Saharan Africa, before finally being "resettled"—along with several hundred other Somali natives—in a subsidized apartment near downtown Lewiston.*

*Already by then, immigration was a loaded issue. Not long before, in an open letter to the city's Somali community, the mayor had been cruelly blunt: "Please tell your friends and relatives to stop coming." A neo-Nazi hate group had gathered to protest "the invasion of Maine by Somalis." There were 1,100 Somalis in Lewiston at the time.*

*Today there are more than 5,000. Lisbon Street, the city's main drag, not long ago a succession of vacant storefronts, is now awash in Somali businesses: mosques, community centers, falafel restaurants—one of them, the Mogadishu Store, where the Somali flag and American flag hang side by side in the window, is owned and run by Shukri. Said, a US citizen now, founded the African Community Office in town. Four of the couple's eight children are graduates of Lewiston High; one is an accountant, another a doctor in Michigan. The high school's Blue Devils, most of them Somalis, were state soccer champions in 2015.*

*It's been a long road from there to here. In the months just after the mayor's 2002 letter, says Fatuma Hussein, another Lewiston "resettler," "you wouldn't believe this was America." But even that didn't kill her faith in a future.*

*"I just remember myself saying, over and over, 'the sooner you get used to us living here, the sooner we can all get along.'"*

The first Westerner Said Mohamud ever met was a young American named John, who came to his village—Dhusa Mareb in central Somalia—in the early 1960s, when Said was six or seven years old. John was a Peace Corps volunteer. He had blond hair and blue eyes, and was often funny. With the help of the villagers, he built a two-room schoolhouse of wood and clay, where he taught the village children to read and write English. The children liked him, or wanted to; they called him Uncle John. At the same time, they were confused.

"We had been taught that people with white skin and light hair and colored eyes—they are the devil. They have horns growing from their heads. They are very bad."

Said himself has skin the color of dark chocolate. He is small and lean, in his late forties, though he looks younger. His black hair is close-cropped and receding; his eyes are very large. He speaks English with a phonetic, book-learned exactness ("peopl-ee," "color-ed"), smiling often, always widely, showing teeth the color of new piano keys.

The first time we met, outside the Lewiston, Maine, city hall on a weekday in early August 2003, he was wearing a red paisley tie over a white dress shirt with no jacket, dark pressed pants, and brown oxfords. He was returning from a job interview, he told me: this one with the Lewiston school system to teach high school chemistry (he has a doctorate in chemistry, from the University of Padua in Italy, and speaks five languages), though there had been many other interviews, he said. So far he had found nothing—"but there is time, something will happen for me." Meanwhile, he was taking a course in computer programming at a local college, and working to improve his English skills.

He lives, with his wife, Shukri, and their seven children—ages two through nineteen—in a rent-subsidized five-bedroom walk-up in a neighborhood of warehouses and cracked pavement a few blocks from Lewiston's downtown. The living room is a 12-foot square of worn carpet, with two stuffed chairs and a sagging sofa covered in a faded yellowish bedspread—all of it dwarfed by the silver, giant-screen television that covers most of the front wall. ("It is so the children will not argue, so they will stay quiet," is all Said will say about it when I ask.) In an alcove just out of sight, fifteen-year-old Abdirahman, a handsome, gangly six-footer who plays guard for the Lewiston Middle School basketball team, sits quietly in front of a computer screen.

Said, when I met him, had been in Lewiston only eight months, though Shukri and the children, he tells me, had come more than a year before that. Exactly how they all came here, and what transpired during that year-long separation, turns out to be elusive—for reasons, as near as I can tell, that involve a mix of pride, pain, and cultural outlook. But some things, the fundamental things, are clear: that Said, some 12 years ago, was separated from his family in the chaos and carnage of Somalia's latest tribal war ("People are dying in front of you, everybody is having a gun in his hand, you are stepping over dead people, it is unimaginable"), during which his year-old daughter was shot to death in Shukri's arms; that his family, like tens of thousands of Somali families, were held in a series of refugee camps; and that, for the last half of the 1990s, Said worked as an itinerant bookkeeper, homeless and without papers, through half of the east African subcontinent—Kenya, Uganda, Rwanda, Ethiopia, Zaire.

He washed up in 2000 in Alexandria, Virginia, by way of Johannesburg and Mexico City (there was a black market passport involved somewhere along the line here, but that's as precise as he'll be)—then on to Atlanta, which by then had become a processing center for Somali refugees. It was in Atlanta that he was reunited with Shukri and the children. There was a "disagreement" not long after ("These sorts of things we do not talk about"), and the family came north to Lewiston alone—part of a resettlement of some 1,100 Somalis, all of them relocated from other points in the US, who have come here since early 2001, most in the first 18 months alone.

Said meanwhile, still in Atlanta, took a job as a night-shift manager at a CVS, earning enough to buy himself a 10-year-old Toyota. At some point the couple reconciled, presumably by phone, and Said joined his family in the Park Street apartment in January 2003.

Eight days later, on January 11, an extraordinary thing happened in Lewiston. More than 4,500 people from all over New England, in defiance of a neo-Nazi group that had planned a rally to protest the 1,100 Somalis in the city, gathered at Bates College's gymnasium, in Portland, in a solidarity march. The hate group, whose leader, Matthew Hale, had planned to give a speech in the city that day ("The Invasion of Maine by Somalis and How We Can End It"), in the end managed to attract only 32 protesters, most of them too cowed to give their names. The speech was never given (Hale, arrested for soliciting the murder of a federal judge, was unable to attend), and the hate group limped out of town muzzled, embarrassed, and escorted by police. And, for Said and Shukri and hundreds more like them, Lewiston became an overnight Promised Land—or at least that's what most of them will tell you, and no doubt try their best to believe.

"Before the rally there was a lot of fear," says Said. "A lot of [us] were afraid. We did not know what would happen with so many people in one place. . .

"But then we *see*. These people are *good*. They come to support the Somalis. They don't know the Somalis—who knows Said Mohamud?—but yet they come to support us. They take it in their hands"—and here, for effect, he balled both hands into fists, leaned forward on the couch, and shook them—"and they say, 'These people are under our authority, it is not possible to mistreat them. We must take *care* of these people. They are not so far from us.'"

All this he shared with me over two long afternoons in his living room. We weren't always alone. On the first day, at a point about two hours in, Abdirahman appeared as if from nowhere, without a word, with a small, neat tray of orange sodas and pastries for two, then vanished just as fast. Half an hour later—again without warning—one of the most beautiful little girls I've ever seen, with tight black braids, half-dollar eyes, and a smile so pure you wanted to cry, crawled confidently into her father's lap, where she squirmed happily and played with the buttons on his shirt. She was Amina, he said, and she was 4 (which would place her birth in 1999, itself a mystery, but Said would only smile and shake his head when I inquired).

Shukri joined us the second afternoon. She is tall, heavyset, lighter skinned than her husband, with an almost perpetual shy smile and a wordless, natural-seeming warmth. Her English is halting—she served cookies instead: a Somali pastry ("made from flour, egg, sugar, olive oil, and a kiss from heaven") that she had baked and sold the week before, three for a dollar, in clear plastic packets at a Lewiston Somali women's center. She pressed these on me proudly and, when I smiled my appreciation, sent me home with my pockets filled.

For close to two hours that second afternoon, with Amina an on-and-off presence—crawling across her father's lap, sitting quietly in her mother's—the two talked as a family with me, sometimes directly, other times with Shukri relying on Said: about their losses, their differences, the sadness they feel for their country, their hopes for a better life. They spoke, a little reluctantly, about their lives as Muslims—Shukri practices Islam, her husband does not, but both are conditioned by its teachings—and about the fear they share that their children, growing up American, will be seduced away from the values of family and work. ("They see how the boys wear their pants—so low—and the big hair and the loud music. Then they come home to our house. It is hard. They are between cultures," said Said.) Shukri, speaking almost without help, told me about her family—listing them on the fingers of both hands—who have been scattered since the war began: her parents in Atlanta, brothers and sisters in London, Saudi Arabia, Kenya, Somalia, Ohio, and Kentucky. And her in Lewiston. "In Somalia before the war, we live all together, four generations," she said.

---

Somalia, on the eastern coast of Africa, is a piteously poor, drought-stricken, chronically war-torn nation of seven million Sunni Muslims, ungoverned and ungovernable, whose only lasting loyalties are to family-based clans. Three-fourths of its people are pastoral nomads, herdsmen who crisscross the country (about the size of Texas) in endless pursuit of grazable land. War and poverty are the only constants. Literacy is scattered and only recent. Those who can manage it—like Said—seek their training and education abroad.

Thirteen years ago, in what was the latest in a succession of savage tribal wars—coupled with the worst drought in memory—Somalia became a massive killing field, with some half a million dead before the carnage was done. Another two million Somalis were internally displaced, and

800,000 fled the country, landing in refugee centers—then diffusing—throughout Africa and the world.

Nearly all those in Lewiston today (or in Portland, Minneapolis, St. Louis, Atlanta, or wherever else they've landed) have lost someone; some have lost whole families. Whatever futures they had, or were working toward, in their home country—Said's degree in chemistry, Shukri's job teaching school—are largely valueless here. Most, when they arrive, speak little or no English. Few own property beyond their furniture and clothes. Then there is the food they eat, and the god they worship, and the blackness of their skin in this once all-white city in this whitest of all states, and those strange, bright-colored robes and headdresses they wear.

Certainly all this is part of what Said was talking about, part of what he meant when he said about the good people of Lewiston that they knew they "must take care" of their Somali brethren. He was talking about brotherhood, about doing unto others. He was talking about compassion. And given the savagery he had fled, it's not hard to see how the spectacle of 4,500 men and women marching on behalf of civil justice—on behalf of *him*—would leave a powerful mark.

But there's more to it than that, and he knows it—he was just smart enough not to say so to a writer with a notebook in his lap. He's a man who has lived half a lifetime with hatred; he's lost his future to it, and his daughter, and his homeland, and six years of his life. He walks the streets of Lewiston every day, reads the papers, and speaks the language better than most. And he knows that, for all the good intentions of last January's marchers, there are still at least as many Mainers who wish he and his people would just take their strange clothes and their problems and go home.

"When my grandparents came here, they worked, they didn't ask for handouts," one Lewiston-area resident, Marc Cyr—asked his reaction to the Somalis' presence in town—told a reporter the day of the January march. Many others said the same, and still do. Some say worse. ("These people are the enemy—make no mistake," a Portland man told the same reporter. "If they get the chance, they'll probably slit your throat.")

There have been rumors, almost since the day the first black face arrived in town: that every new Somali family was given a $10,000 check to start out; that Somalis were given vouchers for free cars; that Somali applications for housing and welfare were being processed ahead of non-refugees'. These were serious stories, which in time grew to truths—which were fed, at least sometimes, by sworn sightings: of Somalis pricing cars in a local dealership; of Somali women in a Lewiston Walmart, carts piled high with groceries, shamelessly passing food stamps back and forth; of the three Somalis leaving a pharmacy with a bagful of free drugs, their prescription order signed by a black man wearing a gold watch who refused to identify himself.

All the while, more black faces were arriving. Along Lewiston Street—the sad, mile-long strip of discount stores, missions, pawn shops, adult bookstores, and boarded storefronts that is the downtown's only real commercial strip—Somali men in long colored *macawis* skirts and women in flowered robes and *hijabs* (traditional headscarves) began to mix with the merchants and the drunks. Before long, an empty store-front in the 200 block had been quietly rented and adapted as a mosque, bringing worshipers who now came in daily streams. A second store-front, this one around the corner on Bartlett Street, became the city's first Somali *halal* market, selling food permitted by Islamic dietary laws. Not long after, there would be a community center, a second halal market, then the Red Sea Restaurant. And all the while, the city's backlog of rent-able housing—which, at least to start with, was plentiful and cheap—was filling with black African families headed, most often, by single mothers waiting, like Shukri, for husbands who had been separated by war, bureau-cracy, politics, or work.

For any city, this would have been a remarkable thing. For Lewiston—a city of 36,000, the poorest in the state—white and working-class to its core, the impact has been cataclysmic: the largest short-term influx of refugees, as a percentage of population, since records have been kept in New England. From any standard you choose to apply—cultural, social, economic—Lewiston is as ill-suited to the overnight absorption of 1,100 dispossessed black Muslims as any city, anywhere, you could name.

Said was happy here, he told me. His family was settling in—Abdirahman at the high school, an older daughter at UMaine, the younger ones in day care or grade school. If he and Shukri could only find work here (she was interviewing for a job as a cook), he felt sure they could make a life.

"In Atlanta, everywhere there were drugs and gangs," he said. "A lot of crime. And the teenagers, they are very easy [with sex]. The boy says, 'I love you, come [to bed] with me, I make nine dollars an hour, I will take care of you.' That is a very bad value, I think. . .

"Lewiston is better. It is a small town. You can rise up. You can get attention here. The crime is very low. The education is good. It is a very good place, I think, to [raise] your children."

You hear this almost anywhere you go in the Somali community—in or out of Lewiston. Three years ago, if you were a Somali yourself, in Atlanta or Minneapolis, newly fled from your war-ruined country, it is a message you would certainly have heard—by word of mouth from relatives, on the Internet, through the network of unseen "elders" who seem to be everywhere and nowhere at once: that the state of Maine had low crime and cheap housing, that the schools were good, that the cities were small and clean and surrounded by country; a peaceful, affordable, morally upstanding place.

The first families began arriving in February 2001, mostly from Portland, where the only available housing was in shelters. Very little notice was taken. In early summer the numbers increased; with the weather warming and people beginning to venture out, the black faces and bright robes drew more attention, though even then, remembers assistant city manager Phil Nadeau, "the calls we got were as much curiosity as unhappiness."

Then came 9/11. It's hard to know, really, how much this had to do with the sense of things in the city, though it wasn't long after—about three months, Phil Nadeau says—that the calls to the city council began to get more pointed, and the first rumors—the free-car vouchers, the $10,000 checks—began to be heard around town.

"We told them what there was to be told," Nadeau says. "We told them these were legal immigrants who were here because there was no more room at the inn. That there were vacant units in town, and they needed a place to live."

The rumors, of course, were false—there have been no special handouts. But, as with most rumors, there was a critical mass of truth: that the coming of the Somalis was a heavy hardship to a city already stretched beyond its means. And that if they were to eat and sleep and learn English even in part at Lewiston's expense, it stood to reason that the needs of others in the city were going to go unmet.

By early spring 2002, a year after the first Somalis arrived, the city's annual welfare budget had doubled, with 200 families—including 339 children—receiving food and housing aid. At the same time, only a tenth of the adult Somali residents were reported to be working (in many cases because of a lack of English skills). At Lewiston's Adult Learning Center, where half the students were now Somali, conditions were so grim that classes were being held in a stairwell.

This is a city with no fat to spare. The last of the mills have been gone for 30 years—though some of their husks still remain, as do the great-grandchildren of the French Canadians, the last great wave of immigrants, who came here 150 years ago to man them. The jobs today are few and low-paying; two hospitals and a college are the main employers. The city's tax rate is among the highest in the state. And there are fewer and fewer to pay it—a tenth of the population has left since 1990.

So, at least for some, there was anger. "An undercurrent of resentment," the mayor called it at the time. Others were more explicit. "Somalians Are Fed Before American Veterans and Maine's Homeless. Call All Elected Officials. Tell Them We Will Not Feed Foreigners Before Vets and the Homeless"—so read the block-lettered sign on the front lawn of a local resident, James Teehan, who told a reporter later by way of explanation, "I was so irritated, I had to do something."

<hr />

A hundred and fifty years ago, when the first French Canadians came to Lewiston to work in the mills, their children were beaten for speaking

French in school. Today, a local bank teller named Debbie, asked what she knows of the language of her grandfathers, is unashamed to say:

"*Ça va bien*," she says, and laughs. "Isn't that something? That's it. That's all I know."

Said does not believe it will happen this way with his people. There is a word Somalis use, he told me: "*Abtirsi*—it means remembering your origins, holding on to the traditional values, to what you come from. It is very important to us." He believes, he said, that if Lewiston's Somalis can do this—can hold on to their values and ways—the Somalis will be happier and more successful, and the two cultures, American and Somali, "will not be so different in the end."

To make his point, he told me about a wedding: two or three weeks before at the Fireside Inn in Lewiston, where a Somali woman named Nima had married a local man named Mack. It was a festive occasion, he said—an American dance band, recorded Somali music, and more than 100 guests. "It was the first," he said. "There will be others, I think."

The same evening he told me this, at the Red Sea Restaurant on Lisbon Street, the newest Somali business in town, my waitress was a tall, silent woman in her thirties in a long flowered dress. Her head was scarved. She was white. Her name, she said, was Aleesha. It was a new name, she told me, only several months old: "My Muslim name. I am training to be one."

She was going to the mosque every day, she said, to try to learn the Koran. It was hard going: "I don't speak the language. So I have to write down the phrases on pieces of paper and try to memorize them. Everyone else knows them all by heart. It is embarrassing sometimes." But her teachers—Abdi Rizak Mahboub, co-owner of the Red Sea, and Roda Abdi, who owns the halal market on Bartlett Street—had been very patient and helpful, she said.

I asked what has made her want to be a Muslim.

"Their peace," she said. "They are such a peaceful people. It is a peace I want in my life."

~—◦—~

The flow continued through the first year and most of the second, at the rate of at least 40 new arrivals a month. Then, on October 1, 2002, the mayor, Laurier Raymond, apparently emboldened, raised the stakes. In a letter, written in English, to the leaders of the Somali community and reportedly delivered by fax, he asked that the migration cease: "We have been overwhelmed and have responded valiantly. Now we need breathing room. The Somali community must exercise some discipline... Our city is maxed-out, financially, physically, and emotionally."

The letter, said the *New York Times* two weeks later, "exploded like a grenade." The Somalis accused the mayor of trying to incite violence; the governor defended the mayor ("I know Larry Raymond and he is not a racist"); the people were split, but very vocal (a pro-Somali rally, an anti-Somali petition). CNN aired the story. Two weeks later, in early November, Matthew Hale's World Church of the Creator declared its support for the mayor and received permission to gather in Lewiston January 11 to demand "the expulsion of the Somalis" from the city. A counter-rally, calling itself the Many and One Coalition, began forming within days. Among Lewiston's Somalis, there began to grow a long-remembered fear.

"In Somalia, we have no government, no protection. The police, the soldiers—you cannot trust who are your enemies, who will shoot you and who will not," Said explained to me early on our first afternoon. "Before the [rally] in January—so many people marching, and the police with their guns. Some of the people were afraid."

But there was no cause for fear that day in Lewiston. Hands were held, signs were waved, songs were sung; there were cheers, chants, speeches, laughter and tears. A black state senator called the day a "defining moment in history." Muhammad Ali, 38 years after he fought Sonny Liston in the Lewiston Armory, sent a letter defending the right of the Somalis "to live anywhere in the United States that they choose." Six children of different faiths led an auditorium full of men and women in prayers, accompanied by a Micmac flutist.

It is half an hour before sunset on an early August evening, warm and still bright with a leftover haze in the air. In the courtyard nearest to where

I am parked, between two so-called townhouses of Lewiston's Hillview Apartments, several girls and one boy, all between six and nine years old, are busy playing. The boy and one girl are white, and wearing T-shirts of no particular color. The other girls are black—Somali—dressed in small, bright-colored robes that wrap around and hang almost to the ground. Still, amazingly, they have no trouble running. Sometimes, when the boy and the girl in their T-shirts come close in their running to the Somali girls in their robes, they seem so drab it is hard not to notice.

Across the way, a tall white boy sits in a window with his long legs hanging over. He looks like a statue. In the doorway next to him, a Somali woman in a flowered robe is helping a younger boy, her son or grandson, lift his bicycle over the lip of the doorway into the hallway of the building. The older boy jumps down from his place in the window, disappears briefly, and a second later is lifting the bicycle above the shoulders of the younger boy into the hallway. The woman stands very still and smiles as she watches them both.

It is getting darker now. All around the courtyard, the doorways are filling with mothers. The children scatter, regroup, then scatter again, each time laughing louder—it is some joke or game I cannot make out in the dusk. A mother calls out from a doorway. The children scatter and regroup. The robes and the T-shirts, on each successive regrouping, are harder to tell apart.

# A New Hampshire Love Story
## *November 1997*

*On the east side of New Hampshire state road 103, about a mile north of the town I used to live in, there is a large rock with a faded, spray-painted message in white letters: "Chicken Farmer I Still Love You." No one at the time seemed to know the story behind it, except that it had been there as long as anyone could remember.*

*Until one day it was gone—effaced, painted over. A week later, just as suddenly, it reappeared.*

*This was too wonderful and mysterious for me to stay away from. There had to be a story there. There had to be lovers—or at least one unrequited lover. And he (or she, or they) must still be around. The flame must still be alive.*

*Was it? Is it? I don't know—I never found out for sure. But the message is still there, still on its rock, and every year or two (I swear) it gets freshened with a new coat of paint. So how do you argue with that?*

Twelve feet or so off the east edge of State Road 103, which runs north-south through the town of Newbury, New Hampshire (population 1,500 or so), there sits a squarish brown-gray slab of rock roughly the height of a man. Its southern face is flat, nearly smooth, at a billboard angle toward the traffic, coming north.

About 25 years ago, across from the rock on the west side of the road, there sat a tidy white cedar-shingled house in whose backyard, as it is remembered, a dozen chickens pecked about. Their eggs made breakfasts (and a tiny sideline business) for a family named the Rules—whose daughter Gretchen was pretty, smart, wistful, and sixteen.

There was a boy—a shy boy, also wistful, also a farmer, whose name is forgotten today, who pined for Gretchen Rule. He cast about for ways to tell her or show her — without telling or showing himself—then he hit upon the rock.

"CHICKEN FARMER I LOVE YOU," he wrote on it, in eight-inch high, spray-painted letters, one moonlit, high-starred night—or so the story goes.

And the girl saw and guessed the author (though it was only, really, a guess)—and the town and the passing motorists smiled, made their own guesses, and went on about their ways.

The message endured for years, though brambles grew up to obscure it, and the letters, once so bold and white, began to fade. Gretchen Rule went away to Harvard, then on to life. The boy, whoever he was—or is—became a man. The rock grew into a relic, a love note out of time.

One night, ten, perhaps 12 years ago (no one saw it happen, and no one today can say for sure), the brambles were cut away. And the message was repainted and renewed: "CHICKEN FARMER I STILL LOVE YOU."

The rock became a landmark. "It's your first left past Chicken Rock" the locals were wont to say. "Chicken," "love" and "farmer" were the first words one Newbury kindergartner—today a teenager—learned to read. And every two years or so, barely noticed, the letters would be freshened and the brambles cut away.

Then, in late April 1996, an unknown caller complained of "graffiti" to the New Hampshire Department of Transportation. By nightfall the same day, a three-foot square of rust-colored primer was all that was left of a shy boy's long-ago love. The *Concord Monitor* offered its requiem: "Love Message to Chicken Farmer No More."

A week passed. Then with the coming of dawn on April 30, the new sun rose on New Hampshire's stubbornest love: "CHICKEN FARMER I STILL LOVE YOU."

The same message, the same eight-inch letters. But bolder this time: thicker-lettered, almost crude, and painted rather than sprayed. As though written by an angry and defiant hand.

In Newbury, the townspeople, inspired now as never before, took steps to assure that their landmark would live on. "A Petition for the Status Quo," they called it, and filled it with 192 signatures in the space of a day. The DOT responded with a letter. The Chicken Rock's message would be forever safe.

And somewhere, surely, a shy, forty-ish man must have smiled.

# Inferno: The Worcester Fire
## *October 2000*

*"No one can know what we [went] through except for us," a Worcester MA firefighter would tell reporters five days after the deadliest fire in the city's history. "Nobody knows what it's like in a building like that except us."*

*The building is gone today, in its place a large red firehouse, the home of Engine Six, Ladder One of the Worcester Fire Department. In front of that is a small bricked-in circle, at its center a stone sculpture of a kneeling fireman facing a raised block of granite topped by a fireman's folded coat and helmet.*

*The simple, quiet eloquence of this memorial seems almost a rebuke against the catastrophic pointlessness of that night, December 3, 1999, when six firefighters, smoke-blinded in a massive, deserted warehouse, lost their lives in an effort to save the lives of two homeless drifters believed—wrongly—to be inside.*

*I spent most of two weeks with the friends, wives, bosses, and fellow firefighters of those six men—including an afternoon, with full gear and air pack, inside the state's Live Fire Training Facility— trying to find my way through what happened that night inside that hellish warehouse, how and why it was that some men lived while others died. What I came away with, I'm afraid, was closer to awe than understanding.*

It was late afternoon—somewhere around four-thirty—on December 3, 1999, and it was already more dark outside than light. On the corner of Franklin and Grafton Streets in downtown Worcester, a block from the I-290 overpass, Bill McNeil of Bill's Place Diner was getting ready for the early-supper crowd. Across the street from him and one flight up on a mattress in a corner of the second floor of the abandoned Worcester Cold Storage and Warehouse Company, a homeless, pregnant nineteen-year-old named Julie Ann Barnes, with an intellect that would later be described as "somewhat below average," was crayoning pictures in a coloring book. Next to her on the mattress was Tom Levesque, thirty-seven, also homeless, also in the words of an acquaintance, "kind of slow." The two were arguing, Julie Barnes would say later, over sex.

*"I lay on the bed and started coloring . . . He started to lay on top of me. pushed him off."*

The warehouse was a behemoth: a great, five-storied, ugly brown box—disused, unlighted, nearly windowless, the length of a football field—that began life, nearly a century ago, as a slaughterhouse and meatpacking plant. Over the years, there were storage rooms added, scores of them, and meat lockers the size of living rooms with ten-inch-thick metal doors. On all five floors it was the same: freezer lockers and storage space surrounding massive, columned open rooms—the old slaughter rooms, in one of which the man and the teenager now shared their mattress—all connected by a single, narrow, wrought-iron staircase with three or four turns to a floor.

Some years ago, to keep in the cold, the owners had added six-inch cork insulation over 18-inch brick walls, then coated it with Sheetrock sprayed with petroleum-based polyurethane foam.

There was a candle next to the mattress, the couple's only source of light. One of the two accidentally knocked it over, into a pile of Julie Barnes's clothes. The clothes caught fire. The two tried to stamp out the flames with their feet.

"But we couldn't. He hit it with a pillow, but the pillow caught on fire."

Probably they panicked. Then, at least briefly, Julie Barnes went searching for her cat and dog. But the warehouse was too massive and mazelike, and she soon gave up the search. The two then left the warehouse together and walked to the Common Outlets Mall, three blocks south, where they went to the Media Play arcade and listened to rock CDs.

"My cat and dog was in there," Julie Barnes, captured by a video camera with Tom Levesque just behind her, would tell a convenience-store clerk the next day. "And all my clothes got burned. I wasn't nowhere around."

———

At the hair salon where she works in a town just outside of Worcester, Michelle Lucey was finishing a regular client's color and cut. It was nearly six already, and she was booked until eight. Her two boys, Jerry and John, were at home with a sitter, having supper. By the time she got there, it would be close to nine; their time together ("watching TV, telling stories, catching up") was certain to be brief. Her husband, a fireman, was working nights this week and wouldn't be home until tomorrow morning at eight.

It was a busy life she led: school, soccer, the salon, the housework, getting the kids from here to there. It helped that her clients, most of them anyway, had been with her awhile and were willing to adjust to her hours, which changed according to her husband's. He worked a crazy schedule that changed from week to week.

"I'd arrange my appointments totally around Jerry's job. If he was working nights one week, I'd work days so someone would always be there for the kids. But it was hard. Sometimes a whole week would go by, we'd hardly see each other at all."

Saturday night was their time. "Date night" she calls it, then adds, "It was special," and smiles widely, without embarrassment, as though the words alone could somehow bring it back.

"We'd always go out, sometimes to J. P. Fisherman's in Leicester, sometimes somewhere else. Have a few drinks, go dancing, maybe with another couple, maybe just us. Whatever. Just be together. The kids, they didn't get it. 'You guys going out again?' they'd want to know. And we'd explain it to them, that Saturday nights were Mom and Dad's time to be man and wife."

It had always been this way for them: the hard work, the hectic days, the precious, squeezed-in hours alone. Ever since they met, as eighteen-year-olds in 1980, at the Big D market on Sunderson Road in Worcester. Jerry worked as a stock boy and Michelle was a cashier. He was driving a

1970 banana-yellow Plymouth Duster he'd bought with his savings from a newspaper route. Five years later, they married. By that time, he was driving a truck for Coca-Cola and she had finished hairdressing school.

"Things were never easy," says Michelle. "But we always found a way to make them work."

This particular Friday, Jerry had left the house before dawn to go to his second part-time job at the Massachusetts Fire Academy in Stow. From there, in the late afternoon, he'd gone directly to the Central Street station, where he was filling in this week for a man who was away.

"I woke up for some reason . . . I guess I had to go to the bathroom. And he was just leaving, just heading out the door. I met him there. I kissed him. I said, 'I love you, have a good day.' And that was it. He was gone."

———

At the Central Street fire station in downtown Worcester, just north of the Centrum, Captain Bob Johnson had been in the kitchen since a few minutes after four. It was nearly six now, and the meal was almost on the table: vegetables, a salad, a big loaf of fresh bread from Girardi's bakery, and 25 pounds of roast beef.

"I came in early to make it," Johnson remembers. "It takes some time to cook a roast big enough to feed 16 guys."

He is a large man of fifty-three with thinning gray hair and a direct, no-nonsense way. He was born and raised in Worcester and has been a fireman for 24 years. The cooking, he explains, is just something he enjoys.

"We spend a lot of time together, 14 hours a day some weeks, more time than we spend with our families. So mealtimes, they get to be pretty important. Breakfast, supper, whatever . . . the meals are a pretty big deal."

As he talks, other men wander in and out of the room—to relay messages, ask questions, or offer suggestions of things that need to be done.

It is a warm afternoon in mid-April, four months since the night of the 25-pound roast; the bays to the street are open, letting in a gentle breeze. In one of them, a man in a T-shirt is mounted on the side of a giant red ladder-truck polishing a length of brass; at a table toward the back, out of the way of the trucks and equipment, three men are sitting with their feet up, sections of the local paper in their laps, talking about the Red Sox, whose season is just two weeks old.

Roughly the same 16 men were here that evening in December. Captain Johnson and John Davies were both on Engine One; Bert Davis and Yogi Connole were on Ladder One; and Lieutenant Dave Halvorsen worked the Rescue squad. Charley Murphy, Bob McAnn, Bert Davis, Mike Coakley, and Tom Dwyer all worked Group Two out of Central Street that night, plus Jerry Lucey, Michelle's husband, and a firefighter named Paul Brotherton, who cooked omelet-and-potato breakfasts, watched monster movies with subtitles sometimes until three in the morning, and had six sons between the ages of six and fourteen.

The shift was only minutes old. Bob Johnson was in the kitchen, applying final touches. A second man was setting the table; Paul Brotherton was slicing the roast. The others were scattered: talking, doing odd jobs, reading the paper, finishing a shower, watching the news on TV.

"Jesus Christ, what's with those skinny little slices? Cut us some *meat*, will you?" It was Yogi Connole, pointing in mock derision at Paul Brotherton's half-carved roast.

"What are you, the portion police?" the other man shot back.

The two men continued their banter. The others, one by one, sat down to their plates. The roast began its turn around the table, then the vegetables and bread.

Someone was talking about Christmas, and how hard it was to shop for kids; another man said how it just seemed to get more commercial every year. The plates began filling. There were the clicks of cutlery on china, then that odd, brief semi-silence that always seems to drop over the beginning of a meal.

Then—at 6:13 p.m. exactly—three short, loud blasts from a box on the wall of the station. Then a longer, louder Klaxon sound, followed by a woman's voice: "Box 1438. Reported fire at 266 Franklin."

Bob Johnson and his men were the first to reach the scene, 6:16 is his best guess. The roof was giving off smoke. Beyond that, there wasn't much to see.

"I went in with John Davies, Paul [Brotherton], and Jerry Lucey," says Johnson. "We climbed the stairwell to the roof and checked every floor on the way. We weren't wearing our masks. The air was still clear, there was no smoke, no flames, no need [for masks] at that time."

What they *did* find, says Johnson, on the roof, enclosed inside a skylight that formed the top of an old elevator shaft, were "embers, bright red, and thick as rain," which told them, he says, that "something big was happening" and that it had "a pretty good head start." They just didn't know yet where it was.

Mike McNamee, as district chief for the south half of the city, was the commander in charge of operations that night. Arriving three minutes or so behind Bob Johnson's Engine One, he and his men found fire on the second floor of the building—on the opposite side of the fire wall from where Johnson's men had looked—but otherwise his impressions were close to the same.

"There was light smoke on the upper levels, but not so much that we had to wear our masks. We were talking to each other, walking freely, trying to determine how far the fire had gone."

Sometime around 6:26 p.m. (though Captain Johnson says, "things were crazy; it could have been later than that"), Bill McNeil, the owner of Bill's Place, the diner across the street, flagged down a policeman to tell him of some homeless people who, he thought, might be living in the warehouse. They came by his diner sometimes, he said, asking for coffee or water; he'd given one of them a job briefly the summer before.

The message went out on the radio. Jerry Lucey and Paul Brotherton, still with Bob Johnson and John Davies on the warehouse's upper floors, split off to take up the search. ("It was never talked about," says Johnson today. "The report came in, and they just left. They were working Rescue—saving people was what they did.") The other two men continued down the stairs.

"We got to the second floor. There was this huge room with big columns, and at the end of it, about 50 feet down, a metal door . . ."

Several other firemen were on the second floor by then. One of them, Yogi Connole, approached the door as Johnson watched.

"He touched it, he maybe pushed it open an inch—and WHOOOM! The flames just grabbed hold of it, just sucked at it, *sucked* at it, like some sort of suction machine, they were wanting that oxygen so bad."

When firemen talk about fires, it is often as though they are talking about something alive—an animal, even a person—perhaps because nothing inanimate could command as much respect.

"It was starving in there. Starving for air. And that door—Yogi's holding onto it with everything he's got, and he's a pretty big guy, six-foot-two, probably 250 pounds—and those flames, they're wanting to just suck it right out of his hand."

They brought up two hose lines, a 1¾-inch and a two-inch, turned on the power, and aimed them at the door. Yogi Connole, still holding on, looked back at the men behind him and screamed, "Put on your masks; it's gonna get ugly!" then let go of the door and jumped back. Within seconds, remembers Bob Johnson, "there was fire everywhere you looked."

Still, even at that point, it remained controllable: formidable, always dangerous, but not yet truly fearsome. The sort of thing they trained for, that they saw and fought at least several times a year.

Then something happened. More than one thing, probably. Some sort of freakish chemical chain reaction. There are several theories, though no one would claim to know for sure.

What seems most certain is that at some very specific point, the flames reached the polyurethane that coated the old cork insulation—and everything, inside of seconds, went to black.

"It took about four seconds," Chief McNamee says. "Four seconds. From flame on the lower levels and light smoke on the upper ones, to just black, hot, boiling smoke. Everywhere, all five floors, total blackness. Just like that."

Then there was the other thing. It happened later, five minutes, ten minutes, there's no agreement on when. Some say it was a "flashover," a simultaneous igniting of every combustible thing at once, a single, explosive moment at which the radiant heat in a space or room has pushed all its elements—walls, floor, doors—to the edge of their tolerance, and they all erupt as one. This, if it happened, would have sounded like a huge, booming shudder of air being released—a sound some men that night claimed to have heard—and would have appeared as a rolling, hungry wall of fire.

"Something catastrophic happened in that building," says Bob Johnson. "Something *incredible*. Who knows what? And the velocity of it, just the velocity. So intense. I'll never forget it. I've never seen anything like it in my life."

Sometime around then, 6:45 p.m. is his best guess, the bell on his air mask sounded: five minutes left in his tank. He turned, made his way downstairs, and was outside switching tanks, chugging water, when he heard the first Mayday come in. It was from Rescue One, Lucey and Brotherton. The caller said that they were lost, that they couldn't find the exit, but that they thought they were "two floors below the roof."

It was a little after seven when Michelle Lucey, still at the salon, got a call from her brother telling her there was a fire in the city. "He didn't sound especially concerned," she says. "He said he just wanted me to know. I didn't think too much of it. Not then." She knew the dangers, she says. Her husband had told her the stories: about how fires got started, and how fast they built; how "it gets so hot in there sometimes that the linoleum in somebody's kitchen will be sticking to your gloves." Even about the time or two, she says, that "he didn't think he was going to be coming out."

But she didn't worry. She didn't see the point: "He ate and slept the fire department. It was most of what he thought about, and all he ever wanted to do. It was his friends, his dreams, it was how he spent his time. Was I going to stand in the way of that? Would you?"

Michelle's last client had left half an hour before. She was cleaning up: sweeping, tidying, getting ready to close shop. Shortly before eight-thirty, she phoned a friend of her husband's—also a fireman—who, with his wife, was expected at a Christmas party she and Jerry were planning at J. P. Fisher-man's the following Saturday night. She hadn't heard from them. She wanted to confirm that they were planning to attend.

"He said, 'Do you have the TV on?' I said no, I didn't, I was still at the salon. There was this really long pause. I said, 'Mark, what's happening?

What's going on?' He said, 'Michelle, go home, make some calls.' There was still hair on the floor of the salon. I kept sweeping, I couldn't help myself. About halfway through, I realized I was crying . . . I knew it was Jerry. I knew right then he was gone."

At the fires scene, from the moment of the first Mayday, the rules changed. With two men missing, the fire was no longer the focus; it was a rescue operation now. Thirty-five men crawled all five floors of the building on their hands and knees, blind as bats ("The only thing you could see was your finger, if you touched your face mask"), banging axes, beating tools, shining beams, holding onto the ankles of the man just in front. The smoke was dense, black, and boiling ("Like being inside a tornado," one man said); the flames cracked like gunshots; there was the sound of wood crashing; the temperature at the ceiling was near 1,000 degrees.

Bob Johnson, on the fourth floor, ran into a column, swiveled, banged into a wall, and was lost ("Now I'm scared. I'm not looking for my friends anymore, I'm thinking I'm gonna die") Chief McNamee, a floor below him, went through one door, then another, then—"for a terrible long moment"—couldn't find his way back out. Dave Halvorsen, from Central Street, was "hopelessly lost" until he spotted a beam of a light. Another man, Mark Fleming, crawling the floor, lost, afraid, and nearly out of air, would tell reporters six days later, "It seems like it's still the same day, the same call." There were some unspeakable terrors endured.

"No one can know what we [went] through except for us," a still-raw Mike McNamee said five days after the fire. "We fight together, we laugh together, we cry together, we eat and sleep together—and nobody knows what it's like in a building like that except us."

It was somewhere around seven when the second Mayday came in. "We're lost. We're running out of air. We're near a window." But there were no windows above the first floor.

Chief McNamee told the caller (he thinks it was Paul Brotherton, though he says he can't be sure) to hit his post alarm, which would have sent out a screeching signal audible to anyone nearby. Seconds later, the chief got a radio call from dispatch saying that they had picked up a signal that there was a firefighter down.

The caller had hit the wrong alarm. "Paul—Paul or Jerry, whichever one it was—the carbon monoxide may have gotten to him already by then."

There was one more communication, which the chief will only paraphrase. "He said they were on the floor, buddy-breathing [sharing a single air tank, because the other had run out]. He said to please help them, to please come quickly. He sounded a little frantic. He sounded scared."

Kevin Maloney, another firefighter, is a close friend of Jerry Lucey. He was once a diver for the fire department. And when he thinks of his friend's last moments, this is what he likes to believe they were like:

"Once, on a dive in Lake Qunisigamond, 70 feet down, I ran out of air. I thought it might be the end. It was kind of a peaceful thing, though, coming up—fighting to swim, to stay alive, but at the same time knowing it could be over, saying goodbye to all the people I loved. . . . I think maybe that's how it was for Jerry. I hope so, anyway."

Chief McNamee, from the base of the warehouse stairwell, began dispatching searchers, linked now by rope tethers, to the third, fourth, and fifth floors. Two members of a ladder crew, standing near him, were on the radio, trying to raise their mates inside.

"'Ladder 200 to Ladder Two.' 'Ladder 200 to Ladder Two.' 'Ladder 200 to Ladder Two.' Four times I hear this. Each time, there's no answer. And I know I've lost two more."

This time it was Tim Jackson, lover of Korean lilacs and Harley Davidsons, father to three sons; and Tommy Spencer, a liturgical minister, soccer coach, and baseball trivia buff, also the father of three. "I gotta call it," Mike McNamee said then. And he did. Standing in the doorway, his short, compact, fifty-one year-old body blocking access to the stairwell, he said simply, to all who approached, "No more."

"What do you mean, '*No more*?'" It was Paul Brosnahan, Tommy Spencer's friend—shrieking, frenzied, disbelieving—who could have picked up Mike McNamee, if he'd chosen, and moved him aside as easily as a chair.

"I mean, we've already lost four. No more."

No one will say much about what happened then ("Some things are just too private" is what Dave Halvorsen has to say about much that went on that night), but Paul Brosnahan did not challenge the chief. No one else did, either. It's safe to say that men were screaming, men were crying, that the agony of those moments was as monstrous as the worst you'd imagine it to be. But no one challenged Mike McNamee in the extraordinary decision he made. Four men were lost already to what he would call "the building from hell." There would be no more.

At somewhere around eight, he sounded the "evacuate" alarm, a long, deep, plaintive wail from the trucks. "I honestly don't believe so," he says, when asked if any of the men inside might have still been alive to hear.

With all the men now outside, he ordered a roll call. Jay Lyons and Joe McGuirk from Engine Three, the first an apprentice bagpiper, the second a father of two, both men in their thirties, failed to answer. So now the number was six.

At that point, says Bob Johnson, "The grief took on physical stuff. It got physical. I can't even say what I mean."

Michelle Lucey returned home a few minutes before nine. Her mother, sister, and brother, in quick succession, phoned. Six men were missing, no names had been released, there was no reason to suppose that Jerry was one of them. But she knew.

Between ten and eleven her brother arrived. "Just don't let me see a fire chief's car pull up here," she said to him. Minutes later, one did.

The police drove her and her eleven-year-old, Jerry, to St. Stephen's Church on Hamilton Street, two blocks from the fire, where the families were being taken to meet with each other and with counselors, priests, and friends. (The firemen had their own church, Our Lady of Mt. Carmel, where they would gather for prayer, aid, and simple grieving for most of the next eight days.) "There was a lot of hugging and crying," she says. Sometime during the night, some of the wives—but not Michelle—were escorted to the fire scene, a full inferno now with 100-foot flames, where the search for bodies would begin the next day. What she mostly remembers, she says, is "the faces of those men. And their smell, their smoke-smell, like my husband when he sweated. I'll never forget that smell."

Around one in the morning, "when I knew there was no hope left," she took her son and went home.

———⌣———

In the city of Worcester, maybe in all of New England, there has never been anything like what happened next. For eight days, 400 men, bone-weary, with shovels, trowels, sieves, gloved hands, and garden rakes, sifted the rubble of the mammoth warehouse—bent steel doors, burnt timbers, twisted metal stanchions, an acres-wide field of ruin 40 feet high in spots—for the bodies of their friends. They worked through rain, 50-mile-per-hour winds, and no sleep. For eight days, aided by an 80-foot crane that bit off whole slabs of the warehouse's innards and dropped them at their feet; by police helicopters; and for a while, by a body-sniffing dog, they raked and shoveled and sifted. The Red Cross fed them. There were counselors, masseuses, and cell phones in a tent across the way to ease their aches and terrors and keep them in touch with their wives. If they left at all, it was only for naps, and there were few enough of those. Thirty hours at a stretch was common. Some worked 50.

For the first two days, nothing but clues: an air tank, a belt buckle, a nylon helmet strap, the rumors of a hand. Then, at a little after ten in the morning of the third day, the first body—Tim Jackson's. They brought him out, covered, on a stretcher, from the northeast corner of the warehouse's second floor. Half the men went to attention; the other half saluted. Every helmet came off. The hoses went to a trickle; a giant wrecking ball was lowered instantly to the ground. Many, spontaneously, knelt in prayer.

Over the next six days, one by one—no two were found together—the remaining five bodies came out: Jay Lyons, Joe McGuirk, Tommy Spencer, Jerry Lucey, Paul Brotherton. Each time, the family was summoned from where it waited, in blue tents by nearby railroad tracks, to take part in a spontaneous ceremony over the body's covered remains. Each time but for the last one, when the ceremony was concluded, the body search resumed.

And behind them in the streets were men and women from Worcester and beyond. Hundreds of them, as reverent as worshippers, behind barricades in the darkness and rain, most with black ribbons or buttons pinned to their chests with photos of the dead men; some—the children especially—hugging gifts: the wreaths, poems, photos, stuffed animals, badges, fire hats, tributes ("Firefighters Saved My Baby"), and crayoned prayers ("And flights of angels sing thee to thy rest") they had brought to pile on the huge red fire-engine shrine that, by the third day, was buried already beneath the crude memorials of a city that seemed desolate in its grief.

Local teachers assigned their students essays on heroism. Impromptu prayer vigils took place almost nightly on Grafton Street. Constance Morrison, the head of the Red Cross for central Massachusetts and a Worcester native, put in 20-hour stints outside the warehouse directing volunteers. "It is my pleasure to do this. This is my city. We have grief in our hearts."

On Thursday, December 9, six days after fire, the six fallen men were honored in the largest single event in the history of the city of Worcester, which was watched by millions of TV viewers nationwide. Fifteen thousand mourners, including the president and vice president of the United States, filled the Centrum, with another 35,000 left to march or gather out-side. Thirty thousand firefighters, most in full dress—from Dublin, Ireland; Lexington, Kentucky; Washington, Anchorage, London, Jersey City, Milwaukee, Windsor, Ontario; and Kittery, Maine—marched for an hour through dead-silent streets.

It was a true hero's goodbye. There was a color guard at full attention with chrome-plated fire hooks and gleaming silver axes; and bagpipers, backed by snare drums, in full-kilt tartans playing "Amazing Grace" and "Minstrel Boy." Even, from a church tower three blocks south, a six-foot-six church sexton, Charles Ketter, in full Nigerian funeral robes pulling on the ropes of a 200-pound church bell, which pealed twice every minute for most of the afternoon.

When Bill Clinton and Al Gore arrived together in the Centrum, the crowd was respectful, but not terribly impressed. "They noticed," says one fireman, "but they didn't exactly knock themselves out." When the

Brotherton family arrived—Paul's wife, Denise, and their six boys—five thousand people stood up, five thousand people stayed standing, and not one of them sat, until the last of the Brothertons sat down.

The next day, at 6:13 p.m. on December 10, the one-week anniversary, the hoses and wrecking ball went silent, and helmet-less firefighters stood at attention at the edge of the warehouse's now-collapsed north wall as bagpipers played "Amazing Grace" in a pelting, windblown rain.

On Saturday, December 11, at 11:20 p.m., Paul Brotherton's body, the last of the six, was pulled from what was left of the second level of the warehouse. It had been eight full days and nights. "And now," as city fire chief Dennis Budd told reporters at the scene, "we've brought everybody home."

About 500 people—firemen, police, relief workers, and civilians—were there when they brought the body out. All stood at attention as the stretcher bearing the remains passed between two long rows of firemen, who held their helmets over their hearts.

Then a remarkable thing happened. Some 200 firemen, most in groups of ten or 12, walked slowly to the perimeter of the wreckage, mounted the ladders still perched against it, climbed to the second-floor deck of the building, turned, and saluted the crowd. The warehouse, blackened, half-gone, still smoldering, was lit by searchlights. The crowd on the street, deathly quiet, stood in black.

And then, after it all—after the salutes and the silence, and the days of crying and searching, and the bearing away of the last man—what happened, though strange in the telling, must have seemed the most natural thing in the world. They cheered. The firemen first, beginning with those on the warehouse deck, then the families in their cluster under the ladders, then the crowd.

"It was to say to the building, 'You did not beat us,'" said Lieutenant Donald Courtney to reporters the next day. "It was to say, 'Hey guys, it's over, you are strong.'"

## The Aftermath

In Worcester, both the scars and the tributes are deep and likely to be lasting. Julie Barnes and Tom Levesque were arraigned on six counts each of involuntary manslaughter and held on $1 million cash bail. This amount was later reduced (to $75,000 for Barnes and $250,000 for Levesque). Levesque remains in jail, and Barnes resides in the custody of a family in Maine, pending a court date. Both have pleaded not guilty and are being represented by court-appointed attorneys. Both, following independent psychiatric evaluations, were judged competent to stand trial. The warehouse, by early spring, was gone without a trace. Razed and flattened, its remains were carried away in trucks. The site is now a football-field-size expanse of new gravel, enclosed behind a fence. "Looking at it now," says Kevin Maloney, "it's amazing how small and innocent it seems."

The firefighters' union is working to raise $1 million to fund a memorial—a statue or perhaps a small museum. The location has yet to be determined. "Anywhere but the warehouse site," Maloney says.

The city of Worcester, in its proposed 2001 fiscal plan, cut six positions from the fire department budget (from 469 to 463). Maloney, in addition to his feelings about the significance of the number six—which he simply calls "ironic"—says he "can't help but be struck by the incredible discrepancy between the support we've had from the people and the priority our city administration apparently attaches to our work."

The *Worcester Telegram and Gazette* established a fund to benefit the six firefighters' families. Donations soon exceeded $6 million.

The healing continues, and it takes many forms. Mike McNamee, the chief who ordered the evacuation of the building when, to his knowledge, there were four men lost inside, calls it "the hardest decision I will make in my lifetime" and admits to "some very bad moments, some dark times" in the aftermath. Still, he says, "Placed in the same situation, equipped with the same knowledge, I'd make the same decision again. I've found some peace in knowing that."

"It'll be a long, long time before all the wounds heal," says Bob Johnson, who, five months after the fire—"to get some kind of closure"—was making arrangements to listen to that Friday night's radio tapes. "I've got to do something to put it behind me. I just keep on fighting that fire in my head."

Paul LaRochelle, Jerry Lucey's partner and closest friend in the fire department ("There was no greater guy in the world"), is the new owner of Jerry's prized Harley Davidson, which Michelle gave to him as a final gift from his friend. His first ride was on New Year's Day; he biked to the cemetery to say a prayer at Jerry's grave. "I told him, 'Now we'll always be together,'" he says thickly, through his tears. "'Now I'll always get to ride with you.'"

Michelle is holding up. The key, she says, is "just to stay busy. There's less time to miss him that way." She continues her work at the salon part-time, nearly every day. Several times a week, there are firefighters' functions to attend: city council meetings, meetings on the disposal of hazardous waste (another of her husband's many causes), benefits, memorials, and speaking engagements. There was an appearance in Washington to tes-tify on be-half of firefighting funds and a guest appearance at an April Red Sox game (at which Kevin Maloney sang the National Anthem and Tommy Spencer's son threw out the first ball).

"I speak for him," she says. "I represent him. It's the closest I can get to him being still alive."

Her two sons are coping, each in his way. "John [at eight, her younger one], he's the more expressive, the more out there with his feelings. I can say to him, 'Listen, if you see me crying, you can come and give me a hug.' And he will . . ."

Her eleven-year-old, Jerry, she says, is quieter and harder to bring out. "He just watches and listens, and takes things in." Still, for all the sorrows he's witnessed and the vigils he's shared in, and whatever private loss he must feel, there is no shaking one thing: He wants to be a fireman one day.

"I'd be the proudest mother in the world," Michelle Lucey says.

# The Redemption of Julie Barnes
## *January 2002*

*This story, which should best be read as a sequel to the last one—*
*"Inferno," the story of the Worcester MA warehouse fire—seems, in the*
*years since I wrote it, to have unwritten itself. At the time, in early*
*2002, it carried a message of silver linings: that no loss, no matter how*
*horrific, was beyond the chance of delivering a measure of redemption*
*But a simple Google search tells me now that, at least in the case of*
*Julie Barnes, the message is different today.*

*Still, there is a story here. I think: of generous hearts, of hopeless-*
*ness turned to hope, of youth and change, and choices, right or wrong.*
*The postscript that follows the story will bring the past into the pre-*
*sent—and from that you can judge for yourself.*

She was a child without a chance in the world. Homeless, pregnant, pen-
niless, mentally slow, beaten and abused, living in an abandoned warehouse in the dead of winter with a vagrant batterer twice her age who
forced himself on her daily—a nineteen-year-old with the mind of a ten-
year-old, whose only possessions were her clothes and coloring books, and
whose only friends were an orphaned dog and cat.

And then even they were gone—dead, in the fire she was accused of
setting—and she was in jail, charged with a crime she hadn't the means to
understand. She would deliver her baby, alone, six months later, chained
by her feet to the bed.

Her name was Julie Barnes. I first heard of her two years ago last
month, when the story of a fire in a Worcester, Massachusetts, warehouse,
and the six firefighters whose lives it claimed, briefly led the national
news. TV images showed a dazed, dirty, frightened-looking teenager in
sneakers and blue jeans and her older codefendant, Tom Levesque, heads

bowed, in handcuffs and leg chains, standing before a judge in the dock of a Worcester court. Their story was too simple to be doubted: A candle had been accidentally kicked over, next to the mattress they shared on the second floor of the converted slaughterhouse, while Julie was busy coloring in her coloring book.

The two were charged with manslaughter. Julie was ordered held on $1 million cash bail (eventually reduced in several stages to $25,000). I was at work at the time on a story of the fire, though it was the dead firefighters and their families, not the homeless couple, who were the focus of my piece. I told a friend that I thought the charges against Julie were unfair but that she might be better off in jail than on the streets. For a child so luckless it seemed the best that could be hoped for.

---

"One day I'm in prison. The next day I'm in *Maine*."

It is an early afternoon in mid-August, two summers after the warehouse fire, hot and nearly cloudless outside. On the couch across from me in the Ellsworth home of Tim and Debb King, the chubby, wide-faced teenager—she is twenty-one now, but looks no older than sixteen—sits grinning widely, proud of the perfect truth of what she has just said. She says it a second time:

"Prison one day. The next day, *Maine!*"

She flings her arm widely to signify the full expanse of her meaning, to make certain I understand that "Maine" is now her term for all that is good in life. Then, just as quickly, her arm drops, the grin leaves her face, and she is back to the magazine in her lap, which is open to a photo spread of Jus-tin, the lead singer of 'N Sync, who, she has told me earlier—actually reddening—is *"so, so, so good-looking."*

The Kings' adopted daughter Jennifer, a shy, elfish-looking eighteen-year-old with a perpetual half-smile, sits briefly on the arm of the couch, looking over the older girl's shoulder, wordlessly sharing the pleasures of Justin's wonderful good looks. A fourteen-year-old niece, Sabrina, pretty and talkative, sits cross-legged on the floor. Nate, the Kings' four-year-old grandson, toddles in, oblivious, and plants himself on Julie's lap, briefly displacing the magazine. She kisses the top of his head loudly, then takes it in both hands and plants a kiss on the end of his nose. Nate laughs and squirms. The girl beams, plainly delighted:

"They all love me *too much*," she says. But it's clear her meaning is her own.

Julie Barnes is Julie King today. That happened, officially, before a probate judge in the Ellsworth, Maine, city courthouse, at 10:55 in the morning, last August 14, a week before I met her—though it was no more than a formality by then.

It is an extraordinary story. If you believe in miracles, you could say it is that.

It began, as such stories often do, with the smallest sort of coincidence—when Tim King, Ellsworth's city manager, scanning the *Boston Globe* for news of the Celtics only weeks after the Worcester fire, happened across a picture of Julie Barnes in court.

"I can still see the moment," Tim says today. "I can see it as clear as day." He is a beefy, balding, open-faced man in his late forties, with a plain, no-nonsense manner and an optimist's easy smile.

"That picture. Her face, her eyes, her expression, *everything*—it was like looking at Jennifer. I said to my wife, 'Debb, Debb, come here, you've got to see this.'"

Debb King looked and agreed: The resemblance was uncanny. She did some checking. And yes, remarkably, it was true—the two girls were sisters, born of the same mother, separated by order of the state of Massachusetts five days after Jennifer's birth. Jennifer, adopted by Debb and her then-husband as an infant more than 17 years earlier, had known she had an older sister but knew nothing of her fate. Julie had been told, years ago by her mother, that her younger sister had died.

Both girls (like their mother, Evelyn Menard) had been mentally slow since birth. Jennifer had grown up the way all children should—happy, carefree, wanting for nothing and nourished by love. Julie, beaten by her father, molested by her stepfather and a boyfriend of her mother's, taken by court order from her mother as a seven-year-old, and homeless since 18, had endured—and now, in jail, was still enduring—a life of unpardonable hell.

Debb King is a tall, blond, buoyant woman with a quick smile and a certain, earnest manner. The first steps she took, in those early weeks two years ago—a phone call to Julie's lawyer, some letters to state senators and reps—were meant, she says, "only to see that Julie was OK, that she'd be treated fairly. The idea, at that point, was to stay behind the scenes."

But one thing led to the next. And on the Sunday after Mother's Day, the King family, including Jennifer, first introduced themselves to Julie, then eight months' pregnant, in the visitors' quarters of the Framingham state women's prison.

On June 8, 2000, Julie, alone and in leg chains and with three guards at the door, gave birth to a seven-pound, 14-ounce baby boy. She named him Joshua. Five hours later, Debb and Jennifer, who'd found out too late to be there in time for the birth, were taking turns holding Joshua at the end of Julie's hospital bed. (Within 24 hours Joshua was taken from his mother and remanded by the state of Massachusetts to the care of a foster family in Worcester, where he remained as of early last fall.)

The next goal was bail money. Eight weeks of phone calls, Rotary Club addresses, a TV appearance, meetings with church groups, letters to the press—and by mid-July 2000, the $25,000 was in hand.

On Friday, July 14, Julie arrived for the first time at the Kings' home, officially in their custody pending the outcome of the manslaughter charge. "She was tired and disoriented," Tim King remembers. "It was a confusing time for her, for all of us, I think. The charges were still hanging. We were still getting to know each other. You couldn't call it a euphoric day."

Two months later, in September 2000, the charges against her were dropped. And Julie Barnes was home to stay.

It has not been an easy time, say the Kings. For the first month or two, she carried herself with her eyes to the floor, had a difficult time accepting affection (especially from males, including Tim), and would barely talk at all. It was longer than that before she stopped eating with her fingers and talking in the language of the street. She would take baths, but never a shower—she had once been molested in the shower. She was obsessed about the doors being locked at night. ("She was afraid someone would take her away," says Tim King.) On car trips, incessantly, whenever the gas gauge showed less than half full, she would pester the driver to stop right away and fill up.

"We couldn't figure that one out at first," Tim says. "Then it came out—it seems her mother's boyfriend, when she was a little kid, he'd take her on a drive, then pretend he'd run out of gas. He'd molest her, right there by the side of the road."

These days, though, life is good. Julie is talkative now and full of laughs. She showers routinely, worries less about door locks and gas gauges, gives and receives hugs and kisses freely, and calls her new parents Mom and Dad. She has a regular job, at the Holiday Inn in town, cleaning rooms and making beds; she earns $7 an hour and swims in the pool most days after work. She is learning from Debb how to spot a bargain, how to work a computer, and what a budget is. Once a week she visits a counselor, where her "drawing therapy"—some memories are too painful to speak out loud—is gradually unlocking the horrors. She works on her hand-writing through letters to her mother, is improving her reading skills with movie magazines, and has learned to eat lobster ("At first she wouldn't touch it, but she's a real Maine woman now," says Debb), to make tacos, and to cook macaroni and cheese. Along with her sister Jennifer she shares in the daily chores.

She visits Joshua for two hours every second Friday, at the Department of Social Services in Worcester, where she feeds him, changes his diapers, and joins him in toddler games. She started parenting classes last fall and hopes to win him back—but the state of Massachusetts has opposed it, and that will one day be up to a judge. In the meantime, she is very, very loved:

"A child like this," says Debb King—referring, by implication, to both Julie and her sister Jennifer—"a child like this is a blessing and a wonder. You *keep* her longer. She's five years old a few more years. A teenager a few more years. She doesn't leave you as soon. And the love she gives us. And to see these two sisters together—it's such a gift for us...

"Those firemen [who died in Worcester]—it wouldn't have happened except for them. None of this would have happened. We wouldn't know Julie today. Julie wouldn't have us. Jennifer wouldn't have a sister."

But Debb King knows, too—as everyone knows—it can't possibly last forever. Julie is twenty-one. The street, and prison, are behind her. The goal now is a place, and a life, of her own. It's a goal her new parents share, that they're building toward every day: her own place nearby, with some serious supervision involved.

"But you could come and visit. And I would invite you," Julie says. And everyone in the room nods and smiles.

"But not always, only sometimes.... Sometimes when you call, you'll say, 'Hello, Julie, this is Mom and Dad. Can we come for dinner?'"

"And I'll say, 'Whoops, whoops, wrong number. No Julie at this number.' And that'll be no visit for my new mom and dad."

She roars at this. The whole room roars. Still laughing, she seems about to pitch forward from the couch. Then she looks up at us, from her bent-double posture, and barely manages the words:

"I'm pretty funny, huh?"

"You're a *gift*, Julie," says Debb King, beaming. "You're an absolute, positive gift."

## Postscript

*Sadly, the Cinderella story didn't last.*

*Not long after she moved in with the Kings in Elllsworth, Julie took a housekeeping job at a local Holiday Inn. While there, according to media reports, she met a man and fell in love. In 2007, against the advice of the Kings, the two were married and moved in together. A year later they had a son, Matthew. They have since broken contact with the Kings.*

*"We were there to help change a path for her" Debb King told a reporter for The Worcester (MA) Telegram in 2009. "But now she's chosen her own... Maybe that was the change that was supposed to come out of all this."*

*In the fall of 2015, according to a brief listing in the* Ellsworth *(ME)* American, *the couple were divorced. I've been unable to trace Julie further.*

# "Something Bad Was Going to Happen"
## *September 2002*

*It has been nearly three months, as I write this, since the last school shooting. But I know—we all know—that the next one will come: tomorrow, next month or next year. And we know too what will happen then: "thoughts and prayers," endless exacting probes of the shooter's life and psyche, lots of earnest chatter about the terrible ubiquity of guns. Then, soon enough, will come the next shooting.*

*In New Bedford MA in early November 2001, a shooting was to happen. The plans had been laid (it was to be "bigger than Columbine"), the guns and ammunition gathered, the date selected by the five students involved.*

*Except it didn't happen. Not because of security guards, metal detectors, on-site heroics or any of the other safeguards we're forever talking about. It didn't happen because a teacher had earned a student's trust.*

*"She listened. And it seemed like she cared," the troubled, parentless eighteen-year-old would say later to police. She was to be one of the shooters, she told them. There would be many deaths. Instead, several nights before it all was to happen, she had arrived at the door of the teacher's home, frightened and in tears, to warn her of the plan.*

*This is a story about that teen, and that teacher, and how one came to care and the other to trust. And maybe about one way to make other bad things not happen.*

*"Every year I meet another Amy," the teacher said not long ago. "We can prevent a lot of problems if we take the time to hear what our children are telling us they need."*

She is the high-school teacher we all remember. The one with the eagle eyes and the brittle voice and the steely stare that withered you from half a room away. She was your nemesis. She docked points for missed commas, gave detentions for "hallway rowdiness," eyed you icily over bifocal lenses and reminded you that "Education is a privilege, not a game."

Privately you feared her. In the halls, though, between classes, you made bad jokes with classmates that involved crude corruptions of her name. You mocked her frumpy dresses, mimed her shrill, outdated dictums, and pronounced world-wearily (you were seventeen at the time), "The old bitch, she has no life." Still, in the end—always, and you knew it—she had the final word.

She still exists. Her name is Rachel Jupin. She teaches freshman and senior English and a senior writing class at New Bedford High School in New Bedford, Massachusetts. Taped to the front of her desk are two posters: "I don't give out grades. You earn them" and "Thank you for not whining." She chases students between buildings to redress dress-code violations. ("She takes everything a little too personally," a recent student, Elijah Washburn, says.) Last fall, on the first day of school, she began with a question to her senior writing class: "How many in here have heard horror stories about me?" Every hand went up—she'd expected nothing less. "Most students call me a very nasty name," she says, and laughs.

Amylee Bowman was a student in that class. Eight months before, in the only encounter the two had ever had, she'd been written up by Rachel Jupin for a minor infraction in the halls. "I didn't know her, but what I knew I didn't like," Amylee remembers. "I wasn't looking forward to that class."

Then something happened. "I don't know what exactly," says Amylee today. "She was strict, yeah—but it didn't seem like she was trying to be mean. And she listened. And it seemed like she cared. I just started to like her, I guess."

Amylee is eighteen, tall and spindly-thin, with dark-colored, shapeless clothes. Her hair, once bleached blonde, is dark and cut close to her head. She wears no makeup. Except for the softness of her skin, and the shy, fragile curl of her mouth when she tries occasionally—almost never successfully—to smile, she could pass easily for a boy.

Her 18 years have been an odyssey of loss: parents split at birth; a father in New Hampshire who took her in, then threw her out at thirteen; a mother who drops in and out of her life; some off-and-on times with an uncle in Nevada and grandparents in Plymouth, Massachusetts (she is vague about the details of most of this, and seems herself to be confused); a year in a foster home that ended with the death of the only person there who seemed to care; then two years spent careening between her grandparents' trailer in Plymouth and the homes and apartments of her mother's former lover in Fall River and assorted schoolmates and "friends."

She has been beaten, abandoned, and sexually abused by parties she will name only as "some people in my life." There have been alcohol abuses, drug overdoses, half a dozen stints in mental hospitals and various run-ins with police; under the sleeves and trousers of her dark, baggy clothes are the scars of repeated mutilations. ("Sometimes I just need to hurt myself.") In the past four years she had been enrolled at seven schools in three states.

"This is a child no one would have," says Rachel. "Everyone she's ever cared for has left her, or molested her, or beaten her up. It's *no wonder* she thinks she's worthless. It's no wonder how she treats herself."

Rachel Jupin, in her early fifties, is a handsome woman in a teacherly sort of way: short hair cropped efficiently around wide, expressive features; direct, intelligent eyes; a thoughtful smile that begins slowly, then often widens to a beam. We are sitting in the living room of the home she shares with her husband, Mike, an AT&T lineman, in the section of New Bedford they call the West End. It is a cheerful, disheveled old house with small, overstuffed rooms, a sagging porch, a sweet-smelling kitchen, and a hall stairway that Mike began paint-stripping a dozen years ago but has never quite managed to finish. The two have lived here 30 years. The last of their six children, now twenty-two and a parent himself, moved out two years ago.

Amylee sits across from us—head down, eyes averted, hands fidgeting with a small brown reindeer-doll in her lap—in a high-backed, stuffed chair she seems to wish would swallow her. For the first five or ten minutes I am there, she is silent as a ghost, lost in herself, like a small child in a roomful of distracted adults. Then, suddenly, at the end of Rachel's chronicle of her many abuses, she comes briefly—though almost spiritlessly—to life:

"I always screw up," she says flatly. "So then they don't want me. So then maybe I hurt myself. And they make me leave. Or sometimes I run away."

She is quiet again. Her eyes remain downcast. Then she looks up, almost furtively, and turns her head toward Rachel, who nods and smiles and urges her gently to "Just say what you're comfortable with."

"It's my fault," she says then, in response to nothing in particular. "It's all my fault. . . It's kind of like . . . more or less . . . maybe if I . . ." Then her voice drops off to a whisper, and she glances up ever so briefly to meet my eyes before turning her look back to Rachel. "I'm just so sorry I got her involved." Then her eyes drop back to the reindeer-doll and she is silent once again.

⌐⌐

October 15th was Rachel Jupin's 53rd birthday. Her senior writing class met in the morning as usual; "The Persuasive Essay" was the topic of the day. There were some rumors around school that involved a fake fire drill to be followed by a "Columbine-style" mass shooting, but nothing had come of them, and rumors at New Bedford High were as common as anywhere else. Amylee was in her usual seat, in the center of the front row of desks. Rachel remembers that she seemed distraught, that she wasn't her usual self.

"Something was wrong. She seemed upset—I had no idea about what, but I could tell there was something on her mind. I asked her about it after class. She wouldn't tell me. She said she was okay. And that was pretty much it."

Two days later, October 17, a student reported to his guidance counselor that he'd overheard some boys talking in the halls about a plan for some sort of "massacre." The school police were notified. No evidence was found.

On the night of November 4, a Sunday, Amylee arrived at Rachel Jupin's home. She was upset—"nearly hysterical," as Rachel recalls it. "She said she had to talk."

Something bad was going to happen, Amylee told her teacher. She wouldn't say what or when, only that it was a plot ("There are going to be shootings") with several students involved. She wouldn't name names, except to say that one of the shooters was supposed to be her. She cried; the two hugged—then Amylee made a promise: "I'll get you out, Mrs. Jupin. Nothing bad will happen to you."

"It was *going to happen*," Rachel Jupin says today. "I have no doubt at all—these kids were serious. If you could have seen Amylee, heard her voice, seen the look I saw in her eyes. She was terrified. They were going to go through with it."

The next morning, November 5, Rachel Jupin reported what she knew to the school. Amylee meanwhile, unknown to Rachel, took her story to the New Bedford police. Again, the information she offered was halting and incomplete (she was frightened, police records show, of being hurt or killed for divulging what she knew), but over a series of several meetings the details of the plan were revealed: Five students—four boys and Amylee, from fifteen to seventeen years old—were to arrive at the school on the appointed morning with loaded weapons under dark trench coats; on an agreed-upon signal they would run through the halls and shoot everyone in sight. That done, they would climb to the school's roof, where they would drink the liquor and smoke the dope they had stashed, then shoot one another to death. It had been planned, said Amylee, "like a military operation," and was scheduled to happen soon.

It was the usual sad story. The four boys and Amylee, all self-described "freaks" with deeply troubled home lives and an unrequited hunger to belong, would take their revenge against the school "preppies" and "jocks" with a killing spree "bigger than Columbine."

"Amylee states that the plan was to kill as many students and teachers as possible," New Bedford police officer Stephen A. Taylor wrote in his report at the time. "[She states] that she could not go through with this because she cares for Mrs. Jupin . . . that Mrs. Jupin was like a mother to her, the only person in the world who felt love for her . . ."

On Thanksgiving Day, November 22, with the police investigation nearing an end, Amylee was one of 20 guests—children, grandchildren, nieces and nephews—around Rachel Jupin's dining-room table. She was very quiet ("kind of overwhelmed," one of Rachel's grown daughters later said). Those old enough to wonder were told only that she was a troubled teen, a student of Rachel's, with nowhere else to go.

Two days later, November 24—following a police search that revealed a stash of knives, live ammunition, a flare gun, and notes copied from *The Anarchist's Cookbook*—three of the four boys Amylee had named were arrested and charged with conspiracy to commit murder and assault. A fourth was arraigned four days later.

Amylee, although she was arraigned on the same charges as the boys, was allowed to keep her freedom on the condition that she report daily to her probation officer. The state's prosecutor, Raymond Veary, was reportedly thinking of using her as a witness in exchange for reduced charges.

By the middle of the last week of November, the press was on to the story. For Rachel, already undone by the events of the past several weeks, the publicity onslaught was too much to bear.

"TV, radio, the newspapers—they were calling the school, calling me, calling the kids at home. I couldn't take it. I had to get away. They got a sub to teach my classes. I missed the whole month of December."

Three weeks after her arraignment, in mid-December, Amylee moved her clothes and books and drawings ("everything she had in the world—it wasn't much") into the second-floor bedroom that used to belong to Rachel's daughter Danielle. Within a few weeks, her poems and drawings covered much of Danielle's old wall space, vacuuming the kitchen was at the top of her chore list, and Mike and Rachel were answering to Dad and Mom.

❦

"Remember when the stores all started staying open on Sundays—how strange that seemed at the time? It was back in the early sixties, I think," says Rachel.

It is a Saturday in early February. We are sitting, Rachel and I, in Mike and Rachel's little kitchen, drinking coffee around a corner table that looks out on the Jupins' backyard.

"That's when it began, I think. That was the first sign—when families stopped doing things together on Sundays, when they started going shopping instead."

We had begun, of course, by talking about Amylee (who wasn't there at the time)—how lost she seemed, how hungry for love, how frightened of life and of herself—when Rachel, so seamlessly it wasn't clear even that she knew she was doing it, shifted the subject to herself:

"Amylee is *me*, you know. She's me about 35 years ago."

She tells me then about her own childhood in New Bedford: an alcoholic father, an absentee mother she longed for but barely knew, and the divorce that finally ensued. The difference, she says, is that "At the time we were the exception. Today, we'd be the norm."

This leads into the subject of the stores staying open on Sundays, and the breakdown of family life. She tells me about another girl in her College Writing class, whose foster parents have abandoned her and whose brother is in jail; about a freshman boy who had never had a Christmas; about indifferent parents and burned-out teachers and a student who had answered her urging to "Make your mother proud" by telling her flatly, "My mother is a *drunk*."

"'Well, then,' I told her—it was all I could tell her—'Well, then, do it for *yourself*.'"

She seems born to have been a teacher. But it wasn't until after she was 40, and still at an AT&T desk job she'd held for ten years, that her oldest daughter came home one day to announce she'd won first prize at a school dance recital—"and Mom, how come you weren't there?"

"That was it. That was the moment," she says.

Three months later she left her job, and the salary (twice a starting teacher's) and pension that went with it, to enroll at UMass Dartmouth in pursuit of a teaching degree. It would take her five years. Mike worked whatever overtime he could; Rachel worked part-time jobs. "Those were tough times in this house," she says now.

In the fall of 1995, at the age of forty-seven she began her second career. From the first day, she was known as a holy terror—a hard grader, a stickler on school rules and dress codes, a teacher who never let you slide.

"I'd been a mother already 23 years. I knew *kids*. I knew they needed rules, needed order, needed to know what was expected of them. They may think they don't want it, but they do."

But there was always a second side to it. She took an interest. She learned her students' lives and problems; unlike many of the other teachers at New Bedford—a strapped school in a poor city, where many of the 3,300 students come from broken, troubled homes—she was almost never too busy to offer her after-class time. She even—most shocking of all in this age of political correctness—was often seen hugging her kids.

"Kids need to be touched. They need *hugs*. So many of them, they get none of that at home. They're starved for it, really starved. Yet there are so many teachers—especially the male ones—who are afraid to touch a kid. They're afraid of that whole thing of sexual harassment, of what someone else might say. We're so *paranoid* in our society about showing caring, about showing anything like love. But love is critical. It's everything. It's amazing what love can do for a person. If you don't think anyone loves you, why is it even worth going on?"

It seems to have worked. Last September, in that senior writing class, when every student answered yes to Rachel's opening-day question—how many had heard Mrs. Jupin horror tales?—she followed it with a second: "How many here are sorry to be in my class?" Not a single hand went up.

—◦—

It is now the last week of April. Rachel and I are speaking on the phone. I hear Amylee in the background. They are about to sit down for a tutorial on *The Canterbury Tales*. (Amylee, expelled from school for being arraigned on a felony, is now being tutored by Rachel at home.) It has been a tough couple of months, Rachel says. There have been some "incidents"—another self-mutilation toward the end of February, and the night, not long before I called, when Amylee came home stoned on dope.

"I reported her. I called her probation officer. She knew I would. She knows the rules. She knows what to expect by now."

Amylee is on house arrest, with a sensor secured to her ankle, in Mike and Rachel's home—allowed to leave only to see her probation officer, attend Sunday church with the Jupins, hold down a part-time job at Grossman's, and keep appointments with a therapist. She is taking medication for her bipolar disorder and, Rachel says, doing her chores daily. The state still seems likely to grant her immunity; as of press time a trial date for the four boys had not been set. With another several months of Rachel's tutorials, Amylee hopes to earn her high-school diploma.

"It's *her* life, she has to live it," Rachel says when I ask what she thinks will become of Amylee. "But now at least she knows what the path is. And she knows that someone cares. That's a pretty good start, don't you think?"

# The Man Who Loves Lowell

## *November 2011*

*Life today is lived mostly in transit. We change jobs, change marriages, upgrade or downsize from place to place to place. Which has its benefits—we see more of the world, in most cases, than our grandparents did—but there's a lot lost, I think, in the process. Friends, neighbors, churches, work groups, book groups, Little League teams—everything becomes short-term, elastic. There's no continuity anymore. This year's neighbors are next year's Christmas-card list.*

*Which is why this story was such a delight to write. It is about a man who is the antithesis of all that. He is a poet, living in a mill city. His father was a millworker there, his grandfather a butcher, his great grandfather a carpenter, whose immigrant father arrived 150 years ago—five generations, all in the same town.*

*His poetry,—his whole life, in a way—is a celebration of this. He writes mostly of things now long gone: the mills, the neighborhood churches, the butcher shops, the old markets, the neighborhoods them-selves. He know the city like he knows his own face, every corner, every little crevice. He sees history in a just-paved parking lot. "People were here," he reminds me. "Lives were lived here." It's a reminder we all need to hear.*

Mr. Alphonse Hudon, / wearing a blue parka and dress hat, / leans on his cane on Pawtucket Street, / checking the freshly tarred walk /
and grove of short pines / along the Northern Canal. / "Looks good, doesn't it?" I ask. / And he says, "I liked it better the way it was," / which opens up a line of talk . . .

The poem goes on to tell of the conversation the two men had that day: Mr. Hudon, the older man, telling the younger one—the poet—how he used to know his father, and his grandfather before him, and an old neighbor named Mr. Marquis, who, 60 years ago or so *("before the wrecking cranes pulled up")*, owned a filling station near the spot where they're talking. The young man recalls a house he knew as a child, a block or two away, with a tree growing through its porch roof. *"Oh yes,"* the old man remembers, *"that was Mr. Marquis' house. / And there was a monkey there, too . . ."*

Mr. Hudon is probably gone by now. He was old already then, and those lines were written years ago. And the village he remembers has been gone now more than 40 years—its only memorial a bronze plaque on a granite slab squeezed onto a narrow spit of grass a block south of the Merrimack River in Lowell, Massachusetts, a minute's walk from where he and the poet had their talk: *"On this site grew the heart of the Franco-American community. Hard-working French Canadians came to fill the mills of Lowell . . ."*

The slab's granite, the inscription says, was cut *"from one of the last blocks to be torn down."* And around the plaque's sides, a border of street names, a fleur-de-lis at each corner, and two dates: *1875–1964*.

It was the poet himself who first brought me here, on a summer day more than a year ago, to deliver on his promise to show me the city of his poems. He's been writing them now going on 35 years, since before he finished college: poems about bars and laundromats and textile mills—"cotton was king" here, but there were wool mills, too—about boxers and politicians, God, death, young lovers, work, baseball, the weather. Nine collections—*Strong Place, What Is the City?* and more—plus essays, co-authorships and, most recently, *Atop an Underwood*, a popular collection of Jack Kerouac's early writings.

At the heart of nearly all of it is this city where he was born. It is both his muse and his dearest subject, and the cause around which he builds his working days. His devotion to it defines him. I may never have known anyone who loved any place more.

His name is Paul Marion. We'd come that day from our offices at the University of Massachusetts at Lowell, where Paul wears a suit and tie and plans community outreach projects, and I write and teach part-time.

For more than five years, we'd worked in the same office—although we didn't anymore—and I had come to value his warmth and wit, his vast knowledge of the city, and his love of the Red Sox. And at least once every summer for the past eight years or more—because as much as he follows the Red Sox, he loves their farm club, the Lowell Spinners, more—we've sat together in the box he rents for the season at LeLacheur Park on Aiken Street, just three rows back from the field, and shared beer and kielbasa while the sun drops behind the scoreboard.

It was around that time last summer, a week or two before our Spinners outing, that I went with him to the little granite memorial. Our tour had begun several days earlier, when we'd met after work at his house. It's a grand house, in an un-grand part of the city, a mile or so south of the memorial: six bedrooms, Italianate, all brick and stone and high windows, built 150 years ago at the peak of Lowell's textile ascension, home to the agent of the old Appleton Mill, the city's largest at the time.

It's bifurcated today—with Paul, his wife, Rosemary, and their 13-year-old son, Joseph, in one half; the other half the home of his in-laws, who have lived there 50 years. Rosemary grew up in the house; her great-grandmother once worked there as a maid, before her son, Rosemary's grandfather, bought the place nearly 80 years ago. Joseph, both parents tell me proudly, is the fourth generation of their family to live there.

They explained all this to me over beer and peanuts in the oversized dining room, while Paul—who seems alternately proud and embarrassed by the grandeur of the home he's married into—came and went with family photos: of his grandfather the butcher, pictured in an apron in front of his market; his father the mill worker ("People always said he looked just like Sinatra"); Doris, his mother, who sold coats and dresses for 25 years in a women's department store downtown. He was in his element, and it showed: telling stories, shuffling photos, eyes alight, between what may be his two favorite subjects in the world, his family and the city of Lowell.

He talked about his father's job in the textile mill—the filth, the long hours, the years and years of daily drain. "I don't know how he stood it," he told me. "I got a job there one summer as a kid, cleaning the drains in the scouring plant—where they scour the dung out of raw fleeces with nothing but hot water and lye. The stink was unbelievable. I think I lasted two days." This took him to the subject of Lowell's mills in general—the wool uniforms for World War II soldiers, for the Union Army the century before—and from there to the immigrants who manned the spinning machines and the looms.

"The Irish were the first ones," Paul said. "Then the French, the Canadians—my great-grandfather, Joseph, in 1880, he was one of the early ones—and then the Greeks after that. But the Irish ran things for a pretty long time. The French were second. It wasn't till '36, I think, that we had our first French mayor . . ."

The talk turned more personal later that evening, over dinner at an Irish pub downtown, where he shared with me, between interruptions (you can't sit down with Paul for long in many places in Lowell without someone calling his name), some of the quiet sadnesses his family had borne: his shopkeeper mother, Doris Roy Marion, who had never finished high school but who once boarded a silver railcar from Boston for a training program with Charles of the Ritz in New York, then caught the flu and came home ("I found the training manual years later cleaning out her dresser"); his father, a shy, quiet man who mapped out retirement trips to California and watched symphonies on TV ("kind of a closet intellectual without the education"), but gave his whole life to his mill job and died of cancer at 62.

"They were good people," he said to me. "Good working people. They dreamed dreams. But all they ever knew of life was work."

It was a side of Paul you rarely see, outside of his poetry. He's an affable man, very gentle in his ways, with wide brown eyes, a round face, and a story or clever remark about almost any subject you could name. There's a dreaminess about him, too, that comes across the first time you meet him—from his eyes, his slight smile—it's hard to know from where. You have to make the time, and do some digging—or hit just the right nerve—to get to where the poems come from.

I remember the first time I saw this. It was four or five years ago; I was teaching a class in freshman composition and had assigned a Paul Marion poem, "Majestik Linen," about a worker in an industrial laundry somewhere in Lowell, seen through a window on a Sunday-morning walk: "*She turns back to her work, what most of us won't see / unless we're in the Flats at the hour of the early Mass, / following the drone of automatic washers / to a sunrise service recognized worldwide . . .*" A student in the class, a boy of eighteen or nineteen who rarely if ever shared his thoughts, raised his hand to tell me, with what seemed like genuine wonderment, that he recognized in the poem—he was very sure of it, he said—his mother's place of employment.

I told Paul about it the next time I saw him. His delight was as plain as a child's. "That's wonderful," he said. "He saw through the poem to his mother. He saw that place as a subject of literature. That made it matter for him. That gave it dignity."

———

Around the same time I was teaching that course, I moved to Lowell from a small town in New Hampshire about an hour away. I had worked at UMass Lowell nearly five years by then, and had a pretty good sense of the city's past and present: the mill girls and millionaires of the 19th-century boom years; the slow obsolescence; the bottoming out through the '60s and '70s; the wax-and-wane cycle that followed; the flood of Cambodians that followed the Khmer Rouge genocide.

I knew about the blight, the muggings, and the gang violence, but also about the galleries, the small museums, the repertory theatre, and the artists' lofts downtown. I knew the city had been down and up and down again enough times to develop a sense of tragedy. But I liked that you could sit in deep cushions in the Caffé Paradiso and eat Italian pastry at 11 o'clock at night, and that there were real-imitation gaslights on Palmer Street, and that you could go to a pro baseball game for eight dollars, and that some of the streets still had cobblestones.

I liked what the city was on its way to becoming: a place where people honor the past but don't cling to it, and where a future is unfolding as you watch. Half a mile from the cobblestones is the 6,500-seat Tsongas Arena, spanking-new, of brick and glass, which has hosted Bob Dylan, Liza Minelli, Van Morrison, and the Boston Pops, along with Serena Williams, the World Wrestling Federation, and the World Men's Curling Championships. The old mills and boardinghouses are today's condos and artists' lofts. Walk a mile along the river and you'll see everything from the ruins of 100-year-old coal sheds to the site of the UMass Lowell's new nanotechnology center. Something exciting is happening: a newness, a kind of hipness peeking out from under the drear, that makes you want to be a part of it.

Part of Lowell's appeal, too, was Paul and other people like him—other artists, because the city is full of them. I was hoping that I might find some of the same gritty, life-grounding energy he was always talking and writing about. I did find the energy, but in the end it wasn't enough to hold me—other things came along—and I left after only two years. I've sometimes wondered since, though, whether I gave it enough of a chance.

It's several days after our pub dinner. We're standing now on the little grass island, deciphering the memorial, talking about the city's immigrant past. On one side is a company parking lot, mostly vacant now; on the other, the rear wall of the university's glass-and-concrete recreation center. It's late afternoon, warm and nearly cloudless, but even now the sidewalks around us are empty. It seems an unlikely place, I tell Paul, to memorialize anything. "Yes," he answers, "but here is where it all was."

This starts him on the stories. He's so full of stories, and of their connections to one another and the lessons he sees in them, that when he goes to tell you one, it will start out clear and linear, like anyone's family story, but then branch out and loop back and link up with others, until what you thought was a simple piece of cloth is suddenly a tapestry.

The monument, he tells me now, was placed here by the priests of St. Jean-Baptiste parish, "to mark the passing of Little Canada," their name for the neighborhood. The church, he says—now standing empty—is on Merrimack Street, one street over from Moody, where his grandfather's butcher shop was ("His store is a parking lot today"). On every street in the neighborhood—Aiken, Cabot, Cheever, Coolidge, and the others, all the streets named on the monument—"the tenements were as dense as Hell's Kitchen in New York." They were so dirty and low-class, he goes on, that his mother, from the Centralville neighborhood on the other side of the river, "wouldn't be caught dead here as a girl"—but still somehow wound up with his father, who grew up on Cheever Street. This starts him on his father, and the work he did grading wools: "a rare skill," he says to me now as his thoughts near the end of their looping—and there's something like pride in his tone—"to be able to grade the wool, one fleece from another, based only on its look and feel . . ."

The stories go on, sometimes sideways, just as often backward in time: about his father, a machine gunner with the Fourth Infantry Division, who marched across Germany, then came home to grade fleeces in Lowell; his father's father, Wilfrid the butcher; Wilfrid's father, the carpenter Doda, who married Rosalba, a weaver on a textile loom; and before Doda, Joseph, also a carpenter, who came south in the 1880s from Quebec. He can trace it back all the way to a merchant named Nicholas, from Normandy, who came with his bride to New France—Quebec— and settled there and raised a family, around 1665.

They're all gone now. His father's mill is gone—all the mills are gone—along with the butcher shop, St. Jean-Baptiste parish, the department store. Little Canada was bulldozed in the '60s—a late victim of urban renewal, which had already taken the Greek Acre and other neighborhoods—to make way for public housing. The downtown emptied: the stores, the Strand Theatre, the sidewalk markets, all shuttered or moved to the malls. Buildings, whole blocks, were burned or flattened; parking lots replaced businesses; the population fell by a quarter; unemployment reached 12 percent. "Somebody ought to drop a bomb on this place," a high school history teacher told Paul's brother's 10th-grade class in the mid-1960s. It was the city's darkest time.

"They were here, and then they were gone," Paul is saying now. It's early evening. We've been driving, for the past 30 minutes, the little grid of streets just east and west of the Aiken Street Bridge, the neighborhoods' old dividing point, and have come full circle back to the monument's little grass island. I've had the full tour, both sides of the river: the parking lot where Wilfrid's market once stood; the shuttered old neighborhood church; a blighted, prewar building complex, North Common Village, where men in undershirts sit in clusters on front stoops; the four-story red-brick fortress, St. Louis School, now in its 103th year, where, Paul once told me, his mother and Jack Kerouac, both Centralville natives, were schoolmates nearly 80 years ago; Paul's birthplace on Orleans Street, still a tidy two-family.

"We can't have those tens of thousands of lives just erased," he says. He's standing a foot or two back from the monument as he says this, sweeping an arm, almost angrily, right to left across his chest to take in the little island, the street and the land behind it, and the river, a block away to the north. He's been talking, for the last several minutes, about the mills that used to line the shore here: "the armies of workers who tramped through them—Irish, Greek, French Canadian, Swedish, any country you could name," and how their lives and stories, their comings and goings from this place, were what made him, in the end, want to write his poems.

"*People* were here," he says to me now, stabbing a finger first at the granite slab, then at the air and sky beyond it. "There are *people* inside that piece of stone. Lives were lived here. That had richness. That had value. That deserves to be counted."

All that history and geography / in a supersaturated marker, / tucked between evergreens on Aiken Street. . . / You stuck an arm out the window / to touch the next tenement. / You heard one tongue for blocks . . .

In a short essay at the end of his latest collection of poems, Paul quotes from Joan Didion, describing the relationship between another writer—James Jones—and the place and time he wrote about: "A place belongs forever to whoever claims it hardest, remembers it most obsessively, wrenches it from itself, shapes it, renders it, loves it so radically that he remakes it in his image . . ."

I'm sure I've never known a writer who has claimed any place harder, devoted himself more obsessively to its literary incarnation—and *re*incarnation—than Paul has Lowell. The difference is that whereas most artists (Twain, Faulkner, Whitman, William Kennedy, Russell Banks) seek to render a place, however lovingly, as a canvas on which to play out some larger truths, for Paul the place itself—and its people—seems the highest truth of all.

"It's a sort of alternative kind of preservation," he once said of his poetry to a reporter. "The whole world is in Lowell. It's so various. Every drama you can imagine, every human condition, is here." And so he captures and freezes them. Two hundred years of ghosts, like layers of old-growth timber: the wool grader; the Little Canada butcher; the laundry worker; Mr. Hudon out on his remembrance walk through the vanished neighborhood. It's not nostalgia he's after; he's a preservationist. He walks the city on Sunday mornings—it's an old habit, he says—as though it were a boneyard, in search of sightings, fragments, to fuse together somehow and recast. The bones become his poems, his verse documentaries, his version of the granite marker but more alive by far.

And as they're read or heard—or assigned in classrooms by teacher-advocates like me—they achieve the goal of all good documentaries: "People have to care about a place. That's where you begin, by getting them to care, by talking about heritage and shared purpose—a common past—by taking the story of Lowell's people, its folkways, out into the neighborhoods. . . That's been the constant for me, always: using culture as a social glue."

This hunk of rock on Earth / states its case for the record, / like the metal message boards / shipped out with satellites, / telling somebody out there who we are.

# Broken-Hearted Town
## *May 2003*

*It's an old story, and classically American. A town is born around an industry—gold-panning, coal mining, steel making, textiles, chocolate, glass—thrives for a decade or two or six, then, for any of a hundred reasons, languishes and slowly dies. You could almost chart our country's history in the stories of these towns.*

*Berlin, New Hampshire is one such town. Born in the 1830s with fewer than a hundred residents around a pair of sawmills on the banks of the Androscoggin River, it grew over the next century into a miles-long grid of pulp and paper mills. More workers arrived by the month, many of them immigrants—Swedish, Russian, Norwegian, French Canadian. A school opened, then churches, an opera house, an art gallery. The population swelled to 20,000. Generations of families succeeded one another in the mills. As recently as the 1970s, as one local woman recalls it: "That's what a guy did when he got out of school. He went to work in the mill, he married his girlfriend, he raised his kids."*

*This is the story of one of those men, and of the girlfriend he married, the family they raised together, and the thirty-two years of slow erosion that pursued them. It is the story of the simple pride and grit that allowed a family, and a town, to survive what most of the rest of us would call progress.*

The signs were there. You had to be a fool, or a dreamer, not to see them. First the bottled-water people stopped making deliveries. Then, in January, there were rumors that some of the loggers weren't getting paid. By early spring, the credit unions had stopped getting deposits. Then a company tax check to the city, for $50,000, was returned unpaid by the bank.

Paul Belanger should have seen it coming. A maintenance supervisor in the pulp mill, 32 years with the company—when a chipper or bleacher went down or needed fixing, it was his job to order the parts. And by mid-summer of 2001, even that had stopped being a sure thing:

"In regular times, I could order $2,500 of equipment, ten times a day if I needed it, without a signature. By July, it had got so I couldn't buy a postage stamp without a signed okay."

And still he didn't see it. Or wouldn't. There was "no way in hell," he told his wife, Gina—"Not after, *what?* 120 years?"—that the mill would ever shut down. Nearly all of his co-workers felt the same.

"They were all members of the club," Gina says today. "I call it the Oopy-Doopy Club. That's where, no matter how bad the news is, the answer's always the same—'Oopy-doopy, everything's gonna be fine,' 'Oopy-doopy, there's nothing to worry about.'"

On August 12, 2001, 100 workers at the pulp mill in Berlin, New Hampshire, were sent home by the owners, American Tissue, Inc. Other cuts followed within days, both there and at the company's paper mill, eight miles downriver in Gorham. By the end of the first week in September, except for a skeleton crew of about 40 workers, both mills had been shut down—the first time in 113 years.

Eight hundred ten workers were idled, nearly all of them men, most in their forties and fifties, with an average of 24 years on the job. More than half had spent their lives in Coos County—as had their fathers and mothers, and many who came before those. Most had wives and mortgages, and payments due on RVs or snowmobiles, or camping tracts on Blue Mountain, or retirement homes somewhere south. Some hunted. Nearly all fished. A night out was Mr. Pizza's in Gorham. An anniversary weekend was the Holiday Inn in Portland, 60 miles southeast. They bowled and camped and went to church with high school classmates, who were godfathers to their sons. A lot of their wives were nurses in Berlin. Most of their kids were grown and gone. Fewer than half, except maybe for some time in the army, had ever earned a living outside the mill. Or ever really wanted to, or imagined that they would.

Three and a half weeks later, at nine in the morning on Thursday, September 6, 2001, five days before the planes hit New York, the line of frightened workers at Berlin Savings were told gently by tellers that their paychecks were no good. The afternoon before, the last paper machine in Gorham—Number 9 at the Cascade Mill—shut down, and the last floor workers went home. At least one of them, a machine-tender in his forties named Ronnie Donato, returned to the mill later that day, breaching security lines:

"He went back," says Paul Belanger, "to turn his machine three or four more turns, to ease the pressure on the bearings so they wouldn't get flattened or freeze up. That was *his* machine. Had been his machine 20 years."

———

Paul Belanger's mother's father, Eugene Lessard, walked 130 miles into Coos County from the family farm in Quebec, as a teenager, sometime in the 1920s. He took a job in the tube mill of the Brown Paper Company, in which he would work the next 45 years. Paul's father's father, Joe Belanger, also of French Canadian descent, was 36 years in the mill before he punched in one morning in 1953 and dropped dead at his machine. He was 54 years old. His son, Paul's father, began at the mill in 1946, straight out of the army tank corps in France. He retired 30 years later, as a boiler operator in the pulp mill, when his knees began to go bad. He is 80 today.

Paul graduated from Notre Dame High School in June 1968, joined the National Guard, spent six months at a machine shop in Nashua, and began work at the mill in October of '69. He was 19, and earned $2.20 an hour. He would turn 52 the month it shut down.

There are a thousand family histories like this in the New Hampshire North Country. There used to be *many* thousands. For a long time now, there have been fewer every year, though there will probably always be some. But the story lines end differently today. The sons don't grow up to make paper anymore. Most of them don't even stay around.

———

Gina Belanger is tall and broad-shouldered, a handsome, powerful-looking woman in her mid-forties with distinct, almost pointed features and eyes that narrow and dart, then widen suddenly, when she talks.

She talks quickly and smiles often, looking sideways from time to time at her husband, who sits next to her at the table off the kitchen in the mobile home in Gorham they have shared for 15 years. Now and then she touches his forearm lightly; when she stands to go to the kitchen, she gives a squeeze to his shoulder on her way out.

They met 27 years ago, in an old beer bar called The Tavern that was built into the back of the pulp mill and was heated in the winter by its steam. Paul was twenty-six, divorced, with two young daughters; Gina was nineteen, a year out of Gorham High School and studying to be a nurse. "It was an instant kind of thing," she says, and smiles slyly at her husband, who smiles also, but sheepishly, and keeps his eyes fixed straight ahead. "No need to tell the full story—just say it was an instant kind of thing."

They married the next year—Paul was making $4 an hour working nights—and had their first daughter a year or so after that. For Gina, the future seemed assured. "It was a different time," she says. "To be able to say, back then, you know, 'My husband works in the mill'—from the perspective of a woman in this town, well, that was about as good as it got."

Paul, by that time, was a first-class pipe-fitter in the pulp mill in Berlin, where the logs come on trucks to be sectioned, debarked, diced into chips in a chipper, "cooked" in a "digestor" as tall as a three-story house from which they emerge as a syrupy mush, then washed, filtered, and run through the bleachery—from where, still thick as mashed potatoes, they are sent through tubes to the paper mill in Gorham, to be dried and smoothed and treated with additives, then thinned, cut to size, and wound into 8,000-pound rolls. He would work there the next 26 years.

It is a process he enjoys explaining. His hands, as he does so, move almost ceaselessly: quick-chopping to depict the action of the chipper, balling into fists to show how the logs are crushed into pulp, then whirl-winding, then flattening, then forming an index-finger steeple to suggest the thinness of the paper sheets. He seems to relish my questions. Each one is answered slowly, patiently, sometimes with a story or example, other times with a prop—an envelope, a salt shaker—from the table in front of us. It is as though paper-making were, for him, some dearly loved hobby—like gardening, say, or bird-watching—and he had stumbled unexpectedly into an interested audience.

"For Paul it's an art form," Gina will explain to me later. "And it's not only him. We know men, some of the old guys, who can pick up a piece of paper off the table, scratch it once between their fingers and tell you it needs a little flock [filler] in one end. . .

"It comes from having your heart in something—it doesn't matter what it is. Paul's a pipefitter. He can look at a machine and tell you where the hot spots are, or if this or that elbow is ready to blow. . . Everybody's heart is somewhere. My husband's heart is in the mill. My husband *is* the mill." And here she stops, and her eyes widen. It's clear that I am to understand: there is no false sentiment here. "He's a piper, he's a factory guy. A French guy. Like his father, like his grandfather. The mill is in his *blood*."

⌘

In July of 1829, the town of Berlin, New Hampshire (formerly known as Maynesburgh), on the west bank of the Androscoggin River, made up of eight families totaling 68 persons, officially came into being. The town had two small sawmills, built of shingle and clapboard, one owned by Thomas Green, the other by his sons, Daniel and Amos, at the head of Berlin Falls.

By the early 1890s, now with two giant mills—C. S. Peabody and E. Libby & Sons—working 400 men around the clock, the town had grown to 3,500 and was adding to that by the day. A third company, Glen Manufacturing, had begun making paper from wood pulp (until then it had been made mostly from rags) and was turning out 60,000 square feet of newsprint every minute, much of it for the *Boston Globe*. Berlin by now had two opera houses—one included a billiard hall, art gallery, and roller rink ("open Tuesdays and Fridays for the ladies of the town")—at least two grand hotels, two churches, one school, and several dozen outlying farms.

In 1888 the Berlin Mills Company was incorporated by a man named William Wentworth Brown, who sent his son, known as H. J., to oversee operations. The same year, the company began making paper; by 1896 it owned 300,000 acres of North Country timberland and was cutting

60 million feet of pine and spruce per year. Its payroll was as high as 1,200 men, not including its 450 river drivers, who, for a month or more each spring, drove the logs downriver to the mills.

The spring drive was an annual event. Visitors would come from 50 miles around, line the banks of the Androscoggin, and watch the mile-long clogs of timber, wrestled by teams of men with 16-foot poles, pass through the runway of the dam and drop into the rapids below. "It was not unusual," one writer reported, "to witness a log 40 feet long, or more, stand up perpendicularly [*sic*] in the seething waters."

By the mid-1920s, the population had reached 19,000. The Berlin Mills Company—now simply the Brown Company, which would be owned for decades by three generations of Browns—was the largest employer in town. The family prospered, and in prospering made itself loved. Its mill workers, by the late '20s, were earning an average of close to $30 a week. A school had been built on company property, and in part with company funds. There were mill-hosted dances, ball games, picnics, and opera-house plays. The family home on Church Street, a marvel of porches and cupolas, was a centerpiece of the town. (Gina Belanger, whose great aunt, years later, would serve as housekeeper there, still has her little-girl memories of "old Mr. Brown's enormous bed, raised up on a pedestal like a throne.") The relationship between the town and the family was as close to feudal—in the best sense—as industrial America would allow.

But the zenith had been reached. The demand for paper was being answered now by others. The glut of North Country lumber mills, coupled with the region's remoteness from its markets to the south, was making it harder by the year for the companies to meet costs.

During the Depression the Peabody Company closed; its mill would become a steam laundry. International Paper left town overnight in the fall of 1930—the old stone foundation, half-buried, still stands behind the ball field in town. The Brown Company, the last survivor, was bailed out at the 11th hour by the state.

The years since have been a slow erosion—but so slow it has been possible, for those who wish to, to forget that it was taking place at all. The Brown Company, freed of local competition, survived the Depression, repaid its state financing, and at times seemed once again to thrive. The war helped, and then the postwar boom. At least through the 1950s, the market for paper held steady. And as late as the early '70s, there was a job waiting for most any local boy who came out of high school in Berlin or Gorham with nowhere else to go. And most looked no further. The money was good, the living was cheap, the work wasn't taxing—and it was what your father had done.

"My last year of high school, I think half the guys in the senior class went to work in the mill right from graduation," says Gina Belanger. "And a lot of the rest went later. That's just how it was. That's what a guy did when he got out of school. He went to work in the mill, he married his girlfriend, he raised his kids. . .

"For girls the choices were different. You could get a job in the towel room [at the mill]—but there weren't that many jobs there. Or you could go to work at the Converse factory in Berlin. Or you could be a nurse. That was about it. Or you could leave town."

In June 1964 Orton Brown, known widely as O. B., the man with the pedestaled bed, the last of four sons of William Wentworth Brown, died in Berlin at the age of 94. A month earlier, on the Androscoggin, the last logs were piked on the river's last timber drive—the wood henceforth would be hauled downriver by truck.

Four years later the Brown Company, no longer profitable, was sold to Gulf and Western. The layoffs were modest. In 1980 it was resold, then 15 years later sold again. Each time there were fewer men left working, and fewer families left in town. Somewhere around the time of the third sale, the old Brown mansion was razed.

In 1999 came the fifth owner, Pulp and Paper of America, a division of American Tissue. It was two years after that, in September '01, that Paul and the rest were sent home. Berlin's population had shrunk to 10,000. And of the 1,800 men who had been there when he started, only 860 were still there to let go.

On a morning in early March 2002, six months after the closings, in a giant, mostly empty warehouse space above A&B Electronics in Berlin, a man named John Collins, an employment counselor, was sitting at a desk in a little prefab office shaking his head and repeating himself. He works for a group called Southern New Hampshire Services, in Manchester, 150 miles and about half a century south. He has come here to help counsel the out-of-work mill workers. He's been in town four weeks, he says, and has never seen anything like it in his life.

"It's amazing. Amazing. They're all the same age, nearly all in their fifties. They're all men, all born here. They all work the same job, in the same plant, their whole lives. . . Their houses, too. They've all lived there forever. And their mortgages—would you believe $148 a month?

"And they all say the same thing—'My father worked here, my grandfather worked here, it's the only work I know.' And then the $148 mortgages. Amazing. It's like going back in time."

The space we were sitting in is the new headquarters of the Workers' Assistance Center, formed with federal dollars after the shutdown to give aid and counseling to the out-of-work men. Three months earlier, it had served as a clearinghouse for some of the toys and holiday turkeys that had been collected for mill workers' families by the fire departments, third-grade classrooms, and marine posts from around the state.

Today, though, it is a cheerless space, far too large for its purposes. Here and there along the walls, middle-aged couples sit with counselors behind five-foot partitions, discussing career prospects, retraining seminars, or ways a week's food budget might be stretched. Except for the hushed voices that seep occasionally from the cubicles, the place is as quiet as a church.

The man in charge is Ray Blais, head of Local 75 (Maintenance and Production), himself an idled worker with 24 years in the mill. His job here, he tells me, and that of his co-worker Christy Langlois, and the several people—like John Collins—who are sent here from agencies downstate, is not so much to find jobs for the workers as to convince them that they ought to be looking for work at all.

"'I'm just a dumb old paper-machine worker with 24 years in the mill. What do I know? What other work could I do? There's nobody gonna hire me.' That's what a lot of them are saying. That's what we're up against here.

"So you try to convince them they're not dummies, that they need to look for work, that they've got skills they don't even know they have. So *then* what? Then comes a story in the paper says the mill's gonna reopen, that some new buyer is coming around. Then the next day the story is different—'No Buyer, No Prospects.' So what are they supposed to *think?* 'I'm 51 years old, my 25 years are more or less wasted as far as retirement—so do I move out of town? Put my house up for sale? Take job education? Or wait around and hope the mill gets bought, then that the new guys will hire me back?'

"Think about it. Financial, mental, emotional—that's an *incredible* amount of stress."

The stress, or a lot of it, was there already. Coos County, for years, has led the state in just about every measure of social and economic misery. Berlin is first among New Hampshire's cities in population loss. It has more than double the state's share of teenage mothers; one in ten of its families, and one in six of its elderly, live in poverty.

And that was before. The numbers aren't in yet for what happened when the mill went down, but it would be hard to overstate the effects. The loss in taxes alone to the city of Berlin—$4 million, or more than a quarter of its base—cut eight percent from police, fire, and school budgets and, for a time, left the city's librarian working for free. "It's like dropping a bomb in the middle of Coos County," John Gallus, a local realtor and state representative, told the *Union Leader.*

Cathy McDowell, executive director of the Family Resource Center in Gorham, prefers a more personal analogy. "It's like when your parents die," she says. "They're gone, and you're alone, and that's when you know—*you're* the one now."

She is a slight, middle-aged, saucer-eyed woman, one of those rare, tireless human-dynamo types who seem always both impossibly harried and utterly at ease. Probably as revered as anyone in the county since the death of Orton Brown, she is out in front of everything at once: director of the Family Resource Center—a "network of providers" that serves as day-care center, family health center, and pretty much whatever else it needs to be; leader of a group of health and human-service workers, Concerned Community Providers, who give their time to the unemployed; and key member of a local business group—Androscoggin Valley Economic Recovery—whose main mission is to recruit companies willing to move their operations north.

She came to the region, a young wife with her new doctor-husband, nearly 30 years ago, stayed, "came to love it," and raised a family there. Over the years, as she grew more involved, the stink of treated pulp stopped being called "the smell of money" (then was purged by the EPA); the Converse factory closed, then Bass Shoes and Valley Lumber and the old Gam Stitching plant; a doctor-drain stripped the county to two pediatricians, and Main Street grew empty and ugly, full of abandoned old brick buildings sided in asbestos and boarded windows and 20 years of grime.

And then, less than three years ago—most cruelly—three of the region's four Catholic churches, home to a century of worshippers, closed their doors almost at once, leaving 1,700 families, many who had never gone anywhere else on Sundays, without their spiritual homes. And the region grew poorer and older, as people took their dollars to Portland and the young departed and the population fell.

But through all those years of slippage, as long as the mill stayed open there was one thing, says Cathy McDowell, that never seemed to change: "There was always that sense of, 'We make paper . . . this is how we see ourselves, this is who we are.'"

Then it closed. And for all the money problems—teacher layoffs, medical crises, food-pantry shortages, a kids' hockey program that had to depend on the generosity of its opponents for ice time and skates—the worst costs by far, says Cathy, have been in the hearts and minds of the men.

"They've lost their pride. They've lost their sense of identity. It's hard to know how much more drinking they're doing—Coos County's alcohol abuse is already the highest in the state. But domestic violence is up 17 percent [immediately after the shutdown], so that should tell you something. And you can see the effect on the women; you can see it just talking to them. Their men are home and out of work, with nothing to do with their days. There's a sense of hopelessness. It's a pretty palpable thing. . ."

For Paul and Gina, things could have been a lot worse. Paul, the day he got his notice, was earning $18 an hour plus overtime and benefits working a rotating shift at the mill. Gina, trained as a nurse, was a drug and alcohol counselor. Paul had some income as a National Guard reservist. Two of their three daughters were at least mostly on their own. There were some savings. The mortgage on the mobile home was paid.

But the savings wouldn't last and Gina's earnings weren't enough, and Paul was too young to retire. Unless the mill found a buyer and reopened, they would move south and look for work.

"We talked about it," says Gina. "And talked and talked. But in the end there's only one answer—what *else* can we do?" Even so, she says, it was unthinkable.

"Paul's two daughters live here. And his parents—two years ago they lost their church, Angel Guardian, that they'd been going to all their lives. And now *he* goes? Just picks up and walks away? And so many friends, a lifetime of friends—how do you leave a *life?* What do you do with a 14-year-old dog? Who will take care of my mother's headstone?"

For others, the pain was far worse. There were those like Roland Caron, a worker in the pulp mill for 23 years, with two children in college and no way to keep them there. Or Ted Miller, 18 years in the mill, who gave up and moved his family to Florida with no job waiting and no buyer for their home. The hospital was losing nurses who were moving south with their husbands to find work. And everyone seemed to know someone who had lost his family's home to the bank. "You'd have to say," says Paul, "that there are a lot of people in a whole lot more trouble than us."

The crisis was well broadcast. And at least in the short term, there was all kinds of outside help. Both Berlin and Gorham received state assistance; for the workers themselves, there was a $4.5 million federal grant. Schools and offices took up collections. The Shaw's supermarket chain trucked in over 70,000 pounds of canned goods to a local food bank, to be distributed to families in need. An anonymous gift of $5,000 was sent for library books. Just about every social service in the region got involved.

But something else, something quieter, was happening too. For 150 years, from the early 1850s until long after most of the rest of America had passed beyond the time of smokestacked factories and men with lunch pails working at machines, a vast part of New Hampshire had drawn its life from its timber and its mills. There had been fewer men lately and only one mill, and the profits were smaller, and there were always some—the naysayers—who said it couldn't last. But the fact is, it had. And it did. And 150 years is a very long time.

Then it ended. The machines stopped, and the men went home. And for the first time in six generations, as Cathy McDowell depicts it: "We had to face the question—'Who *are* we, and why are we here?'" And there may have been no one around, unless it was Cathy McDowell herself, who faced it more searchingly, or with more effect, than a mill worker's son named Steve Griffin.

Gina remembers him from high school in Gorham. He was two years ahead of her. She recalls that he was "kind of quiet, and seemed bright. You got the sense that he was one of those who probably wouldn't end up in the mill."

She was right about that—though his father had worked his life there, and his grandfather, and most of the men he'd known growing up. But his father was the exception: a mill worker who steered his sons away. And when Steve Griffin talks today about his father, though he doesn't seem to intend it, the pride is audible:

"He was in quality-control at the Cascade plant. He put the three of us through college doing that. And right from the start he said it—it wasn't going to be the life for us."

So Steve became an accountant instead. And ten years ago he went to work for Isaacson Structural Steel, which had been started in 1960 by a scrap dealer named Eli Isaacson and by the early '90s was one of the larger employers around. Six years ago, when old Mr. Isaacson's health went bad, Steve and a partner bought him out. Today he is president, and the company, with 175 employees, is—after the mill, the hospital, and the state prison—the fourth largest in Coos County.

He is a smallish man with sandy, receding hair. His voice is soft and mostly flat, but he is not stinting in his answers. He is careful and exacting in his statements—an accountant—but the subject is dear to him, and it shows:

"When I was a kid growing up, even after then, there was this invisible iron curtain between the [two] towns. Berlin was pulp, Gorham was paper; they were big, we were small; they were stink, we were clean air. The schools were rivals, the towns were rivals. It was a pride thing. It was just this mind-set we had. . .

"But Berlin was always the place to go. And Friday nights were big, really bustling; it seemed like the town never closed. It's different now. It's been different for years.. . . There's been this erosion of pride. . ."

———

In early August of 2001, a week or so before the mill closed—but well after American Tissue had bounced its last check to the town—Steve Griffin sat down with his partner, Arnie Hansen, the president of the local bank, and the owner of the largest car dealer in town, to talk about what they could do. "We knew the closing was coming any day," Steve says, "and that it would kill the valley if we couldn't come up with a plan."

So the men pooled their money—more than a few thousand dollars, he won't say just how much—to hire an economic-development expert. At about the same time, Gorham's mayor, Bill Jackson, came up with $335,000 in state and federal redevelopment grants. The group then hired a planning firm, which began looking into options—downtown redevelopment, expanded tourism, small business, a casino, a federal prison. By now—it was December by this time—the mill had long since closed, and the original band of four had grown to 12, then 21. They called themselves AVER—for Androscoggin Valley Economic Recovery—and included, among others, a retired selectman, a hospital administrator, a lumber executive, a motel owner, a social-services leader—Cathy McDowell—and the former manager of a mill. They were, by any standards, the North Country's best and brightest; and their focus, which had begun as strictly economic—attracting new companies, retaining the old—broadened almost by the week.

"Education, health services, tourism, governance, we started looking at all of it. But it wasn't just us. Other people started getting involved, mill people, business people, a lot of them that had never been involved before. And the [Berlin] city council, once the mill closed down, well, they were just a lot easier to work with after that. The closing changed everything. There was a whole different mind-set about things."

Over the next six months, from the winter after the shutdown until the late spring of 2002 the headlines in the *Berlin Daily Sun*, which had begun as a litany of miseries—job losses, tax-revenue losses, local relief efforts, the insolvency of American Tissue—began to show a change. A council vote on new school funding. A Main Street renovation project. A new, 25-job employer. A yes vote on a prison referendum. The hiring of a city grant writer. A radio promotion for a catchy new slogan, "It Is Better in Berlin."

By the spring of 2002, the AVER people had begun dreaming out loud. Steve Griffin saw a region-wide school system, a resurrected downtown with a modern assisted-living complex at its center, and a tributary of the Androscoggin running through a newly vibrant city green; Cathy McDowell spoke of bookstores and crafts shops, an explosion of artisans and telecommuters whose discovery of the North Country ("Wow, this is a pretty cool place. I could run a bookstore here.") would create an all-new tipping point. Bill Jackson, the Gorham mayor, saw a new four-year college, a regional health center, a meshing of the two towns' services, an end to local rivalries.

"It comes down, in the end, to the question: 'Why are we here?'" says Cathy McDowell today. "The values, the connections, the beauty of the land. Not having to lock your doors when you leave, never worrying about your kids at night. These are the things we all treasure, that we're all trying so hard to save. They're the answers to the question. We just never asked ourselves before."

~

From the first day, there had been rumors. This or that company was looking at the mill. So-and-so had made an offer. There was a buyer in the wings. No one knew whom to listen to, whether to believe what they read in the papers, whether to relocate, retrain, or stay put. "It was just a damn roller-coaster," says Ray Blais.

In May 2002 the seesawing ended. Fraser Papers, Inc., of Connecticut, the sixth owner in 34 years and the third in the past eight of the old

Brown Company mills, was approved by a US bankruptcy court. By mid-July, the Cascade Mill in Gorham was back up and running, with 450 men. The pulp mill in Berlin remained idle, with no sure opening date. A consolidation had been announced already by Fraser. Of the 860 laid-off workers, 160 would not be coming back.

Paul Belanger was among the fortunate. He returned to work in June, with the first group called, as maintenance supervisor of the Number 3 and Number 4 machines at Cascade. The product was book paper. Of the six-man crew he'd been part of in the pulp mill, only four, he says, would be returning to their jobs.

"You want to know the hardest part of my week?" asks Gina. It is a late afternoon in mid-August. Paul has just returned from his shift at the mill and sits between us at the kitchen table.

"The hardest part is when I go out and run into some old friend, some woman I've known my whole life whose husband got laid off with Paul. 'Hi,' I'll say, 'How you doing? Is your husband back to work yet?' And already I'll know that he isn't, and might not be again. But mine is. That's tough."

It's a small town, she explains, and people feel one another's troubles. "On the one hand, you don't like to see your friends struggling. But then we've been taking it all for granted, all of us, way too long. . . So now we're learning our lesson—that way is broken, and it's got to be fixed. We're going to have to change, or we'll die.

"I'd want this to be a place my daughter could live. But there are no jobs here for her, so she's going to end up downstate. The young ones, the good ones, all leave. . ."

⎯ ⌣ ⎯

A little while later, Paul asks if I'd like to see the pulp mill while there is still daylight. We drive north in his pickup, along the west bank of the river. It is a little before six in the afternoon; on the far shore, the white and green of a million birches, planted decades ago to replace the hardwoods stripped to feed the Brown Company mills, rise unbroken in the late sun toward the foothills of the Moosuc range. Paul, never talkative, seems happy for the silence, the small mission of our drive. "Another week or two, gonna start seeing some color on those hills," he says at one point. "Gets real pretty for awhile, then it's gone."

The pulp mill is a fortress. Scarred red brick, flat and massive, at the center of a maze of stacks and silos and ugly, modular outbuildings that seem to breed on themselves. It is old—even the dirt seems old—with corners that have gone round with age and high-up irrelevant windows so crusted with grime it is hard to tell them from the walls. There is soot everywhere, and discarded things: paper, pylons, old gear wheels, bark chippings, half-sawed tree trunks that lie rotting against outside walls. It has been empty now a year.

We begin outside, at the flume, where the logs arrive from the trucks—600 tons a day—then follow what would be their path: up the metal belts, idle now, into the wall of the mill, then down into a trough, as long as half a football field, in which the logs, in other days, would be pushed along by surging water. Today, instead, a family of bats crisscross between metal stanchions. The sun outside is dying now. There is no other light.

"This is where they come," says Paul. "They go out *there*"—and he points, and looks, toward somewhere above and beyond the end of the sunken trough. It is hard, in the gathering darkness, to know just where he means.

"Not much left of them then," he says. "They go out as brownstock—slush." He speaks quietly, as he always does. He seems not to notice the quiet, the dark.

# About the Author

 **Geoffrey Douglas** is a former reporter, columnist, editor and publisher, and the author of four nonfiction books; the 2005 film *The Game of Their Lives* was made from his book of the same name. A long-time contributor to *Yankee,* he is the author of more than 100 magazine pieces, many of them widely anthologized. A former adjunct professor of creative writing at the University of Massachusetts/ Lowell, he was a fellow at the Bread Loaf Writers Conference and has served as writer-in-residence at several schools and universities. A native of New York City, he lives with his wife in western New Hampshire.